Hold Fast to Dreams

Hold Fast
to Dreams

*A College Guidance Counselor, His Students,
and the Vision of a Life Beyond Poverty*

Beth Zasloff and Joshua Steckel

THE NEW PRESS

NEW YORK
LONDON

Requests for permission to reproduce selections from this book
should be mailed to: Permissions Department, The New Press,
120 Wall Street, 31st floor, New York, NY 10005.

Quotation on page vii from "Dreams" from *The Collected Poems of Langston Hughes*
by Langston Hughes, edited by Arnold Rampersad with David Roessel,
Associate Editor, copyright © 1994 by the Estate of Langston Hughes.
Used by permission of Alfred A. Knopf, an imprint of the Knopf Doubleday
Publishing Group, a division of Random House LLC. All rights reserved.

Quotation on pages 16–17 from *Song of Solomon* by Toni Morrison, copyright © 1977
by Toni Morrison. Used by permission of Alfred A. Knopf, an imprint of the
Knopf Doubleday Group, a division of Random House LLC.

Published in the United States by The New Press, New York, 2014
Distributed by Perseus Distribution

ISBN 978-1-59558-904-0 (hc.)
ISBN 978-1-59558-928-6 (e-book)

CIP data available.

The New Press publishes books that promote and enrich public discussion and
understanding of the issues vital to our democracy and to a more equitable world.
These books are made possible by the enthusiasm of our readers; the support of a
committed group of donors, large and small; the collaboration of our many partners in
the independent media and the not-for-profit sector; booksellers, who often hand-sell
New Press books; librarians; and above all by our authors.

www.thenewpress.com

Composition by dix!
This book was set in Adobe Caslon

Printed in the United States of America

2 4 6 8 10 9 7 5 3 1

For our parents,
Joseph and Tela Zasloff,
and Steve and Barbara Steckel

Hold fast to dreams
For if dreams die
Life is a broken-winged bird
That cannot fly.
                    —Langston Hughes, "Dreams"

But experience has taught me that you cannot
value dreams according to the odds of their coming true. Their real value is in stirring within us
the will to aspire.
                    —Sonia Sotomayor, *My Beloved World*

CONTENTS

Authors' Note

Thinking about college is like thinking about life.
—Scott Way, at age 16

We wrote this book to document the struggles and triumphs of students like those Josh has worked with during his eight years as a college counselor in the New York City public schools: young people whose stories are too often left out of the national conversation about college or reduced to grim statistics. It is not a how-to book or an application guide. Through the lens of Josh's work with ten students, we try to bring to life what it is like to be a low-income student of color trying to get to—and through—college in America today.

The ten students' stories begin with their work with Josh in high school. As Scott suggests, "thinking about college" spurs big and difficult questions about who they are and what they can become. The students' narratives then expand into an exploration of the educational, professional, personal, and spiritual choices they face after their high school graduations. In their reflections and memories, students capture the experience of coming of age in a society where the American dream of opportunity through education often clashes with another defining American narrative: that of poverty as a vicious cycle that only the most determined young people can break.

This book was written as a husband-wife collaboration—roughly divided as Beth doing the writing and Josh doing the

research. It was also written in partnership with students who
spoke about their experiences in interviews, welcomed us to their
homes and campuses, and reflected back with us on documents
from their application processes, including essays, letters of recommendation, and e-mail exchanges. Josh has stayed close with
all the students in this book, and in interviewing them he has
continued the counseling relationship that is also our subject. The
book shifts between Josh's memories and those of the students. As
much as possible, their stories are told in their own words.

In agreeing to participate in this project, each of the students
expressed a hope that this book would help others. We are incredibly grateful to all of them for their courage, generosity, and
insight. All of the ten students read and commented on the manu-
script to ensure that their experiences were represented accurately.
Four students and their close friends and family members are
given pseudonyms. For Aicha Diallo and Santiago Hernandez,
this is due to ongoing concerns related to immigration status; for
Santiago, we have also changed identifying details. Ashley Brown
and Dwight Martin expressed the desire to maintain their privacy.
For the remaining six students, real names are used.

1

Riding Backward:
Nkese and Dwight

Just before beginning a new job as college counselor at the Secondary School for Research, a public school in Brooklyn, New York, Joshua Steckel was greeted by a member of the upcoming senior class with this e-mail message:

> hi im nkese (pronounce nik-a-ce) im glad that you email me because many of seniors need help with the college process. me for one because i have many college applications sent 2 my houses but i havent filled none. SO i appreciate and look forward 2 workin with you in da comin school year

Josh was intimidated, both by Nkese's apparent low skill level and by the hope her message expressed. Her e-mail, a response to one he had sent introducing himself to the senior class, voiced the expectation that he would fill a need he wasn't sure he could. He had no experience working with low-income, inner-city kids beyond the few scholarship students he had counseled in his previous job at Birch Wathen Lenox, a private school on New York City's Upper East Side. He didn't know what it would be like to guide this set of students through the consuming drama of the college application process, or whether the success he'd had placing wealthy students at elite schools would translate to the task that lay before him: helping students who would mostly be the first in their families to go to college.

Josh wrote back to Nkese that he looked forward to meeting her and that he would appreciate her help contacting the other seniors. "i already spread da wrd 4 u," she replied within seconds.

The Secondary School for Research, where Josh began in the fall of 2006, was one of three schools located in the John Jay building, which occupies most of a block on Seventh Avenue in Park Slope, Brooklyn.[1] The old John Jay High School had been shut down as part of the city's plan to replace large, failing schools with multiple small, nurturing schools housed in the same building. The population of the Secondary School for Research in 2006 was 46 percent Latino, 40 percent African American, 8 percent Asian, and 6 percent white. Eighty percent of students were economically disadvantaged by federal standards and received free or reduced price lunch. Kids came mostly from neighborhoods outside Park Slope, including Sunset Park, Flatbush, Bedford-Stuyvesant, Crown Heights, and East New York.

The old John Jay High School had a history of violence: in 1997, the *New York Times* reported, it had "more assaults, robberies, and acts of drug and weapon possession than any high school in the city."[2] When Josh began, incidents had decreased to levels on par with many other New York City public schools. But John Jay's reputation still lingered in the upper-middle class neighborhood. The pizza shop across the street from the school building posted a sign reading, "No students allowed before 5 p.m.," though at lunchtime, a pizza shop a few blocks away was crowded with the students from the highly regarded elementary school nearby, PS 321. At the end of the school day, police officers gathered outside the John Jay building to herd students to the subway.

Students and parents had to pass through a metal detector to enter the John Jay building. They emptied their pockets, removed their belts and jewelry, then placed their backpacks on the conveyer belt. If the light was red, they needed to step to the side and spread their arms as uniformed New York Police Department safety officers passed wands over their bodies. In response to a recent cell phone ban by schools chancellor Joel Klein, students also had to hand their phones to safety agents or school aides, who would put them in Ziploc bags and returned them at the end of the day.

Jill Bloomberg, the principal of the Secondary School for Research, was a vocal critic of the metal detectors. "We take our students extremely seriously," she is quoted as saying on the website Inside Schools. "We say 'we are educating you because the future is yours. We're going to hand the world to you.' But scanning says 'we don't trust that you're going to come to the school without a weapon.' "[3] The building now had safety statistics equal to or better than schools without metal detectors. But the process for removing school metal detectors, once installed, was complex and difficult. On top of this, the principals of the other two schools in the building, the Secondary Schools for Law and Journalism, wanted the metal detectors to stay. Security agents occasionally found weapons, and the scanners, these principals believed, kept everyone safer.

At Birch Wathen Lenox, the Upper East Side private school where Josh had been a college counselor prior to coming to the Secondary School for Research, conflict over the school entrance had centered on complaints that parents were blocking the lobby with their Bugaboo Frogs, the wide, brightly colored strollers that cost over $700. Josh's office had been located just past the entrance desk, across from the headmaster's study. The Birch Wathen Lenox college counselor played a central role in the school administration. Parents saw college placement as the final evaluation of the time and money they had invested in their children's education and looked to Josh as the expert insider who would secure their child's spot at an elite college.

Josh had started at Birch Wathen Lenox as a teacher, then worked as college counselor for three years. Though he formed strong attachments to his students and wanted to help them, he grew increasingly uncomfortable with the ways his advocacy gave a leg up to students already in a position of significant privilege. As he learned more about the field of college admissions, he felt drawn toward work with students for whom the issue was not college choice, but college access.

In hiring Josh, the principal of the Secondary School for Research, Jill Bloomberg, aimed to provide public school students with the kind of intensive one-on-one support and advocacy that Josh had given his students at Birch Wathen Lenox. In the New York City public school system, there is no position called "college counselor": at most schools, the work of supporting students with their college admissions process is neglected or folded into the jobs of already overworked guidance counselors. At new small schools, however, principals have increasingly sought ways to establish the role. Jill used a salary line in her budget called "Community Coordinator" to create a full-time position for Josh. Jill knew that many of her students, by virtue of their race and family income, were not expected to graduate high school, much less go on to college. A central part of her mission was to build a school culture in which all students saw themselves as college-bound.

The three schools in the John Jay building shared the college office, which was three flights down from the rest of the Secondary School for Research. Josh knew that this distance would make it difficult for him to get to know the students and start his work with them. One of his first goals was to interview each senior for the counselor letters of recommendation he would write. As part of his training at Birch Wathen Lenox, Josh had attended the Harvard Summer Institute on College Admissions, where he learned strategies for producing successful application packages. Quotes from individual meetings with students were "like gold" for his letters of recommendation, Josh was told by the counselor from Milton Academy, an elite Massachusetts prep school.

Nkese took the first step in arranging to meet a few days after school began. She wrote in an e-mail,

I would like to set up a meeting sometime next week wed at lunch. In this meeting i will bring about 13 different college application that was sent to me. This way i can discuss my option.

Nkese wore her hair long and straight and dressed in close fitting, brightly colored clothes. She had a direct, confident manner, and Josh had the sense that she was sizing him up: his curly hair and crooked glasses, the clutter of cardboard boxes and makeshift cubicle partitions that separated his desk from those designated for the other two schools. Josh had been concerned that his office would have too little privacy. At Birch Wathen Lenox he had grown to understand the college application process as a fraught, vulnerable time for students and parents, a moment of transition when they looked back on their lives. Though he had no formal training, he had found himself in the role of psychological counselor, mediating family confrontations and emotional breakdowns.

Nkese set down the applications she had brought. They had been sent to her home by colleges that relied heavily on mass-market mailings, attracting students by making them feel as though they had been recruited. Josh said that before they discussed specific colleges, he'd like her to speak about herself. What were her interests and goals? What had her experience of the school been like? Who was in her family?

Nkese spoke readily, and Josh took notes on his white legal pad. Nkese had been born in Philadelphia. When she was very young, her family had lived in a large apartment in a neighborhood she remembered as quiet and safe, on Chestnut Street. Her father was a chef at a hotel and then worked at an airline. When Nkese was five and her brother Rasheed was four, their father was killed. Nkese did not want to say more about him.

Three years later, the family moved to Brooklyn, to the small apartment in East Flatbush where they now lived. Nkese's mother, Peggy, worked a night shift as a nurse's aide, and usually arrived home around midnight. Nkese and Rasheed shared responsibility for housework and for taking care of their younger sister, Risa. Nkese also worked up to fifteen hours each week at McDonald's to earn extra cash.

At the age of thirteen, Nkese told Josh, she had decided that she would be "the girl who gets out of the 'hood." Her test scores in elementary school had been "through the roof." In middle school she had been admitted into a specialized program, but, she said, she was distracted by socializing. She knew by eighth grade that she "had to shape it up" if she was going to make it to college. "I used to say I was going to Princeton," she said.

Nkese had started at the Secondary School for Research in ninth grade determined to "do something constructive" for her future. But instead of the high school experience she envisioned, Nkese found "a lot of confusion." In 2001, three existing middle schools had been combined into one and moved to the John Jay building. As the old John Jay High School was phased out class by class, the new school would grow into a school for grades six through twelve. In 2003, when Nkese entered ninth grade, this new school, the Secondary School for Law, Journalism and Research, was divided into three separate schools. Students and staff still remaining from the old John Jay were randomly distributed among the three schools.

The result, in Nkese's account, was chaos. There were "fights through lunch, things of that nature." Teachers came and went throughout the year, and kids "passed their classes by luck." Nkese remembered her first year of high school as mostly wasted time. "I knew there was something wrong with our education, I knew it from day one," Nkese said. "I knew we weren't learning what high schoolers were supposed to learn."

Jill Bloomberg began as principal during Nkese's sophomore year. Nkese saw that Jill was determined to create order and structure at the school and was willing to involve students in making change. In the absence of student government, Nkese and her group of friends took it upon themselves to be the voice of student opinion. Nkese would create surveys and petitions that she would distribute among her peers, then present her findings to the school leadership. Nkese and Jill often disagreed, and Nkese felt bitter when her proposals were not accepted. She felt that the administration "really treated us like kids, and we had to fight for everything."

In tenth grade, Nkese said, "we advocated for a little bit of flexibility in our schedules. That was something that most high schoolers have, and we didn't see why we didn't." In eleventh grade, Nkese focused on what the school lacked in preparing students for college. An after-school program offered an SAT class for the Secondary School for Law, and Nkese pushed to open spots for students from the Secondary School for Research. She knew from TV, she said, that she should take the SAT in eleventh grade and was angry that, the previous year, she had been advised to wait until twelfth.

One of Nkese's strongest desires was for Advanced Placement (AP) classes, a campaign she and her friends had also waged during their junior year. Josh had spoken with the principal, Jill, during the summer before his arrival about the decision to offer AP courses. The Department of Education was creating shared AP programs in buildings that housed several high schools, and the Secondary School for Research could opt in. Jill was ambivalent: she preferred classes that reached students at multiple skill levels to those that pulled out the top performers. Every student should have access to college preparatory classes, she believed, just as every student should have access to college. But Jill had finally agreed to offer the AP classes: as she and Josh had discussed, they were an opportunity to communicate, to students and colleges, that kids at the Secondary School for Research were capable of advanced academic work. To Nkese, this was a chance finally to take what she knew were "real" college preparatory classes, with the same curricula offered by top high schools.

As a senior now, Nkese was proud of the ways she and her friends had helped to improve the Secondary School for Research. The school was "a totally different world from when I was a freshman," she told Josh. This fall, she was enrolled in AP English Language and Composition and AP U.S. History, and now they even had a college counselor. But these changes also drove home the anger Nkese felt when she looked back on the gaps in her high school education. Josh was struck by the way her resentment seemed to extend even to the younger students who would have opportunities she didn't. "Everything we did helped other students," she said when she reflected back, "but at the same time we didn't reap most of those benefits."

Nkese's goal in the college process was to "get out of here": to leave New York City. Nobody in the previous year's graduating class had gone to a residential college. Before Josh arrived, the college process had been handled by the school's general guidance counselor, Alissa Lembo, in addition to all her other responsibilities. Alissa had attended several relevant trainings that year and worked hard to help support students. Sixty percent had been accepted to college, the vast majority to the City University of New York (CUNY), which includes both four-year and two-year options. Nkese said she would not be applying to CUNY schools. There was nothing wrong with them, but they would be like "thirteenth grade," just a continuation of high school.

Josh asked Nkese if there were any schools she had in mind. She mentioned Temple University, in Philadelphia, and the State University of New York (SUNY) at Albany, which her class had visited on a bus trip the previous year, led by a teacher who was an alumna. Nkese had not heard of most private colleges other than those in the Ivy League.

Before the meeting, Josh had given some thought to how strong a candidate Nkese would be at selective liberal arts colleges. Though he hadn't met her, he had looked over her test scores and transcript and spoken with some of her teachers. Josh had been shocked to see the low grades many students received, and Nkese's transcript had stood out, with a cumulative average over 90 percent. Nkese's tenth grade history teacher told Josh that Nkese was the best student she had ever had. Though the teacher had a graduate degree in history, she said that every night she had to "go home and prepare for Nkese," who would read ahead and come to class with challenging questions. Jill Bloomberg described how, during her sophomore year, Nkese and a small group of students organized the most impressive "student action" she had ever witnessed. A white student new to the school had made racist comments and some students were threatening to beat him up. Instead of letting the situation escalate into violence, Nkese and her friends demanded that the principal call an emergency assembly to discuss the issue and stood with the white student on stage as he made a formal apology.

At the same time that they recognized her drive, intelligence, and leadership qualities, the teachers and administrators Josh spoke with about Nkese expressed reservations about her skills and her attitude. Though her SAT scores were just above the school's average, they were unimpressive by national standards: a 400 in Critical Reading, and a 430 in Math, putting her in the lowest quartile nationally. Her English teacher, Menucha Stubenhaus, described the ways Nkese had trouble accepting criticism and help, especially with her writing, which was full of basic grammatical errors. She described Nkese as "sassy" and disrespectful of authority. Menucha had been a New York City Teaching Fellow at the school during Nkese's chaotic first year and was still stung by the moment when Nkese interrupted her class by saying, "Miss, you're thin . . . but you're a little thick in the thighs."

Josh had little sense of where Nkese could get in to college and even less of where she could thrive. But speaking with her in person for the first time, he was captivated by Nkese's passion for education in the face of so many obstacles and imagined she would create a strong impression at admissions interviews. He would describe her, he thought, as what admissions officers call an "impact student," somebody who would build positive change in campus life. Her writing skills would be a concern, but he had not yet seen an example beyond her e-mail messages. He now realized that these were sent from a phone, the primary way students at the Secondary School for Research accessed e-mail, and reflected conventions of text-messaging that were still new to him.

Josh typed up a list of colleges that he thought might be possible for Nkese. Through his work with the scholarship students at Birch Wathen Lenox, he had become familiar with New York State programs that offer funding and support for low-income students: the Higher Education Opportunity Program (HEOP) at private colleges and the Educational Opportunity Program (EOP) at colleges that are part of the State University of New York (SUNY). He had also spent time that summer calling admissions contacts to tell them about his new job and to express the hope that their colleges would continue to work with him. He focused his attention on schools that did not prioritize SAT scores, which he knew would be low among his new students, and those that he knew had made a commitment to recruiting students of color.

The list Josh handed Nkese began, "Mr. Steckel suggests Nkese take a look at . . ." It included Union College, SUNY Binghamton, Syracuse University, and the University of Rochester, all in New York State, as well as small liberal arts colleges in Pennsylvania and Connecticut: Dickinson, Franklin and Marshall, Muhlenberg, Trinity, and Connecticut College. He asked Nkese if she might consider women's colleges or those as far away as Maine. "Sure," she said. "I'll look at anything."

As Nkese remembered, she took home the list and sat down at the family's computer. She was glad to be able to do this while her mother was at work. Peggy had made it clear that she wanted Nkese to stay in New York City for college or at least go to a college no more than three hours away. "When I was younger I wanted to go to school in Boston, that was the dream," Nkese said. "Then I realized it was too far away, and I let it go."

Peggy was very protective and strict with all her children, and especially with Nkese, her eldest daughter. Her parenting style reflected her West Indian upbringing, but her fear came from the trauma of her husband's violent death. She wanted to know where Nkese was at all times and didn't want her to date. Nkese kept the fact that she'd had a boyfriend since the previous spring a secret. While Nkese kept up with her homework and family responsibilities, she and Peggy often battled, especially over Nkese's ideas about her future. Before her father's death, Nkese remembered, "there was a certain life plan: go to private school, then go on to med school." Private school had to be abandoned, but her mother still held on to the idea that Nkese would become a doctor. "I was leaning toward film, psychology, fashion, pre-law," Nkese said. Nkese felt she had always taken charge of her own choices in her education, with or without her mother's support. "I chose the high school I wanted, I chose the junior high I wanted. I can't wait around for other people's approval, I just do what I have to do." Still, she knew it would be difficult to go against her mother's desire for her to attend college close to home.

Nkese typed the names of the colleges from the list Josh gave her into Google and browsed through their websites. Images appeared of students reading on green lawns, peering into microscopes, and rowing on rivers, overlaid with words like "think," "explore," "discover." She remembers thinking how beautiful the campuses looked, and wondering if she could get in.

Then she clicked on a link that showed tuition. All of the schools cost at least $40,000 per year, more than Nkese's mother earned annually to support her family of four. Her father had set aside a small fund for Nkese's education, but it would quickly disappear, and what would she live on? Even with financial aid, she would leave school with enormous debt. Clearly Josh had no idea what life was like for kids like her. How could you do this to me? she thought.

Nkese went back to Josh's office the next day. She told him that she would not be able to afford the colleges on the list. Josh tried to explain how financial aid worked: that it was "need-based" and that concern about cost should not prevent her from applying. He could tell that Nkese was skeptical about what he was saying. But he also felt confident that she was determined to get to college and would do whatever it took to make it happen.

He soon saw how rare this attitude was among the seniors. Once a week, they were now required to attend his college seminar, which was held in the science lab. Josh stood in the front of the room, facing students at three rows of black lab tables. Behind them was a large aquarium filled with piles of leaf litter taken from nearby Prospect Park for a unit on the habitats of insects.

Josh began the class with the question, "Why college?" He distributed a handout in which he had done his best to articulate the value of college for his new students:

College is a place where you develop and explore your potential, where you gain knowledge about yourself and the world around you, and where you acquire the tools and the credentials that will make the dreams you have about your future possible.

College is about your education, first and foremost. A college education helps you acquire a range of knowledge in many subjects, as well as advanced knowledge in the specific subjects you are most interested in; a college education will increase your ability to think abstractly and critically, to express thoughts clearly in speech and in writing, and to make careful decisions.

It's a cliché, but this knowledge is power. Unlike other things in the world, a college degree, and the knowledge it represents, once acquired, cannot be taken away from you. And a college education provides you with credentials that will open doors for you when you enter the world outside of school.

In the next section of the handout, he inserted graphs and data that outlined the economic benefits of a college degree. According to statistics from 2001, a college graduate earned 70 percent more than a high school graduate.[4] The unemployment rate for high school dropouts was four times the rate for college graduates, as reported by the Center for Labor Market Studies at Northeastern University in 2004.[5] The U.S. Department of Labor issued data showing that 70 percent of the thirty fastest growing jobs would require education beyond high school, and 40 percent of all new jobs would require at least an associate's degree.[6]

Going to college would not only benefit them personally, Josh told his new students, but was crucial to building a more equitable society. He cited statistics that had helped convince him to shift away from private school work: according to a Century Foundation study published in 2004, the nation's 146 most selective colleges drew 74 percent of their population from the country's wealthiest quartile, the income bracket occupied by most Birch Wathen Lenox families. Only 3 percent of their students came from the country's poorest quartile, as did the majority of students at the Secondary School for Research.[7] It was these selective colleges that were training the country's future leaders, Josh told his classes, and it wasn't right that they should be filled with rich kids. By applying to college, the Secondary School for Research students would help to work against this injustice and find paths to the meaningful, influential roles in society that they deserved.

In the discussions and writing assignments that followed his presentations, Josh tried to get a sense of how his students were responding. There was a core group of seniors intent on getting started with the college process. Along with Nkese, the group included her close friends Candace Jones, the daughter of a teacher and a pastor, and Boris Komarovskiy, who was born in St. Petersburg and whose ambition, he said, was to own the New York Knicks. There was also a group of motivated new immigrant kids, including Roshney Licorish, who had arrived the year before from Barbados and who loved science; Audry Hines, who had just arrived from Costa Rica and still struggled with English; Emilia Strzalkowska, from Poland, who learned English from the copy of *Gone with the Wind* she carried around with her; and Zhi Chao Zhou, from China, who won the hearts of his friends and teachers with his sincerity and humor.

Another set of students echoed Josh's pitch for why college was important, writing in response to the prompt "Why college?" answers like, "To set a good example for my younger brother," "To get a good job," "To help my family have a better life." But when Josh spoke to many of them individually, they voiced doubt about whether they would go to college at all. Melida Medina, a serious student, told Josh she was not sure her mother would let her go. Melida unofficially shared her mother's job as a home attendant, and her mother relied on the hours Melida worked. Ravell Robinson, a pensive guitar player, poet, and fan of alternative music, talked about his desire to expand his intellectual horizons, but seemed crippled by his struggles as an overweight teen with writer's block and difficulty taking tasks to completion. Erica Silvestri's father was incarcerated and her brother had just returned from college without completing the first year; while Erica wanted to apply, she feared what she might experience herself.

Some students responded enthusiastically to the idea that they could go to college, but didn't seem to understand how their performance in school affected their college choices. Kory Fleurima was charming but often disruptive in his classes. He skipped the first two sessions of Josh's college seminar but sent Josh a message on his Sidekick: "o and one question what are my chances of getting into college with my grades being tha way they are and my SAT scores but I don't remember what my exact score was????"

Kirk Hillaire, a good-looking, soft-spoken boy who loved basket-ball, had reading and writing skills that were below grade level but began approaching Josh with questions about where he could go. Krystle Guejuste was a fierce, engaging student who had led a protest in partnership with the American Civil Liberties Union in response to the previous year's cell phone ban in schools. Josh learned from Jill that early in high school, Krystle had walked into the principal's office to ask if she could enroll at the Second-ary School for Research: the school she attended, she explained, was failing, and she wanted the chance to get a good education. Krystle was one of the most vocal participants in the seminar when she was present, but this was only about half the time. Josh also learned from Jill that Krystle led a life of extreme instability, without a reliable place to live.

Other students simply cut the class, which was not required for graduation, or tuned it out. One of these was Dwight Martin, who always sat in the back of the college seminar, usually with his head down on the table. Sometimes he would get up and leave in the middle of class, other times he would not show up at all.

Josh tried to resist the impulse to ignore Dwight, who was rarely disruptive. Josh's goal, and the goal of the school, was to make college a choice for all students. Many Secondary School for Research students clearly did not see college as a viable option or fully understand how it could benefit them. Josh wanted to ap-proach his new students with the same assumption he brought to his students at Birch Wathen Lenox: that after their high school graduations, they would continue their education in ways that helped them hone their talents and pursue their dreams. It was his job to help every student understand how to make this possible, even those who seemed to show no interest.

One day Josh decided to cold call Dwight, as he had often done at Birch Wathen Lenox to rouse students who weren't pay-ing attention. Dwight jolted up when Josh called on him. His af-fect changed completely, his slouchy, relaxed demeanor becoming tense and confrontational as he stood up. "Why are you blowing up my spot?" he yelled at Josh, and left the room.

Josh was rattled. He spoke about Dwight with Alissa, the school's guidance counselor, who to Josh's surprise described him as a sweet kid who was always looking to help other people. During one of the application work sessions he held during the seminar, Josh approached Dwight and asked why he didn't participate in class.

One on one, Dwight was responsive and respectful. He told Josh that the college seminar made him feel terrible. He especially hated hearing the statistics Josh presented about what life looked like without a college degree: unemployment, low-paying jobs, or jail. This was something he and his friends already knew. He used to think he would go to college, Dwight said, but that was the past. "I used to be a good student," he said. "I used to be a football star." That life had ended in middle school. Dwight blamed his failure on himself, the school, and the pull of "the street."

Josh told Dwight he could still go to college. A number of CUNY colleges were open to all high school graduates, and if Dwight had been such a good student in the past, it must mean he had ability and potential. He could start at a community college and, if he did well, transfer to somewhere more competitive. Why not at least fill out the application? Dwight just shook his head.

Following this conversation, Dwight still did not participate in the college seminar. But he would stop and talk to Josh in the halls, sometimes while he was skipping other classes. Whenever Josh pushed him to apply to college, Dwight would refer back to how successful he used to be, and how college wasn't possible anymore.

Though thinking about the past clearly brought Dwight down, it was something he couldn't seem to stop doing. He reminded Josh of Milkman, a character from Toni Morrison's *Song of Solomon*. As a young child, Milkman sat wedged in a backward position between his parents during their Sunday drives:

But riding backward made him uneasy. It was like flying blind, and not knowing where he was going—just where he had been—troubled him. He did not want to see trees that he had passed, or houses and children slipping into the space the automobile had left behind.

In a later passage, Morrison describes how this uneasy position defines the way Milkman sees his life: "It was becoming a habit—this concentration on things behind him. Almost as though there were no future to be had."[8]

Josh kept encouraging Dwight but knew his words were formulaic. Dwight's oblique comments suggested fear of imminent violence, and he needed a kind of counseling Josh couldn't offer. Josh had sometimes helped boys in trouble at Birch Wathen Lenox. The year before, a student who was the son of a prominent lawyer had begun abusing drugs as a senior, and his family feared he was sabotaging his future. Josh talked to this other boy about the issues he was struggling through, and now he was in his first year of college. But Josh knew little about how to help Dwight, whose problems he had no way to imagine.

Dwight remembered that when Josh first came to the Secondary School for Research, "like anybody new, when they first come into the scene, we're like yeah, whatever, nobody *really* cares about us. It's just like, who's this new guy?" There were the good students, and then the kids like him, who "would cut class and hang out in the hallway." Dwight had once been the other kind of student. But by senior year of high school, he said, "I felt like I screwed up so bad that I couldn't fix it." As he faced the end of his education, he became consumed by regret. "I could have been somewhere great," he said. "It's almost hard to explain it sometimes."

Dwight had spent most of his childhood living with his grandmother in Park Slope. His parents, a police officer and a health care administrator, lived separately from him in Canarsie, a middle- and working-class Brooklyn neighborhood distant from Park Slope and from the gentrification that had transformed many parts of Brooklyn. Dwight's parents had made this split in part so that he could attend PS 321, the highly regarded Park Slope school a few blocks away from John Jay on Seventh Avenue. Dwight's parents came to see him every day, and he remembered elementary school as a time when they rode bikes with him and took him to museums. For middle school, Dwight was accepted to the accelerated program at MS 51, another prized local school.

During middle school Dwight and his parents began to battle. Dwight was growing taller and beginning to experiment with baggy pants and a tougher demeanor. His parents came down hard on him, pushing him to work more in school, warning him about the consequences of making the wrong kinds of friends. Dwight resented their criticizing him and telling him what to do. Though they had stayed involved in his life, he felt they had distanced themselves from him, that they "weren't being parents." Their visits began to turn into fights. Every day, he said, "they used to jump down my throat." He would especially "get into it" with his mother. "I guess it was because me and my mom didn't really click, or I just wanted to do my own thing."

The conflict took on an intensity that Dwight found hard to explain, even to himself. He was frightened by his own suppressed anger. "Do you know how it feels to be so angry at a person and there's nothing you can do about it? I was angry to the point where I wanted to go ahead and punch you in the face. I was mad to the point where I was going to fight. Right here, right now, I don't care if I lose." He found relief when he began to confide in two friends, who told him they had similar problems. The three began cutting school and smoking weed. It was the only thing, Dwight said, that gave him a break from being "so stressed and upset all the time."

As Dwight remembered, the changes in his life that followed were swift and traumatic. At first he was "just hanging out in the street" with his friends. And then: "What happened? We started hanging out with gang members. I'm chilling with Bloods, and Crips." By seventh grade, he said, "we were out there smoking weed, we might go to parties, we might be drunk. We were out doing stuff we really shouldn't have been doing, because we were with much older kids. We saw so many people get robbed, and attacked. I had guns stuck to my head, guns pulled on me. It was horrible."

Dwight was careful to conceal his new life from his parents. "Nobody really knew what we were doing, because then it wouldn't have been allowed. We weren't stupid about it." At the same time, he felt hurt that they didn't seem to notice what he was going through. "That's why I tell a lot of parents, watch your kids. Seriously, take care of them, and make them feel like they can speak to you about stuff. Don't pressure them too much. If you do, make sure you push them in the right direction."

Dwight remembered his experiences through middle school as a painful loss of innocence. "It was a huge turnaround. You get forced to become somebody that maybe you weren't in the beginning. That's kind of what happened to me." There was a time in elementary school, he said, when his friends asked him, "How come you never say 'nigga'?" He responded, "Man, why did our ancestors fight for hundreds of years to get rights, and not to be called that, why the hell would I say that now?" For Dwight, this memory described a worldview that was now lost. "That was me in *fifth grade*. I was just so pure. I never said the n word. I never said nothing. I never *hurt* nothing. Then look what happened. I'm running around just like everybody else, 'Hey, what's up, nigga,' 'what's up, my nigga.'"

By the time he entered high school at the Secondary School for Research, Dwight saw the world around him defined by violence and hopelessness, something that people like Josh were oblivious to even as it surrounded them. "Do you know what it's like to go up against somebody who doesn't care if they lose their own life? Do you know how that would feel? Somebody puts a gun to you, and you're just like, I wish you would, and really mean it? You're not going to do nothing to me but put me out of my own misery. You know how many people are walking around like that? Even Park Slope is bad."

Though Dwight blamed himself for making bad decisions, he saw his story as part of a pattern repeated among his peers. "When you feel like crap at home—even if it's just one person making you feel this way—sometimes when you're younger, you can't get away from it. So what do you do? You run to the streets and hang out with your friends. And even if you're not doing anything, you still get messed with. It's like, where do you go? Cops on my ass, other people who want to rob me, other people who want to fight for no damn reason."

For a young black teen, Dwight said, the experience of anger and meaninglessness was compounded by constant harassment from the police. Once, Dwight said, he was "in a cab with my girl, driving near East New York." The cab stopped at a stoplight, and "this cop pulls up next to the car, saying, 'You're going too fast.' He starts shining the light, and asks the cab driver, 'Who you got back there?' "

The cab driver told the police officer, "It's fine, just a guy and his girl coming home from the movies." The cop responded, "Yo, pull the fuck over," then came inside the car. "He was just rough-housing for no damn reason, throwing me around. That's the type of thing a lot of us go through. A lot of teachers at school, a lot of people, don't understand. It just sucks. I can't even count how many times I was put in handcuffs for no apparent reason."

Dwight said he knew it wasn't only white cops who roughed up black teens under the New York City Police Department's stop-and-frisk policy. His dad was a cop and insisted Dwight carry an ID with his father's NYPD badge number on it, part of an under-standing among police officers that they leave each others' kids alone, or settle it in the locker room. "After they find out my dad's a cop, they kind of sober up real quick, and then I might get let go. I wonder how many beatings it saved me. It's messed up."

Dwight said that in high school he "seemed more hard-core" than he was. Throughout his whole life, he was "just trying to slide by, be all right." In school, his grades were low, but he was doing what he needed to graduate: "I didn't want to work my butt off; I didn't want to be left behind." It was the same thing on the streets. "I always got out of doing anything. I would come up with something, so I didn't have to rob that guy." Dwight never joined a gang, but at the beginning of senior year, as his friends were starting to get deeper into "the life," he felt himself pulled along.

As Dwight sat in Josh's seminar with classmates focused on their path to college, he felt his life hurtling in a different direction, one he felt powerless to stop. "What's my future?" he remembered thinking. "I'm never going to have a great job, I'm never going to go anywhere. Maybe I'll be like every other black dude in the streets. I might sell drugs; I might get killed."

Dwight and Nkese were part of different social groups, but had become close friends the year before, when they were paired up on a bus trip to visit SUNY Albany. The visit had been their first college trip as a class, and Josh had heard about it from Jill, the principal. On the way, the bus had broken down, and the group arrived at the campus over an hour late. The boys had gone into the bathroom when they arrived. At the urinals, several started taking pictures of themselves with their cell phones. An admissions officer was in one of the stalls. When the students gathered for their information session, the first thing they heard was a lecture about their behavior. The class was exhausted by the long bus ride and indignant that all of the students were being reprimanded because a few kids had acted up. When they divided up for campus tours, most chatted instead of listening to the guide. Several kids from the two groups yelled to one another, flashing gang signs across the campus quad.

Though teachers and administrators had considered the Albany visit a failure, for Nkese and Dwight it had been a chance to bond. Nkese remembered that before this trip, Dwight "just seemed like all the other guys: a flirt, and jokey." Though she knew he was smart, he was one of the kids who never did his work. Nkese said that while she "was cool with these people," she "wasn't remotely best friends with them." Sitting next to each other on the long bus trip, Nkese and Dwight "started talking about personal stuff." She told Dwight about her new boyfriend, who went to another school. A lot of her guy friends didn't like him: they thought he was sneaky. Dwight talked about his girlfriend and about his problems with his parents.

Dwight didn't seem interested in talking about SUNY Albany or thinking about college at all. "I knew he had ambition," Nkese said, "but I was like, why don't you do your work? Just do your homework. He was like, 'I don't feel like it. I don't want to be a nerd.' "

After the trip, Dwight and Nkese began talking on the phone and sometimes hanging out outside of school. Their friendship was intense, the nightly phone calls alternating with periods when, for various reasons, Nkese said, she was mad at him and they stopped speaking. Nkese met Dwight's parents and felt confused by all he had told her about his troubles with them. While not well off, the family seemed "better off than most people" and to be close with one another. "Things are not always as they seem," Dwight told her. Nkese tried to involve Dwight in the life of the senior class, but he was "very disconnected from high school culture" and refused.

At the beginning of senior year, Nkese remembered, the friends in her group were focused on getting into college and moving out of their parents' homes. She described the sense of hope they felt as they began their AP classes and college applications. Finally, they "felt like real high school students."

For the AP class in English Language and Composition, students including Nkese, Candace, Boris, Melida, Ravell, and Erica walked down to the first floor of the building, together with students from the Secondary Schools for Law and Journalism. The course was intended as a college-level composition course, training students to analyze a writer's rhetorical strategies and to hone their own. The teacher, who came from the Secondary School for Journalism, announced that he would demand rigor and correctness in their work and behavior. Erica left the class in tears one day after the teacher yelled at her for sucking her thumb, a habit not uncommon among the female students. "Do you think you'll be able to sit there sucking your thumb in college?" he said.

Though Nkese was doing well in her AP U.S. history course, she remembered AP English as "too advanced for me to understand at the time." She saw the gaps in her ability to "construct a proper sentence and understand the flow of ideas." She couldn't follow the passages she had to analyze, and the teacher tore apart her writing. She blamed her education. "I didn't have those foundation skills. If I did get them, I never revisited them."

The hope of the year's beginning faded as Nkese saw that it was too late to recoup her educational losses. But she felt that there was still a chance to create a proper senior year. Nkese was part of the newly established Senior Committee and threw her energy into organizing activities. The seniors wanted to show the administration, Nkese said, that they were "just as capable as adults." For the yearbook, she took charge of the senior photos, learning "to contact companies and let them know what I want and when I want it, and when we should set up a date to talk." Though they would need school approval, members of the Senior Committee settled on the events they would "fight for" that year: a senior trip to Florida, a spring barbecue, a big prom, and a traditional graduation in a big hall. To raise money for these events, the committee organized its first event: a Halloween dance for all three schools.

Josh worked late the evening of the dance. When he left his office the cafeteria was transformed, hung with black streamers and balloons. Aundre Walker, a senior who had told Josh about his work as a DJ at clubs and parties, stood at a turntable mixing reggaeton, pop, and hip-hop, joking with the crowd over the microphone.

Josh stood in the doorway of the cafeteria. In school, his students were often uncertain, negative, slumped in their seats. "I don't do anything, I don't have any interests, I hate school," so many of them had said in their individual meetings. Here, together at a successful event they had organized themselves, he saw another side of them. "Come on, Mr. Steckel, dance," they yelled above the music.

Josh enjoyed watching the students but also felt uneasy. The next morning, many of these seniors were scheduled to take the SATs. Helping students register for a test date and select a testing site had consumed almost all of Josh's time for two weeks in September, but he hadn't made the connection with the date of the dance. The test began at 8 a.m., and students would have to wake up early to travel to their test sites, which, for most, meant making long trips before sunrise by public transportation, something many parents were reluctant to let them do. Lack of sleep would be one more factor driving down their scores.

Nkese had known that the date selected for the dance was the night before the SATs, but didn't see that as a reason to change it. "I wanted to make my senior year more memorable. I'd rather put energy into that than into a test I know I wasn't going to do better on." The after-school SAT prep course she had taken had been "helpful in the sense that it got me acquainted with material. But if you miss the basics you'll never be able to build on them."

Nkese arrived at the test exhausted. "At that time I didn't stay up late on Fridays, so it was weird to go home at ten or eleven o'clock." She remembers that she fell asleep during one of the writing and one of the critical reading sections. "I remember Boris sitting behind me, poking me with a pencil. My attitude was, I just want to get this over with. I kind of wanted to just leave the exam. I don't think I completed the test."

When Nkese received her scores two weeks later, they were slightly higher than her previous test, but still far lower than the averages for students admitted to the kinds of schools she hoped to attend. At that point, Nkese said, she knew for certain "that I didn't have an equal chance of doing as well as I should in the college process. I felt terrible. I was just like, fuck this." Nkese stopped coming into Josh's office and started to slack in her classes and to arrive at school late.

Josh was baffled by Nkese's reaction to the SAT. It felt so extreme. The student who had been the most eager to start the college process and motivate her classmates to do the same seemed now to have abandoned it suddenly and completely, at the crucial moment. He understood that the low scores were demoralizing, but most of the colleges on her list didn't even require the SAT.

Nkese remembered November and December as a "bad season." Her SAT scores, alongside her struggles in her AP English class, showed her that whatever she had done to try to improve her education had come too late. Even if she got into college, she wasn't prepared, and probably wouldn't be able to afford to pay. On top of this, Nkese was breaking up with her boyfriend of six months and conflicts within her social group were intensifying. Two girls who had been her close friends would no longer speak with her, angry at the role she had played in a conflict over boyfriends and a threat from another girl. There were "a lot of phone calls, going to people's houses, a lot of emotional stress, almost a confrontation."

Nkese responded by withdrawing from her social as well as her academic life. She now had a part-time job at Waldbaum's and picked up extra shifts there. "I just kept a low profile, doing my own thing, distancing myself from friends." An exception was Dwight, who was removed from the social drama. He became a steady source of support, "one of those people really cheering me up." Dwight encouraged her to get back on the path to college, saying, "You can do this, you're a smart girl."

Nkese's depression eventually began to lift. A couple of weeks into December, she said, "I did a day. I did something different with my hair, bought more clothes, spent money on myself." On her eighteenth birthday her friends threw her a party. "Once we got there, everybody got me pumped."

Nkese told her friends she still wasn't sure about college. Maybe it made more sense to take time off and look for a way to learn through experience. She was good at drawing clothes, and "very critical" of movies. She thought about seeking an apprenticeship or freelance work in fashion or film. Deadlines for college applications were just a couple weeks away, and she had not even begun.

Nkese's friends convinced her to make one last push. She came to Josh's office a few days before the December break. Her biggest task was the essay for the Common Application, the centralized form accepted by most selective colleges. "Just write whatever comes to your mind," she remembers her AP English teacher telling her, but she couldn't come up with anything. "I'm only going to apply to schools that don't require an essay," she told Josh.

Nkese remembered sitting with Candace and Aundre, both of whom had completed their applications, and feeling frustrated. "Why do you want to go to college?" they asked her, trying to help her get started.

Nkese thought back to the end of middle school, when she had first decided that she would be the girl who got out. It was sort of like now, she told them. All the kids had been angry at the school for making them go to a farm for their eighth grade trip: they wanted to go somewhere more fun, like Great Adventure. They weren't handing in their homework, and their teacher was fed up. He asked what they thought they would do with their lives. One girl said she wanted to be a model. "Too late," the teacher said, "you're not tall or skinny enough. What's your backup plan?" She said she might become a forensic scientist, like on the television show *CSI*. He said it was too late for that, too: "You don't know enough about science." Kids like them, the teacher told the twelve- and thirteen-year-olds, would probably end up pregnant or addicted to drugs.

Candace and Aundre encouraged her to start writing, and Nkese sat down with a pen and piece of loose-leaf paper. At the end of the period, she brought what she had written to Josh. "You wrote this just now?" he said. Josh proofread it with her and made suggestions for rearranging the essay. She titled the final draft "Motivation":

"All you kids are going to do is drop out and get pregnant or get hooked on drugs," my eighth grade teacher said to us. I do not want to be part of that stereotype of young black females. I feel I have something to offer to the world. But opportunities for underprivileged kids like me are limited. For me, education is the only chance I have to make it out of poverty. I want to take advantage of the opportunity to receive a college education. Unfortunately, there are obstacles I have to overcome to achieve the success I dream of.

Growing up in New York City has been very difficult. Prior to my coming to New York City, my father died; this changed my life forever. I came from Philadelphia (at the age of eight) with only my mother, brother, and sister. We left our home and moved to an apartment in Brooklyn. I was not used to living in an urban setting like East Flatbush. I eventually grew into apartment life, even though I had little space to play in with my siblings.

As I became a teenager, my mother was all I had to depend on for emotional, physical, and mental support. Seeing me succeed in school made her happy. I strive to succeed in school because I am motivated to break the cycle of poverty, but my most important motivation is to make my mom happy. Most of my success in school can be attributed to having a solid foundation at home.

It isn't going to be easy to leave East Flatbush. It is my neighborhood, and I have plenty of memories and friends. My neighborhood is my comfort zone; there, I feel that being me is right, because everyone is the same in a way. I know that going to college will take me away from home and my comfort zone. But I want to go to college to introduce myself to the real world and face diversity.

College is going to help me mature into the best woman I can be. I do not want college to change me immediately, and I know it will not. I know that change will happen gradually, over time. My college experience will influence and shape me, but I am not going to college to change my personality. I am going to college to bring me closer to the life I desire.

I want to be somebody. I say that a lot to people. They are just words, because they do not mean anything yet. I don't have the 99 average or a 2300 on SATs, and I didn't have certain educational opportunities because of my financial status. I just have motivation, which is my burning light inside of me. It makes me feel like I can conquer the world.

Susan Sontag said, "I was not looking for my dreams to interpret my life, but rather for my life to interpret my dreams." This quote is very inspirational to me. My success in life will decide if my dreams come true. This is why college is so important to me. I want success, but I need a road to that place. The road starts with college.

Through Christmas and New Year's, Josh e-mailed back and forth with Nkese, helping her edit her supplemental essays and request last-minute letters of recommendation from teachers. By early January, Nkese had submitted applications to Wheaton, Bates, Bowdoin, Simmons, Hobart and William Smith, and Mount Holyoke—all small private colleges—along with SUNY colleges at Buffalo, Oneonta, Geneseo, and New Paltz. Nkese was relieved: the applications were done. But she had little sense of what, if anything, would happen to them.

A few weeks later, Nkese remembered, "someone from a college wrote back to me." "Dear Nkese," she recalled the letter as saying. "I was very touched by your essay. I hope to see you." It was signed Carmita McCoy, associate dean for multicultural enrollment at Bates College in Lewiston, Maine.

Nkese said that the letter "just blew me away. It was handwritten, so I knew it meant something." She had long held on to the idea of college, but it had seemed increasingly disconnected from her daily life, where all the signs were pointing in a different direction. Now, a voice from the world of elite schools, a real person, was responding. Maybe I can do this, she thought.

In January, on Martin Luther King Jr. Day weekend, selective liberal arts colleges often set aside one or two days to interview candidates in New York City. While students have opportunities to schedule interviews earlier in the process, New York City is an important region, and colleges want to ensure that they meet with promising candidates. Interview events target applicants from high schools with whom colleges have strong relationships, as well as multicultural applicants who might otherwise be missed. That year, Josh's students attended interviews with alumni and admissions officers from Skidmore, Hobart and William Smith, Union, Wheaton, and St. Lawrence.

Nkese's first interview was for Wheaton, a small liberal arts college in Norton, Massachusetts, south of Boston. Josh went with her, as did Roshney, who had arrived from Barbados the year before, and Melida, who worked with her mother as a home attendant. They traveled on the number 4 train, as Josh had on his former commute, to the Hewitt School, a college preparatory school for girls on the Upper East Side, where the interviews were held. "This is a school?" one of the students said, as they entered the converted townhouse with its carpeted waiting area, gold-framed oil paintings, and shiny wall sconces. One of Josh's former Birch Wathen Lenox students, dressed in a preppy blazer, was also waiting for an interview. Nkese, Roshney, and Melida watched as Josh greeted him, and as he shook hands with the Wheaton admissions counselor.

Josh had developed a friendly relationship with this admissions counselor while at Birch Wathen Lenox, and now Josh felt anxious about how his new students would be viewed. The Birch Wathen Lenox applicants who had gone to Wheaton had largely been B and C students whom Josh hoped would develop their passions and work ethic within the college's nurturing environment. By comparison, Nkese, Roshney, and Melida seemed like superstars. As seniors, all three were earning mostly A's. Roshney lit up when Josh described his memories of organic chemistry, which he had taken as a student at Duke. She had lived most of her life in Barbados with her grandmother and aunt, who had treated Roshney as a kind of servant, when she wanted nothing more than to be able to study. As a senior, Melida was earning a 90 average while working twenty-four hours each week, including a shift as a home attendant from 8 p.m. to 8 a.m. every Wednesday. But all three brought to the interview the hallmarks of low-income students: low SAT scores, grammatical errors in their speech and writing, and full financial need.

When the interviews were over the admissions counselor took Josh aside. All the students had impressed him, especially Nkese. "We have to have her," he said. "That's funny," Nkese said when Josh told her this. "He said he just wanted to make sure I knew there would be places in Norton I could get my hair and nails done." On the walk to the subway she and the other students seemed to walk taller, Roshney teetering in her borrowed heels.

For admissions offices, February is "reading season." In late January, Josh began making calls to advocate for his students with the specific admissions counselors who would read their applications and present their cases before "committee," where many final decisions are made. Admissions officers are generally more responsive to calls from high schools with whom they have relationships, or, as Josh hoped now that he had moved to an unknown school, from counselors they know personally.

At Birch Wathen Lenox, Josh had approached these "counselor calls" with several goals. One was to check that applications were complete and address any logistical issues. Another was to slow down the reading process: with the admissions counselor's attention on the phone, Josh could ensure that what was compelling about each student came across clearly. The calls gave him the opportunity to respond directly to any concerns an admissions counselor expressed, including those issues the counselor anticipated might arise for other members of the admissions committee.

As committee neared, Josh made follow-up calls to advocate more aggressively for particular students, offering updates about a student's academic and extracurricular achievements. Sometimes he shared information about which students were likely to attend the college if admitted and made a case for why these students would be a good fit. Josh would also follow up after committee to get informal reports of outcomes. Knowing which kids were all set, and which required continued advocacy, would help him to manage his time through February and March.

Josh remembered the first counselor call he sat in on, part of his training at Birch Wathen Lenox. It had been unnerving to understand the extent to which a counselor's advocacy could make a difference in a student's outcomes. He sat across the desk from Curtis March, head of the Upper School, while he called Tulane University in New Orleans on behalf of one of the seniors.

Curtis held the phone a little away from his ear so Josh could hear both sides of the conversation.

"I think he's a little on the weak end," the admissions officer said. "His SAT scores are lower than I'd like to see."

Curtis described the boy's strengths: his interest in the arts, rigorous course load, and impact on the life of the school community. "We have a lot of faith in him," he said.

"You think we should take him?" the admission officer said.

"Yes," said Curtis.

When Curtis got off the phone he laughed. "They'll take him," he said.

For Nkese, Josh called the dean of admissions at Bowdoin College, Bill Shain. At Birch Wathen Lenox, Josh had invited Bill, then dean of undergraduate admissions at Vanderbilt University, to be a keynote speaker for Birch Wathen Lenox's annual college night. The evening program for parents was followed by dinner with Upper and Middle School heads and their spouses at a high-end restaurant, paid for by the school. There, Josh and Bill shared personal and professional stories and cemented their connection. Bill told Josh that he was coming to New York that winter and would be happy to interview Nkese while he was there.

Like the handwritten letter from Bates and the Wheaton interview, the meeting with Bill seemed to transform Nkese's attitude. She carried herself with less defensiveness and spoke in a measured way about the merits of different colleges and what she might want to study. There was a strange power, Josh observed, in these moments of human connection, when adults expressed faith in her future. By the end of January, Nkese had told Josh she had settled on Bowdoin and Wheaton as her first choices and Bates as her second.

As he was in the midst of helping students prepare for interviews in January, Josh received a call from Dwight's mother. She had just realized that Dwight had not applied to any colleges or taken the SAT, and she was very upset. Josh felt responsible: he hadn't even checked and had never called Dwight's home. If Dwight had been a student at Birch Wathen Lenox, there was no way this oversight would have occurred. The deadline to register for the January SAT had passed, so over the phone, Josh helped Dwight's mother understand how he could take the test as a standby student. His mother promised that Dwight would come in to work on his applications.

No classes were held during the last week in January, when many students took the New York State Regents exams, the set of standardized tests required for graduation from public schools. For three days at the end of the month, Dwight arrived at Josh's office in the morning and stayed until Josh left at 5 or 6 p.m. At his mother's insistence, Dwight completed the Common Application, the CUNY and SUNY applications, and applications for several public colleges in North Carolina, where he had relatives. Dwight wrote his personal essay about helping his mother develop a workout plan and his own interest in personal training as a possible career. It was new and surprising to see Dwight engaged in school-related work. He seemed to have little sense of where he wanted to go, but to enjoy the process, sometimes taking breaks to talk with Josh.

Josh was thrilled finally to have Dwight's attention. But Josh worried about whether he was using his own time productively in spending so much of it with Dwight. The North Carolina applications were unfamiliar and full of snags, and he knew Dwight's grades were too low for any of the schools that used the Common Application, which had multiple essays and required intensive work. It seemed more urgent to help other students complete applications due in early February and to confront the next stage of the process that for Josh was new and complex: helping students to manage financial aid applications.

At Birch Wathen Lenox, the end of January marked a shift in the application cycle to which Josh had grown accustomed: applications had been submitted, the seniors relaxed a little bit, and Josh could focus on advocacy with colleges and on work with the juniors. At the Secondary School for Research, the intensity of the application process continued. Through February, Josh's office was filled with students tracking down the documentation they needed for the Free Application for Federal Student Aid (FAFSA), for New York State's Tuition Assistance Program (TAP) application, and for the College Search Service (CSS) Profile. Without sufficient financial aid, any offers of admission would be irrelevant: getting in wouldn't matter if students couldn't afford to go.

Josh quickly realized that he needed to sit with individual students to help them through each task. At Birch Wathen Lenox, most students had not applied for financial aid, and those families that did handled it themselves. Now Josh found himself pushing students to gather sensitive personal and financial information from their parents. Seniors sat in Josh's office to call their parents and ask them, without preliminaries, for the balance in their checking and savings accounts, for the month and year of a separation or divorce, or for information about whether the family received food stamps or other public benefits, prompting confused or suspicious responses. Parents were often reluctant to release private information to colleges and uncertain what results, if any, the process would yield for their children.

Josh tried to meet with parents in person, but this could be difficult to arrange. Peggy, Nkese's mother, needed to sleep during the day before she worked a night shift at the hospital, and she was not returning Josh's phone calls. Though the government's deadline to submit tax returns is April 15, colleges often require students applying for aid to submit them by February 15. Nkese told Josh that her mother had not yet filed her 2006 taxes, so Josh helped Nkese complete her FAFSA and CSS Profile using Peggy's 2005 tax returns. Nkese also had to submit a copy of her father's death certificate: if only one parent's tax information is included in financial aid applications, some colleges require students to prove that it is not possible to provide the second parent's information.

In early March, college results began to arrive. On a bulletin board outside the school's main office, Josh posted letters of acceptance under the heading, "Students at SSR Go to College!" He photocopied each letter, backed it on construction paper, and highlighted the name of the student. At the suggestion of Candace,

Nkese's best friend, he blacked out all addresses: kids did not want this information to be public.

Some of the letters were for students who had dedicated themselves to the process. Boris was offered an $18,000 per year scholarship to St. John's University in Queens. Ravell was admitted to Hobart and William Smith Colleges, Zhi Chao to St. Lawrence University, Emilia to Union College, Erica to SUNY Binghamton, and Aundre to Utica College, all through the Higher Education Opportunity Program (HEOP) and the Educational Opportunity Program (EOP).

But even those who had never expected to go to college were getting in. When Josh told Denise Vasquez that she'd gotten into John Jay College of Criminal Justice, she said, "I did? Are you sure?" Kory was admitted to York College in Jamaica, Queens, and told Josh, "I wish I always knew this was going to be possible." Students expressed a joy that took Josh by surprise, even when the acceptances were from community colleges, which are open to all high school graduates. When Pascal Brooks learned he had been accepted to Kingsborough Community College, he ran a lap around the fourth floor, called his mother from the main office, then handed the phone to Josh so he could assure her the news was true.

As he celebrated with the students, Josh also worried: if students had not been admitted through HEOP and EOP, most aid packages asked students to contribute more than their families could handle. Josh was surprised by the extent to which colleges would "gap" students, leaving them far short of what they needed to accept an offer to attend. Josh had explained financial aid to students as it had been explained to him many times by financial aid counselors: that aid was supposed to cover the difference between the cost of attending the college and what families were able to pay. Josh now faced the task of having to communicate to students which colleges were real choices and which were not, without undermining the pride they felt at getting in.

Josh also felt stung by the rejections received by some of his top students from colleges that had accepted his second- and third-tier students from Birch Wathen Lenox. When he called to ask for explanations, some admissions officers shrugged him off with statistics about selectivity, instead of giving him the kind of real account he had typically received in his former job. When Josh asked why Emilia, a straight-A student, was not accepted to Dickinson College, which the previous year had admitted a Birch Wathen Lenox student who was weaker academically and much less compelling personally, he was told that Emilia's grades from Poland didn't translate and that she didn't seem serious because she had mentioned "roller-blading" as an extracurricular activity.

Nkese's first acceptance was to Wheaton College. She was elated: "I knew that I accomplished something. It just felt like an accomplishment, just getting in." But Nkese was not accepted to Bowdoin, which she found "really upsetting." Bill Shain told Josh that, while Nkese had impressed him personally, her writing was just too weak. Like many colleges that did not require the SAT, Bowdoin had asked for a writing sample to be included in the application. Nkese had submitted one of the essays she had written for her tenth grade history class. Looking at these essays had surprised Josh, especially after her history teacher's praise. The papers were two to three pages long, well organized but simplistic accounts of slavery and colonialism, with significant errors in grammar and diction. The writing seemed out of sync with the teacher's assertion, which he quoted in his letter of recommendation: "She doesn't need an intro history class in college . . . she is ready for higher-level work *now*."

Bates College, also in Maine, not only accepted Nkese but worked actively to recruit her. "I was always hearing from them," Nkese remembered. "Someone was always calling my house." The most meaningful contact for Nkese was from Jason Patterson, then assistant dean of admissions and coordinator of multicultural recruitment. Nkese "sat down with him for about two hours." Jason, a Bates graduate, was African American and had grown up on the Lower East Side. His story resonated with Nkese. "He had great things to say about Bates, and it made me think about it more." She remembered feeling that Bates "actually wanted me to come, like I wasn't just another figure to add to diversity statistics. They weren't afraid for me to be me."

At school, Nkese spoke with Josh about how to decide between Wheaton and Bates. But at home, Nkese's mother Peggy had returned to her original stance that Nkese should stay in New York City. Nkese remembered her mother's reaction to her Wheaton acceptance, which came just after a death in the family: "Can we talk about this another time?" If Nkese wanted to study law, her mother said, she could go to John Jay College of Criminal Justice, part of CUNY. Why did she need to go so far away?

To assemble an aid package for Nkese, both Wheaton and Bates required income documentation Peggy still had not submitted: her 2006 W-2 and federal income tax returns. Josh had been pushing Nkese to get the tax forms from her mother for over a month and continued to press. "My mom and I aren't really able to speak," Nkese told Josh. When she was home, Nkese told him, her mother was at work or asleep, preparing for her twelve-hour shift at the hospital. Josh feared that they were already so far past the deadline that Wheaton and Bates would not offer Nkese an aid package at all, or even if they did, that the package would be significantly less generous because of the late date.

Josh finally reached Peggy by phone. He sensed, in her tone, that she resented his interference in her daughter's life. When he said she would need to submit her tax forms to make Bates and Wheaton real possibilities for Nkese, Peggy said that she was afraid to let Nkese go to these colleges. Maine seemed especially risky: a remote, rural area where there would be psychos in the woods and predators on campus.

Josh assured Peggy that Bates was safe. The campus was self-contained, with good security and with very little crime. "She's not going to be in East Flatbush anymore," he said.

"You don't get it," Peggy said. She explained that she didn't want Nkese living in a place where she would be isolated from those who loved her and vulnerable to racism in a state that was 97 percent white. She knew about date rape and alcohol abuse on campus. Nkese was an obedient daughter, but she still needed her mother's protection and supervision.

Josh felt shaken as he hung up the phone. He was frustrated that Peggy couldn't see what a powerful opportunity this was for Nkese, who had made it clear from the start that she wanted to go away. He was also aware of the stereotypes at work for him in his assumptions that East Flatbush was a dangerous place to live and that the best life choice for Nkese was to get her out.

Trying to buy time, Josh called the financial aid offices at Wheaton and Bates to describe Nkese's mother's resistance. He was able to speak with Wheaton's director of financial aid, Susan Beard, who agreed to extend the deadline. A financial counselor at Bates explained that while the college needed the tax documents to finalize her package, they had already assessed her need and budgeted to meet it in full. Though getting in the tax forms was still urgent, Josh was reassured to know that Bates would be affordable and that Wheaton would work with him as he focused on helping Nkese and her mother make the decision.

Josh believed that the only way to push Nkese to make a choice and get Peggy on board was for both of them to visit the colleges. Josh called Jason Patterson, who was clearly invested in Nkese's coming to Bates, to explain how important it was that she and her mother make a visit. Jason got back to him with the offer of a plane ticket to fly Nkese to the college. But when Nkese was slow to pick a date, Jason grew impatient. Josh asked if they might be able to fund a flight to Lewiston for Peggy as well, but Jason told Josh that his discretionary funding for this kind of recruitment effort was running out and that soon the offer for Nkese would no longer stand.

Wheaton was closer, and the journey there was possible by bus. Josh spoke with the admissions officer for multicultural recruitment, who said that the college could not provide travel funding for Nkese. But he told Josh they could help arrange for a student to host her for an overnight, even though Nkese had missed the scheduled weekend for accepted students.

Nkese came to Josh's office after school the day before spring break to work out the least expensive route to Wheaton. Candace, who had a cousin who lived close by, agreed to go with her. Nkese sat on the desk, her friends looking on, as Josh read the online schedule for the cheap though loosely regulated bus that traveled from New York's Chinatown to Boston's. In downtown Boston, she could catch the commuter rail to Mansfield, Massachusetts, and then the GATRA shuttle bus to Norton, where Wheaton was located. When Josh asked the same admissions officer if someone could pick up Nkese from the Mansfield train station, he said that they couldn't help.

Josh began spring break anxious that Nkese's choices would evaporate. It was doubtful that Nkese would make the trip to Norton to visit Wheaton. Staff at the college didn't seem to recognize how much they were asking of a high school student who had never traveled on her own before. Bates had already committed significant resources to recruiting Nkese, but that's what it would take if they wanted students from backgrounds like hers to enroll. Without a last push to get her to the college, it seemed unlikely that Nkese and Peggy would choose Bates. Josh also feared that Nkese's inaction would undermine his credibility with Bates and Wheaton, colleges he saw as potential partners.

Nkese came to Josh's office after spring break. She had not visited Wheaton. But her mother had relented and given Nkese her tax forms, and Nkese told Josh she had decided on Bates.

Josh was taken aback by Nkese's decision. He doubted she had a real sense of what she would find at Bates, a college filled with affluent, white students from New England boarding schools. Nkese laughed uneasily when Aundre, who was going to Utica, an upstate New York college with a significant population of students of color, teased her about the corny music Bates students would play at parties.

Through May, Nkese's bitterness toward the Secondary School for Research seemed to intensify. This surprised Josh: at Birch Wathen Lenox, an outstanding college acceptance usually acted as a kind of retroactive justification for all that came before. Nkese's college results did not change her sense that her high school had failed her. In classes, she was blatantly disrespectful. Teachers spoke to Josh, and among themselves, about how Nkese would get her "comeuppance" at Bates. "She's going to learn she can't bullhorse her way through the world," he heard one teacher say.

That month, Nkese walked out of the AP English exam. In her memory of the event, this was because she was suffering pain from an ankle injury and could not concentrate. In the proctor's account, after flipping through the test, Nkese began, ostentatiously, to draw pictures in the test booklet and, when reprimanded, began to curse: "I don't give a shit, I'm going to get up and leave." When Nkese left the room, the proctor said, other students followed.

Nkese felt, as the year came to a close, that the school "had taken so much away from us." She had gotten into college, but she knew better than anyone that she wasn't sufficiently prepared. The end of senior year was a great disappointment. She was furious that Jill had rejected the request by the Senior Committee that they rent a hall for graduation. "I did not want to have the graduation in the auditorium," she said. "A lot of us didn't." The senior trip to Florida was also ruled out. "A real senior trip was very important to us, so we felt like high school students." Prom was a battle she felt she won. The Senior Committee had collaborated with the other two schools in the building to hold a combined prom, which would enable them to cut costs and plan an event on the scale they envisioned. Dwight agreed to be her prom date.

In mid-May, one of Dwight's friends told him he was needed for a fight involving members of a Latino gang. Word spread that a fight would happen at the Fourth Street entrance to the school building. Dwight showed up at the time he was told. He and a friend "caught a few kids," then followed the group to join another fight near MS 51, Dwight's former middle school a few blocks away.

When Dwight arrived the fight seemed to be calming down. Dwight remembered someone saying they should end it. As Dwight started to walk away, a guy Dwight didn't know jumped out of the group and punched a rival gang member in the head. A big brawl ensued. Dwight found himself in the center. He got knocked down but pushed his way out. He was "waling on one kid" when another kid got hold of him, and Dwight "held them both off."

Then he felt a blow to his head and fell down against a car. He was hit again with what he realized was a metal bat. There was a loud ringing noise in his head and ears. He felt his body moving and tried to get back up and keep fighting but realized he couldn't.

Dwight touched his face: it was covered with blood. He felt freezing cold. Dwight thought he was going to die right there, lying on the pavement. "I just looked at the sky. I was looking at the clouds pass by."

With his friend's help, Dwight made it to the hospital. Dwight had a concussion but no brain damage. He needed to spend a week out of school to recover, and it was unclear whether he would be able to complete the work he needed to graduate high school on time.

When Dwight returned to school, he remembered that other students were surprised to see him. Some thought he was dead.

Since the fight, there had been a series of violent incidents, with kids being pulled into the bathroom and jumped.

Dwight remembered how strange he found his position. He thought of himself as a guy who was "cool and jokey," not hard core. But he felt completely different at school now. He was guarded and aggressive, suspicious of anyone who looked Latino. One day after gym a kid burst into the locker room, waving a gun. Despite the metal detectors, it was possible to get a weapon into the school through one of the side entrances, and there were areas of the enormous school building where kids could evade security. Dwight was terrified. He hid in a space between the lockers and the windows until he heard the boy leave.

Nkese remembered how scary this time was for Dwight. Before the fight, she had been going through one of her periods of being mad at him on account of some gossip. She "started to talk to him again, to make sure everything was all right." After Dwight recovered, Nkese tried to get him to come to the prom. He refused. "I was really mad at him for that," she said, "and I stopped talking to him again for a couple of weeks."

Nkese finally spoke to Dwight a few days before school ended. He told her he was going to North Carolina to live with his grandmother, who had moved there. He was already enrolled at Guilford Technical Community College, where he was going to study aviation maintenance. "Oh my God, what the hell?" was her response. "But maybe it will be good for him."

At graduation, the auditorium was hot and stuffy in Brooklyn's early summer humidity. The seniors filled the first two rows of wooden seats: girls in high-heeled shoes with mortarboards carefully clipped to newly styled hair, boys in pressed pants and shiny black shoes. Parents, grandparents, aunts, and uncles sat behind them, their arms filled with flowers, babies, and programs they waved as fans. There was an atmosphere of jubilation that was very different from commencement ceremonies at Birch Wathen

Lenox, where families took it for granted that their children would finish high school.

In the cohort of forty-two seniors, all but one had been admitted to college. The exception was a white student who had refused to apply and who planned to work in his family's restaurant business for a year, then consider music school. Thirty-three students (79 percent) had been admitted to four-year colleges, with seventeen students (40 percent) admitted to private four-year colleges. Eight students (19 percent) were admitted only to two-year colleges. The total estimated amount of scholarships and grants awarded to the students over four years of college was $1.8 million. Looking at them, Josh felt they had accomplished something big.

For the first time, the program listed each senior's postgraduation plans. Many Secondary School for Research students were attending highly selective four-year colleges, including Hobart and William Smith, Union, St. Lawrence, and SUNY Binghamton. Candace Jones would be attending Babson College as the recipient of a Posse scholarship, a four-year, full-tuition award for students with "extraordinary academic and leadership potential" who might be "overlooked by traditional college selection processes."[9] Many of the lower-achieving students seemed well placed at CUNY schools.

Some of the students' choices were a disappointment. Melida was going to the College of Staten Island, where her boyfriend was already a student. Late in the process, she and Josh learned that the additional income Melida earned in her mother's name, putting in extra shifts as a home attendant, meant that her mother's annual income during the previous year was above HEOP eligibility guidelines. Without the special consideration available to her through the HEOP admissions pathway, many of the residential colleges Josh thought she might attend were no longer choices, and most of the places where she was admitted were unaffordable. Roshney was going to Kingsborough Community College. She had wanted most to attend St. Lawrence University, where she had been offered over $35,000 a year in grants and scholarships. But her relationship with her mother had deteriorated completely, and Roshney could no longer count on her mother to support her education in any way. Though Roshney's appeal for additional grant aid was approved by the college, it still wasn't a feasible option, and Roshney had to turn her energies instead to finding a stable place to live.

Josh watched the seniors as they got up to collect their diplomas. Dwight, who had thrown himself into his schoolwork so he could graduate on time, walked quickly across the stage. He shook hands with Jill and with the assistant principal, then returned to the auditorium floor in front of the stage, where the guidance counselor and physical education teacher were taking pictures. Dwight turned his head away from the camera. At his seat, he bent over his knees and covered his face in his hands, not wanting to make visible, in public, the emotion that overcame him.

2

With Whom Do You Make
Your Permanent Home?
Mike and Abby

In Josh's second year at the Secondary School for Research, a former supply closet on the fourth floor was painted bright blue and transformed into the new college office. Josh lined the high walls with pennants and with the autumn landscapes and Gothic spires of college posters. "We have an extremely exciting year ahead of us!" he wrote in a letter to students and parents. "I am so pleased to have the opportunity to work closely with our current juniors and seniors in making their college plans."

Michael Forbes and Abigail Benavente were two students about whom Josh felt particularly optimistic. The lists of colleges they had begun to assemble as juniors were similar, including Hobart and William Smith, Skidmore, Union, and St. Lawrence. Both Mike and Abby had been regulars in Josh's office the year before, where they watched him work with seniors and began their own application processes. While neither had initially expected to attend a selective residential college, each seemed enthusiastic about the idea and open to leaving home.

Josh knew that before his arrival as college counselor, Mike and Abby would have been steered toward the City University of New York, which at the time placed students at its various campuses based on academic record and test scores alone. Both students had grades and scores that qualified them for CUNY's most selective campuses, like Hunter College and Brooklyn College, and both mentioned these schools among their choices. The CUNY application process would be far less stressful and time consuming than completing the essays, activity lists, and multiple financial aid forms required by the private colleges Josh was suggesting.

But Josh was convinced that attending a residential college would enable students to grow intellectually and emotionally in ways that wouldn't be possible if they stayed at home. During his own undergraduate experience at Duke, he met his closest friends, discovered a passion for literature during a year abroad in England, and graduated with a stronger sense of who he was. He had learned in his first year at the Secondary School for Research what constricted lives so many students led, managing their schoolwork between part-time jobs and responsibilities for younger siblings, keeping at bay the life of the street, which had swept up Dwight. He did not know how the previous year's seniors would fare at the selective liberal arts colleges where many were now starting as freshmen. But he believed that life on campus would help his students explore academic, social, and extracurricular possibilities beyond the horizons of their current worlds. And he hoped that with the financial packages certain colleges were prepared to offer, students could graduate with minimal debt and an open pathway to the middle class.

Abby came to see Josh in his new office at the beginning of her senior year. Her presence in a room always caused a shift in the atmosphere. She burst in with her huge, dimpled smile and began several conversations at once: with a friend, with Josh, with a teacher who had come in to use a computer, talking until she got out of breath and had to pause to catch it. Abby was friends with students in many different social groups and beloved by her teachers. Josh often saw her helping another student with a precalculus or Spanish assignment or stapling essays onto a bulletin board for her English teacher.

As a junior, Abby had told Josh she had lupus, the autoimmune disorder that most frequently affects young women, especially African American and Latina women, who tend to get it at a younger age and have more severe symptoms. "It's scary, because I know it's something that won't go away," she said. "I'm used to it now." Abby said she was diagnosed when she was twelve, in response to a series of skin rashes that doctors could not otherwise explain. "My immune system was dying, my body was killing itself." Symptoms of the disease, which include fatigue, joint pain, and sensitivity to sunlight, could come and go.

It was easy to forget that Abby had the disease, as energetic as she was. That fall, Abby agreed to stay late after school to help Josh manage the increase in clerical work he faced with a senior class of seventy-five students, double the size of the previous year's. This was the first class that had begun at the Secondary School for Research with Jill Bloomberg as principal and, under her leadership, more students had enrolled at the school and fewer had left. Having begun work with Josh as juniors, many seniors were now prepared to embark on a complex, comprehensive college application process, and Josh knew that he needed to guide them through every detail, filling the role parents play for more privileged students. He would begin by helping every student submit an application to the City University of New York. This would ensure that none would be left without an option, as had almost been the case for Nkese and Dwight the year before. Abby volunteered to spearhead efforts to raise money for a College Fund, which would be used to help the many students who could not afford the $65 application fee CUNY required.

Mike shared Abby's positive attitude and easy manner with adults, though where Abby bubbled with energy, Mike maintained a laid-back calm. When Josh first met him as a junior, Mike had just moved to Brooklyn from Georgia, and he seemed especially young and fresh, with baby-faced good looks and a voice that was still changing, in a school where boys often cultivated a tough shell. He would always come down to the college office with a girl—first Nadine Calixto or Audry Hines, who were seniors, then with Abby or with Chiquita Hamblin, who were in his class. While Josh worked with another student, Mike would lean back in a chair or find ways to help: getting up to submit an online form for Nadine or mapping the best subway route to Audry's CUNY placement test site. He seemed to be trying to find a place for himself in his new school, wanting to look good and do the right thing. Mike wrote with more ease and skill than most of his peers and quickly grasped concepts in math and history. When Josh asked him why he was missing classes and getting lower grades at the Secondary School for Research than he had in Georgia, where he had earned all A's and B's, Mike responded vaguely, saying he got confused about scheduling.

Mike came into Josh's new office senior year with Alice Medrano, his girlfriend since the previous spring. The two were always together now, taking care of each other, wearing the same oversized plastic glasses with "D&G" emblazoned on the sides. Josh asked Mike what he had done that summer. "Oh, nothing," he said. "I went to Atlanta for a reunion with my dad's family. We ran obstacle courses, ate barbecue, had competitions, played softball." He said he wanted to return to Georgia, and he and Josh spoke about college possibilities there: Emory, a highly selective research university Josh knew would be a stretch, and the historically black colleges Clark-Atlanta and Morehouse.

After his initial visit, Josh began to see less of Mike. Though Josh tried to track him down, he got the sense that Mike was avoiding starting his applications. Mike's English teacher, Menucha Stubenhaus, told Josh that Mike's college essay, about leaving Georgia for Brooklyn, was only a series of notes. At the end of October, Josh was notified that Mike was in danger of failing several classes. Josh feared that even if Mike managed to complete the process by the January deadlines, his first semester grades would scuttle his chances for admission at most of the colleges he and Mike had selected together.

Josh learned that Mike was only one of many seniors who had been cutting class and not handing in work, a pattern that continued through November. This behavior contrasted with the resolve so many showed in their approach to the college process. In Josh's crowded office, students worked intently at the computers and hovered around him: "Mr. Steckel, I need help with the SUNY application." "When are you going to sit down with me?" "When will you look at my personal essay?" After hearing reports from teachers about their performance in class, Josh would turn to them incredulously, asking if they realized that colleges would look at these grades before admitting or rejecting them.

Part of the problem, Josh began to realize from students' responses, was that he had insisted seniors take heavier course loads than they had anticipated for the first semester, so that they could be competitive applicants at selective colleges. It was common in New York City public schools for seniors to have light schedules if they had done well in ninth through eleventh grades and were on track to graduate. Now Secondary School for Research seniors were being asked to take math, science, and foreign language courses beyond the credits they needed for a high school diploma. At Birch Wathen Lenox, students had sometimes resented their heavy schedules, but understood that selective colleges carefully assessed the rigor of their course loads, especially during senior year. Students at the Secondary School for Research, who also really needed the additional courses to be ready for college work, had trouble accepting the unexpected burden on top of the stressful, time-consuming application process, which Josh knew could catalyze crises even for students with broad networks of support.

Josh worried that his work might be harming instead of helping his current students. He feared that in pushing them to aim beyond graduating high school and attending CUNY, he had raised the stakes too high. It was as if the balance beam they walked in their daily lives were replaced with a tightrope: there was farther to fall if they didn't make it and still no safety net. Maybe they were performing badly as a kind of self-protection, taking a pre-emptive dive instead of risking one from a greater height.

Josh left school for Thanksgiving break with his faith shaken. As much as he wanted to believe that his students could get to college and graduate, he couldn't be certain. Maybe the students' academic deficits and expectations of failure ran too deep. Even Mike, who had seemed so ready for college and so steady and grounded, had dropped off the map at the crucial moment.

The Monday after Thanksgiving, Josh received a phone call in his office from Alice, Mike's girlfriend. She told him that there had just been a fire at Mike's house. Alice said Mike didn't want anyone to know what had happened, but that he needed help getting his books and homework from school.

Mike returned to school a few days later and sat with Josh in his office. He looked tired but self-possessed, leaning back in one of the chairs by the computers as Josh swiveled around in his desk chair. The fire had started, Mike told Josh, when a man upstairs was smoking in bed and the bed caught fire. Mike joked about how happy one of his younger brothers was that he'd managed to grab his X-Box as he escaped the burning house. "He didn't care about clothes or that we had just gone grocery shopping the day before," he said. Mike had returned to the apartment and tried to salvage his schoolwork, but the papers were rotten and wet.

Josh asked where he was living now. Mike told him that he, his mother, and his two younger brothers were in a homeless shelter in East New York.

Josh couldn't reconcile this image of disaster with the Mike he knew, lounging with his usual relaxed air and well-groomed appearance. It all sounded so terrible. Was there anything he could do? Mike declined Josh's offer to help and resisted his urging that Mike tell his teachers about what had happened and let them cut him some slack. Mike seemed seized by a new stress about keeping up with his schoolwork. "I gotta do my college essay for Ms. Stubenhaus," he said with a groan.

Josh asked if he wanted to try writing about what had happened or if it was too raw and new. "It's not the first time I've been in a shelter," Mike said. At Josh's suggestion, he wrote this down as his first line.

Mike remembered how hard it was to write the essay. He sat in the tiny room he had to himself in the shelter, music blaring from the bodega behind the unit where his family had been placed. He stopped and started repeatedly. He found he could list the events leading up to the fire and his memories of what happened that day but tried without success to arrange them coherently and express his reactions. "I don't like to get into emotions like that," he said.

Mike brought what he had written to his English teacher, Menucha Stubenhaus, in mid-December, a day past the due date. Menucha pushed him to add an "internal narrative" describing his feelings and to try, in his final paragraph, to draw meaning from the experience. Mike made revisions, though he still felt dissatisfied with his final version:

> This isn't the first time I've been in a shelter. I lived in a shelter for three months when I first came to New York last November. My mother was ill with abdominal cancer. She could not work, and on top of that, her job would not give her disability. So my mother had no source of income. When my mother's health improved, she was able to return to work and we moved into an apartment. Now, seven months later, my mother, my two younger brothers, and I are back in a shelter. This time it's not because my mother is sick, but because my house caught on fire, and we cannot live there anymore.
>
> I remember the day it really set in that we were leaving Georgia. I felt like I was leaving everything I had behind. My friends, my school, my house, and even my dog had to be given up. I felt

like all the possessions most dear to me were being taken away. When we hit the highway, the reality of the situation hit me. I wasn't hysterical, because I did not want to upset my mother. I felt horrible inside. I felt like running away and living on my own, because every time I would get accustomed to a place we would end up moving. Something always happens and causes us to move. Mostly economic hardship, because my mother is a single mother trying to support four people and give her three children all of the finer things in life. It makes me feel good to know that she is there for me and my brothers and that she tries her best for us. I admire her a lot for that.

When we arrived in New York I stayed at my grandmother's co-op apartment, while my mother and my brothers stayed with my aunt in her one-bedroom apartment. I slept on the loveseat in the living room, which was barely big enough to fit half of my body, yet it was still better than sleeping on a hardwood floor. I was at the point where I felt like I had no hope. The last bit of hope I had to go on was that my mother told me that in five months we should be able to go back home to Georgia. I thought about that every day. Although I regret it, I even let myself slack in school. The way I saw it was that the grades were not going to count if I was going to leave in a couple of months, so why do work? That was a mistake that I should not have made. Five months turned into seven months, and then a full year. Luckily I opened my eyes to the reality that it was not for sure that I would go back to Georgia. I went to school and tried to pull my grades up. For the most part I was successful, but well aware of the fact that I could still do much better.

It was only two months until we had to move again. My mom couldn't handle living with my aunt. They were extremely cramped in her one-bedroom apartment, with my aunt, her husband, my cousin, my mother, and my two little brothers living all together in that small space. When my aunt's husband struck my brother for sitting in his chair, that was the last straw. My mother came to pick me up and told me to pack a bag with two days' worth of clothes. So at about two in the morning in the middle of February my mother, my brothers, and I were walking around the Bronx trying to find a place called Emergency Housing Services. This is when we first got into a shelter. We lived there for three months.

After my mother was well enough to start working, we moved into a three-bedroom apartment and everyone had their own place to sleep. Things were much better once my family was together again. We lived in that apartment for about eight months. The only problem was that my mother wasn't any closer to being able to move us back to Georgia. I pretty much just let go of the possibility altogether and tried to move on. In my head I thought that there was no point in holding on to it if the chances were very slim. So I made the best of it here in New York. I started to be more social and open with others. My grades began to improve. Then another tragedy happened.

On November 17, 2007, I went out to look for Christmas gifts for my family and my girlfriend. I didn't intend to buy yet, because I had no money. I was merely browsing. So I went around town looking in various stores at gifts I might buy. When I was done, I got on the train and went back home. When I got off the train and climbed up the steps the first thing I saw was a big cloud of smoke a few blocks down and about twenty fire trucks speeding down the street. I remember thinking, "Wow, someone is really stressed right now." I continued walking and as I got closer I realized the fire was on my block. That's when my heart started to beat rapidly. Each step I took my feet grew heavier and heavier. I heard a woman scream, "Oh my God, Reggie's building is on fire." That's when I knew it was my apartment, because Reggie was my landlord. Thousands of thoughts rushed through my head at once. I thought about my mother and my brothers. I imagined them being trapped in the smoldering building with no escape. I ran around the corner and looked up at the burning apartment building that was once my home. I didn't even realize that I ran past my mother and brothers. Before I got to the front of the house I heard her call my name. I ran to her and she hugged me and sobbed on my shoulder. It felt like a weight was lifted off my shoulders to know that she was okay. Then just as soon as I was relieved, I was right back to feeling worried again. I thought about all of my belongings being burned up. I thought about my clothes, my computer, my phone. I closed my eyes and I could see them burning in my mind. My mother told me to take my brothers and go to my grandmother's house down the block. I got there and just tried to keep my mind off of it because I didn't want to upset my brothers or have anyone asking me a bunch of questions afterward. It was almost as if I went into an awake coma. I completely zoned out. The images of what I had just seen kept replaying in my mind. I felt like I had nothing left.

This experience has impacted my life in many ways. My family is in a shelter, which I hate going to and will never call my home. Many of my possessions were destroyed, like my bed, my computer, my games; even schoolwork and textbooks were lost in the fire. I am grateful that my family is alive and well and together. All of my things can be replaced. My family cannot. I know that even though all of this has happened I still have them and I will be all right.

Mike began to come to Josh's office every day to work on his applications and meet with Josh for counseling sessions. This intensive work with Mike was transformative for Josh. He had begun work toward a degree in school counseling at Hunter College, and his fieldwork supervisor kept asking him to "get in the water with the kids," to imagine himself in their circumstances. Josh, who had always done well in high school, asked himself what his grades might have looked like in the face of experiences like Mike's. It required extraordinary character to achieve under the circumstances many of his students faced. What must it take for Mike to get to school every day, not to mention focus on homework, with the stress of not knowing where he would sleep? How could he retain his personal equanimity as his mother battled cancer and his family circumstances grew increasingly desperate?

Josh's desire to help his students go away to residential colleges increased in urgency. If Mike could do as well as he had done in the context of homelessness and instability, how much better would he be able to perform in a place where all those problems were taken away? Josh stayed up one night and drafted his letter of recommendation for Mike in a kind of fever of conviction:

> For many of my students, the opportunity to study at a residential college is like gold. So golden that it often seems unattainable: Why should they believe, really, that there might be a place where they can escape so much of what is difficult about their lives, when such a place has never been available to them before? How could they imagine an environment explicitly designed to enable study and the pursuit of knowledge, when they've grown up in an environment that is so much the reverse that they've hardly had the opportunity to be a child, let alone a student?
>
> I can't imagine a child who would benefit more from the opportunity to study, socialize, live, and contribute within a residential college community than Michael. He has so much to give, and he possesses the intellectual sophistication and hunger, and the writing and analytical ability, to thrive in the most rigorous and challenging academic environment, at our country's most selective colleges. Michael is golden. Look at what he's done already. Imagine how he'll shine when he's not worried about the roof over his head, the bed he will sleep in, the food that he will put on the table, the time and the space to learn and study.

Abby was always at Josh's side as a cheerleader for the college process at the Secondary School for Research. For the College Fund, she spent two evenings wrapping gifts at the Barnes and Noble down the block from the school, soliciting donations to "help our seniors get to college" from Park Slope holiday shoppers. She cooked specialties from Peru, where she was born, for the PTA crafts fair and sold raffle tickets to nearly everyone in the John Jay building, including teachers from the other two schools and the security agents who staffed the metal detectors. Through the fall, she had stayed on task with her own applications and helped her classmates with theirs. Her final push in December was to finish her essay, which was far too long, a jumble of paragraphs that attempted to explain her family's sudden move to Florida, then return to Brooklyn, during her sophomore year.

The news that she had to move had come just as Abby was planning her *quinceañera,* the rite of passage celebrated in many Latino families on a girl's fifteenth birthday. As she described in her essay, Abby's parents told her that her sister, who lived in Florida, was pregnant, and that they needed to go there to support her. Abby learned later that her parents were also facing eviction from their Brooklyn apartment and that this was the reason they had to leave so suddenly.

Abby was very unhappy about having to begin at a new school in Florida. "My classes, the people, everything was so different," she wrote. "I realized that I wasn't in New York anymore and I didn't know how long it would be until I came back." Abby felt left out and alone. "Everywhere I looked I saw people talking, and I just wanted to have someone to talk to. I kept missing what I had left behind. I started acting badly in class, not paying attention and not doing work."

Though Abby at first resented her sister's pregnancy, she grew excited about it. She enjoyed "learning about what happens during the different stages" and putting cream on her sister's belly. "I talked to the baby. I would tell it how I was and about problems I had." But, Abby wrote, as her sister's belly grew, the family's troubles did, too. "My parents and I had no health insurance and I needed medical attention for my lupus."

After several months in Florida her mother received a call that she had a court appointment in New York City to become a naturalized citizen. When she returned to Brooklyn she realized she wanted to stay. Abby, she said, could join her at the end of the school year.

Abby was thrilled to return home but found a new set of problems there. She and her mother rented a room in an apartment shared with two other families and a single man who slept on the living room couch. Abby's sister arrived about a month later, "this time with a huge belly." Abby wrote that she was "excited to see her so big and it was nice to feel her belly and talk to it and feel it kick back. But in one small room, my sister, mom and I were squished."

When Abby's father arrived, things at home became even tighter. For a couple of weeks, her father slept in the taxi he drove. When the owner of the car told him he needed to begin using it at night, her father moved inside and slept on the second couch in the living room, for an extra charge.

Abby was ecstatic when her niece Valerie was born. "I felt as if she were part of me. It was the best feeling, and I thought that the months of waiting for her were worth it," she wrote. But the single room, with one twin-sized bed and a trundle, was now even more crowded.

When she returned to the Secondary School for Research in the fall, Abby remembered, "it was hard to do homework with the baby crying and my sister watching TV. I couldn't go to the living room mostly because the other people living in the apartment were there. It was hard trying to find a quiet place in a crowded house." Abby felt "more comfortable being in school than I did anywhere else." She spent as much time as she could there and threw herself into her work.

In the middle of her junior year, Abby's uncle rented the family an apartment of their own. While he knew Abby's father would have trouble paying the rent, he didn't like to see a new mother and baby living in such cramped circumstances. With the move, Abby's intellectual development seemed to accelerate. In her letter of recommendation, Menucha Stubenhaus, Abby's English teacher, wrote,

> I remember reading an essay she handed in comparing a similar theme in two works of literature she had read. I was almost taken aback at the progress she had made . . . I was greatly impressed and commented to my colleagues that Abigail seemed to be blossoming. Her math teacher remarked that he had noted a similar transformation.

That Abby's skills had crystallized as her home life became more stable struck Josh as an important counterpoint to his fear that students were unprepared for college-level work. He knew Abby as "a learning machine, absorbing absolutely everything around her," as he wrote in his letter of recommendation. That fall she had spent an afternoon in his office watching *The Battle of Algiers*, then discussing colonial regimes with her history teacher. She was the winner of the school's Sudoku competition. She worked as an intern for her biology teacher, Amy O'Donnell, who, to Abby's mother's horror, allowed Abby to bring home one of the leaf litter aquariums full of insects from the science lab at school. If Abby ate up everything an underfunded urban public school could offer, what would her learning look like with the resources and stimulation of a college campus?

Abby, too, felt strongly that she needed to get away. "I didn't want to stay home," she said. "I didn't want to repeat the cycle of just being there, being so tight with money, and so tight with limited resources. I felt like I had to get out of Brooklyn, out of Sunset Park, to actually become something, to actually get to grow."

While for Abby school was a haven, Mike remembered that during the fall of his senior year, before the fire, school became something he just didn't want to deal with anymore. He rarely skipped class, but schoolwork left his mind when he left the building. When he

attended high school in Georgia, Mike's daily life had been cush-
ioned by suburban comforts that gave him the freedom to be a student. He enjoyed school and earned mostly A's. He played football
and attended an after-school program for students interested in
the health professions. He remembered with nostalgia the yellow
bus that picked him up in the morning and dropped him off at his
home at the end of the day.

In Lithia Springs, where Mike last lived in Georgia, his family
had shared a large, two-family house with his mother's sister and
her two children. The house had a back porch and a basketball
hoop in the driveway, and Mike slept in the top floor master bedroom. While Mike's mother, Ebony, worked, his stepfather stayed
home with Mike and his younger brothers, Anthony and Justin.
His stepfather was a disciplinarian who enforced strict curfews,
allowed no visitors in the house, and mandated daily chores. He
was volatile and obsessive, constantly lecturing and complaining
to himself, exploding over a piece of lint on the rug, playing off
fear in his methods of discipline. Mike resented his rigidity but
credits his stepfather for making him a "clean freak." The saving
grace was that Ebony left work every day at 5 p.m. Even though
she and Mike's stepfather fought constantly, her presence at home
made his less oppressive.

When Mike's mother and his aunt got into a fight, his aunt
moved out, and his mother could not afford the rent and bills on
her own. This was the beginning of what for Mike seemed like a
never-ending downward spiral of events. The family moved from
the large house into an apartment complex in the same area. Their
apartment was small, but with "a nice carpet" and maintenance
staff on site. One day a friend of Mike's came to their door. Mike's
stepfather disliked the boy, whom he saw as someone who would
lead Mike astray. His stepfather confronted Mike's friend—"Didn't
I tell you not to come to the door anymore?"—and his friend responded, "You don't own this walkway, I can stand here if I want to."

Mike and his friend walked to the parking lot. His stepfather followed and, after some words, punched Mike's friend in the face. Further enraged by Mike's friend's remarks, Mike's stepfather pulled a kitchen knife from his back pocket and slashed at Mike's friend's face. When the police arrived, Mike's mother urged Mike to say he hadn't seen anything.

Mike already felt as if he were "a bad person," because his friend, who was sixteen or seventeen, had a welt on his face and had just been punched and slashed by a grown man. "I want to tell the cop what happened, my friend of course wants me to tell the cop what happened, and then my mom is also standing there." Mike did as his mother asked. Another friend, also present, reported what she had seen, and Mike felt even worse for what now seemed like a needless betrayal.

Mike's stepfather turned himself in to the police and spent a brief time in jail for assault. His ten-year probation meant he could not leave the state.

When Ebony's chronic stomach pains were diagnosed as cancer, she realized she could no longer afford treatment in Georgia. She moved the family back to Brooklyn, where she had grown up, to find the support of her own family while she underwent chemotherapy, but found instead the tension and conflict that led her to bring her children to the first shelter.

The East New York shelter where Mike and his family would spend three months "was like a really shitty hotel." Inside wasn't much warmer than outside. Rats lived in the cabinets. Mike had to check all his clothes for roaches before he left the unit. Other residents, mostly women with children, left garbage and dirty diapers outside their doors. When Mike and his mother tried complaining that this violated shelter rules, staff shrugged off their protests. They tried themselves to deinfest their unit with roach bombs but with little success. They had a sink and stove, but Mike was too disgusted by the vermin to cook much, aside from pouring cereal and heating up Jamaican beef patties. Everything felt dirty no matter how many times he washed it.

Families were not given keys to their units, which locked when they closed the door behind them. When they entered, they had to ask someone at the front desk to let them in. Ebony had returned to work and was gone from 5 a.m. to 8 p.m. At first staff refused to allow Mike into the family's unit without Ebony because he was under eighteen. This meant that after they returned from school, Mike and his brothers would have to wait for hours in the lobby until their mother came back from work. One staff member helped secure Mike an ID card with a false age. On the whole, however, Mike remembered the staff as rude and hostile to residents. "I don't know if it's because they deal with so much in a day, or because some of the people there give them an attitude. I don't know why these people act like this. They were not nice at all." It seemed to Mike that he was being punished, that the shelter was a kind of jail where he was trapped with all the rodents, unable to sleep.

East New York, where the shelter was located, is the site of frequent gang violence. On one of his walks to the train, Mike was stopped by a young guy whose red bandanna across his face identified him as a Blood. He asked to "see" Mike's phone, and Mike refused to take his phone from his pocket, understanding that the kid intended to steal it. Then the kid asked Mike if he was a Blood. "We need dudes like you, with heart," he said, when Mike responded that he wasn't gang affiliated. Mike felt no attraction to gang culture and did his best to stay away.

Mike didn't tell anybody at the Secondary School for Research where he was living. He continued to attend class and to hang out in the college office. At the same time, through the winter of his junior year, he began to consider dropping out of school. He didn't see how his mother could support the family on her own, working long hours and undergoing chemotherapy. If he found a full-time job, he could help pay for food and bills. Maybe a high school diploma and a college degree would help him in the long run, but at that moment, his family desperately needed money and a place to live.

Mike remembered that as a junior he "liked the idea of college" and enjoyed talking about it with Josh, but "it just seemed like it wasn't for me." Nobody in his family had gone, and he "didn't feel like there was a reason why I should make it when nobody else did." His mother told him he should study to become a doctor, but he felt that she would have understood and supported him if he chose to drop out and get a job. "College was something that you would dream about," Mike said, and "hopefully maybe your kids would be able to do," but that in his current circumstances "seemed unobtainable." Josh assured Mike that he was a strong candidate for generous grant and scholarship funding, but Mike couldn't see why colleges would "support people who really don't have much going for them."

Mike's family stayed in the shelter through the spring. By the time they had moved into the apartment that later caught on fire, he had let go of the idea of dropping out of high school. While he hated feeling selfish, he knew he should pursue his own best interest. He had made it as far as junior year and didn't want to "throw that away." He tried to deal with his feelings of guilt by telling himself that staying in school would benefit his family in the long run, even though it wouldn't relieve the hardships of the moment. Besides, he saw how difficult it was to find even a part-time job. He had applied to several places, but received no calls back.

It was when he began his essay, after the fire and his family's move into the second shelter, that Mike began to take the college process seriously. He had begun to listen to his peers at the Secondary School for Research speak about where they were applying and to notice where seniors from the previous year had gone to college. He knew that while some of his peers had more money and resources than he did, most others came from similar backgrounds. He started to think, "Okay this is real."

For most of the schools to which Mike and Abby were applying, they would use the Common Application, a standardized application for admission accepted by hundreds of selective colleges. The first section of the application students are asked to complete, after entering their name, address, and contact information, is subtitled "Demographics." Questions in this section deal primarily with students' race. The next section, "Family," includes questions about parents' marital status, occupation, and level of educational attainment. The form also asks, "With whom do you make your permanent home?"[1]

Mike put off filling out these sections for as long as he could. It seemed to him that "the colleges were asking more than they needed to be told." Why should admissions officers know that he was the son of a single mother whose education had ended with a GED and who worked a job that didn't keep them above the poverty line? Mike lived not in a "permanent home" but in a homeless shelter in East New York. The language of the question excluded his experience and reinforced his sense that college was not really intended for someone like him.

For Mike, the demographic questions worked against the promise, in the other sections of the application, that colleges would recognize students as individuals. "Some of the questions, okay, that's true, but there's more to me than just that. Everything's not yes or no answers." Answering the questions on the forms felt very different from revealing his struggles in his essay, which he didn't imagine many people would read. Though writing his essay had been difficult, it had given him a sense of self-respect, "thinking about everything that my family and I have been through and how far I've come already in school, to even still be in school." His demographic profile added up to a stereotypical picture of a poor black kid with a hard life. "Maybe identifying that way made me feel like less of a person," Mike said as he reflected back.

Mike's resistance to this section, while common among students at the Secondary School for Research, was very different from the reactions Josh remembered from his private school students. When questions about the demographic section arose at Birch Wathen Lenox, it was usually out of a sense that being a minority offered some students a way to game the system. Most of the white students chose not to respond to the questions about race, which are optional on the form. Several nonwhite students who had been adopted by white parents hesitated to complete the information, sensing that if they labeled themselves as students of color, colleges would accept them for reasons that didn't seem meritocratic—regarding them differently from their peers because of the color of their skin. Sometimes students complained that those who were able to check something other than "Caucasian/non-Hispanic" had an unfair advantage. For Secondary School for Research students, their demographic information did not strike them as an angle that could get them in, but as a barrier that would keep them out, defining them as poor, minority applicants whose parents had not gone to college and who probably were not college material themselves.

Mike and many other Secondary School for Research students also faced emotional and practical challenges simply coming up with the information required by the family section, which for Birch Wathen Lenox students took a short time to complete. The form asks for addresses, occupations, and levels of education for both "Parent 1" and "Parent 2." Mike regarded his biological father as "Parent 2" in name only. Mike was born when his mother was seventeen, and she and his father broke up when Mike was around three. Mike's mother was the family's sole breadwinner, and his father had never supported Mike financially, even during his mother's illness and downward spiral. Mike and his mother were reluctant to include any information about his father, but unless they indicated that Parent 2 was "Unknown," the online form did not allow them to leave these fields empty.

Mike also struggled to complete the Common Application's "Activities" section. Students were asked to list up to seven of their most important activities on a grid and to describe one of them in a short essay. Mike wrote about caring for his brothers, Anthony, who was ten, and Justin, who was nine.

His brothers, Mike said, were smart kids who "rolled with the punches." Anthony reminded Mike of himself: he was laid-back and didn't need much from anyone else. Mike characterized Justin as adventurous and playful. One day, Mike remembered, Justin made a "fishing pole" out of half of a pair of scissors, some Scotch tape, and a broomstick, to "survive in the wilderness." Justin sometimes ran into problems in school for his good nature and gullibility, which Mike attributed to his coming from the South.

Mike's responsibilities for his brothers had intensified after the family's move into the second shelter. The boys had changed schools for the third time, and the after-school program at their new school did not run as late. So in addition to helping Anthony and Justin get ready for school in the mornings, Mike supervised them in the afternoons and evenings. At about 4 p.m., they would all get let into the shelter. His brothers were always hungry, so Mike would make them a second lunch, then "whatever we were going to have for dinner so I didn't have to do it later." He would help them with their homework and take them to play outside, either on the sidewalk with other kids from the shelter or at a playground a few blocks away. When his mother came home, Mike would "put stuff aside for her to eat, then talk to her for half an hour. She'd tell me about her day, then off to bed."

To Mike, what he wrote in the activities section looked woefully thin. "Even though I've done stuff, I haven't done enough," he remembered thinking. He compared himself to students who attended schools with wide extracurricular opportunities, and those who had "volunteered in soup kitchens, or cleaned up the environment, stuff that looks better than 'I babysit my brothers.'" He knew that in spending his time caring for Anthony and Justin and trying to be a positive influence, he was doing what he had to do, but he worried that "people may not understand why."

By mid-January, both Mike and Abby had submitted the Common Application to eight colleges each, completed the supplemental essays required by individual colleges, and attended several interviews. Through the beginning of February, Josh worked with them to complete the Free Application for Federal Student Aid, New York State's Tuition Assistance Program application, and the College Search Service Profile.

For Mike and Abby, yet another stage of the process began in mid-February: applications for New York State's Higher Education Opportunity Program (HEOP). HEOP, funded by the state and run by individual colleges, provides scholarships and support services for "educationally and economically disadvantaged students." Students must meet strict income requirements: for Mike's year, the maximum a family of four with a single parent could earn was $37,150 per year. Each college selects students who show outstanding character, intellectual ability, and potential, but whose scores and academic record would render them inadmissible in the regular pool of applicants. Numbers of available spots for incoming freshmen vary from college to college—larger programs may have forty or more spots, while smaller programs might have ten or fewer.

Colleges refer students' applications to HEOP after they have been processed through the standard channels, and the HEOP offices begin what is in effect a second application process. They generally start by verifying that students are economically eligible for the program. Once students have submitted the necessary financial documentation, their applications proceed to a committee that evaluates their academic and personal qualifications. Students may be required to meet an HEOP counselor for an interview, write additional essays, or visit campus for placement exams or mock classes.

At the Secondary School for Research, students struggled to keep up with all the additional deadlines and unfamiliar requirements. "So many things that needed to be done, such a rush," Abby remembered. "The main thing was, nobody in my family knew what was going on. My sister didn't apply to college, and my brother went straight to the navy. Everything was brand new."

Just a few weeks after Mike had submitted his applications,

staff from the HEOP office at Skidmore, a private college in Saratoga Springs, New York, contacted him for financial information to confirm his economic eligibility. The college indicated that it needed a copy of his mother's 1040 form for the current tax cycle as soon as possible. Mike's mother didn't have the necessary documents: she had just received her W-2 a week or so earlier and only knew that the government deadline for filing taxes was April 15.

Mike began to receive almost daily calls on his cell phone from HEOP support staff, who were also calling Josh. Josh knew that at Skidmore, the HEOP office worked to confirm income eligibility for all candidates before "committee" in March, when counselors would begin to select students for the incoming freshman class for Skidmore's Opportunity Programs. Students whose economic eligibility had not been verified by then would not be part of the conversation.

For two weeks, Mike pushed his mother every day to complete the tax forms. As he described, "I felt animosity toward my mom, even though it wasn't really her fault. She didn't have her taxes sorted out. She would start to give me some story, and I would say that I didn't want to hear the story." Mike's family was still in the shelter, and she was struggling with cancer, three kids, and a fifteen-hour workday. "She understood the urgency of me needing what I asked her for," Mike said, but he felt that she wasn't pulling through for him. If she didn't get the forms in before the beginning of March, all the work that he had done to write his essays and complete his applications, to overcome his own doubts and to stand out as an individual, would be made irrelevant by a bureaucratic detail that was out of his control.

Josh remembered a marked shift in Mike's demeanor at this time. He was not his usual easygoing self, always smiling and tolerant. Mike was edgy and irritable, on a short fuse. The college process, Mike told Josh, seemed to go on forever. He was exhausted.

Mike's mother finally produced the documents he needed to complete income verification for his HEOP applications. Then

Mike needed to wait another month for a decision. During this time his focus shifted to his anger that, while most students had received their placements at the City University of New York, no letter had arrived for him. Several phone calls revealed that Mike's application was reading as incomplete, despite the fact that he and Josh had completed the required forms and submitted his SAT scores and the application fee months earlier. For the first time, CUNY was requiring all students to submit online applications, and Mike's was one of many that were held up by glitches and bugs in the new system.

While he understood Mike's frustration, Josh was puzzled by his obsession with the CUNY application. Josh had been advocating fiercely for Mike in phone calls and e-mails with residential colleges and felt confident that Mike would have good results. Though he couldn't repeat confidential feedback from admissions counselors, Josh reassured Mike that, in April, he had a strong chance of receiving an offer of admission to at least one of the prestigious liberal arts colleges Josh hoped he would attend, with substantial financial support as an HEOP scholar.

But Mike had privately begun to think that Brooklyn College, the CUNY campus of his choice, was his best option, and he needed to know if he had been admitted. Enrolling there would enable Mike to earn a college degree while still helping his family, perhaps through a part-time job. It would also mean staying close to Alice, his girlfriend. Mike remembered his frustration at this time. "It was all these if, if, ifs. Nothing was certain. All these things that were undecided were floating around in my mind."

Since he left Georgia, Mike's life had spiraled increasingly out of his control. He had often imagined living on his own as a way to find independence and stability. Now the possibility of leaving his family seemed increasingly real, but increasingly risky for his mother and brothers. "I needed to have all the options in front of me," Mike said, "so that I could make a decision about what I was going to do with my life, if I wanted to stay or to go away."

3

Take the Brooklyn Out of You:
Nkese and Dwight

Nkese Rankine moved from East Flatbush, Brooklyn, to Bates College in Lewiston, Maine, in August 2007. It was her first time seeing the campus. Redbrick buildings with white wooden columns surrounded a leafy quad dappled in late summer sunlight. Along the walkways, students and families carried belongings in plastic bins and cardboard boxes, balancing blankets, poster tubes, lamps, laptops, and lacrosse sticks. Among the students with blond ponytails and Birkenstocks were a few families of color: a girl in a hijab, a mother with her head wrapped in a brightly colored scarf, a large African family with small children in tow.

The year Nkese entered, Bates was beginning an initiative to increase the diversity of its student body. The college had been founded in 1865 by abolitionists and accepted both black students and women, one of the first colleges in the United States to be co-educational from its origins. In the words of the current college president, Elaine Tuttle Hansen, in her convocation address to Nkese's class, Bates was founded "to create a place of possibility for more than the elite handful who were at that time allowed to pursue higher education." Now, President Hansen told the freshman class,

You have arrived during a period of intense effort at Bates to enrich what today we call diversity in the composition of our

students, faculty, and staff, both in the character of our educational environment and in the ways we engage and serve the
world. We believe that living and learning in a broadly diverse
community fosters the examined life, obliging us to think harder
and expand our horizons. Only by moving outside of our psychological and social comfort zones can our human spirit grow,
cognitively and personally.[1]

Implicit in President Hansen's remarks was the idea that in accepting its largest group to date from "underrepresented populations," Bates was engaging in something different from affirmative
action, usually understood as giving an extra boost to historically
excluded groups. The goal of diversity, as she expressed, was to
raise the value of the college experience for everyone, cultivating
more deeply the growth of the human spirit.

In the language of the convocation address, Nkese heard echoes
from her personal essay, which had described her sense that she
needed to leave her "comfort zone" in East Flatbush and "face diversity" to grow. Nkese anticipated that this shift would be a challenge to her identity, but asserted, "I am not going to college to
change my personality. I am going to college to bring me closer to
the life I desire." She began at Bates determined to "be somebody,"
without letting go of being herself.

Nkese's jolt from her comfort zone began with her move into
Smith Hall, her freshman dorm. As she remembers, she found
herself "thrown into a situation where I lived in two small rooms
with three other girls." One room contained two bunk beds, the
other, four desks against the walls. The first day, "we decided to
debunk the beds so we could all have our own personal space."

As she hung out with her roommates and floormates, Nkese felt
"shocked at how fast everyone was getting into the social scene,"
with its heavy drinking and unfamiliar codes. "I wasn't into partying like that, and for me college wasn't my first taste of freedom in that sense, to just go all crazy." In get-to-know-each-other

conversations, girls sought common ground and common friends, connecting networks of summer camps and boarding schools. Having gone to an unknown public high school, Nkese lacked social currency, even among students from New York City: "People want to know what high school you went to because that reads what your contribution to the conversation could be. So if you went to Dwight, or you went to Fieldston, or you went to Berkeley Carroll, you can contribute something to the conversation. If you don't know how to speak that lingo, you're already cast aside. If you've never been to Europe, you're already cast aside."

Nkese remembered one incident where she became aware that she was consciously being excluded. She had joined her roommates and their friends in the dining hall, and "the conversation was shifting to different terrains, about who knew who—'Oh, you went to her private school? Oh, I'm friends with her!'—that type of conversation." When Nkese tried to say something, the girls ignored her in a pointed way. "I thought they were just being bitchy, so I left," Nkese said. Later, one of her roommates approached her. "I know what happened," she said. "They were mean, and I want to apologize." While Nkese was grateful for the apology, it angered her that her roommate had seen what was happening and stayed quiet.

Nkese remembered "more positive social interactions" from the beginning of freshman year, "because not everyone was like that." But there were "people at Bates who didn't know how to understand difference," who seemed stumped by how to interact with someone with whom they did not share obvious common ground. "So you didn't go to a wealthy private school or a wealthy public school in the suburbs? That's 'different.' "

As an African American public school student from Brooklyn, Nkese felt as though she were speaking a language many of her new peers could not or did not want to understand. One of Nkese's friends, who was also black, described frequently being asked by her roommate to stop screaming. "My friend didn't scream: she has a very low-pitched voice," Nkese said. The roommate "assumed that when my friend took an assertive role in a conversation she was screaming at her and being 'ghetto.'" These kinds of interactions were not "the main reason why I wasn't having a good time at Bates," Nkese said, "but they were a contributing factor."

Even more of a shock than the social scene at Bates was the academic life. Many of Nkese's peers seemed to be professional students, already confident with managing their time and their coursework. "If you went to boarding school," she said, "college is not such a big transition. Period." Nkese found herself with massive amounts of writing and unstructured time she didn't know how to handle. She took long naps in the afternoons and missed meals to finish her work. "Going from writing a paper two hours before class in high school to doing that in college was not good at all," she said.

Nkese's most difficult class was her first year seminar, aimed at helping freshmen improve their writing and critical thinking skills. Nkese had chosen a section titled "The U.S. Relocation Camps in World War II," a "very intense history freshman seminar" with a subject that intrigued her. The course was taught by a professor from Japan ("though her ethnicity has nothing to do with it," Nkese said), who was strict and exacting in her expectations for students' writing. "She said she was trained in the Queen's English, and she wants us to excel. You would get points off if you missed a period in a citation." Though the class was stressful, Nkese appreciated the focused attention to her writing. "She said to students, including me, you speak English, but you don't know how to write English."

Many of the students in the fifteen-person class had weaknesses in their grasp of language and grammar, but Nkese perceived the ways her own deficits stood out. "Everyone sounded so poised," Nkese said. She rarely spoke in class, a big shift from her passionate participation in high school. At the time, Nkese said, "I had a really strong accent." When she would tell students where she was from, she could hear in the response—"Oh, you're from *Brooklyn*"—all the assumptions about race and class she wanted to avoid. "I didn't like speaking in public, because I was like, 'Oh God, I don't want them to think I'm not articulate.' "

Nkese described the day she gave a presentation comparing Executive Order 9066, which established the Japanese internment camps, with the Patriot Act. "There were close similarities," she remembered. "I was scared because I knew this was a strong project to take on. I did the research and looked at the government documents." When she got up to speak, she felt tongue-tied and couldn't begin. Seeing her anxiety, the professor said, in front of the class, "Just pretend everyone here is from Brooklyn."

Nkese remembered thinking, "Oh my God, this is not okay." At the same time, she said, she understood why the professor made the comment. "There was a certain level of discomfort that was very readable on my face, everywhere I went. Everyone was like, 'You don't like it here,' and I'm like, 'Yeah.' " Nkese's unhappiness seemed connected to her sense of being out of place, and her professor zeroed in on this. "She kept telling me, 'I know you're smart.' She said she was going to take the Brooklyn out of me."

Having applied to college determined to get out of East Flatbush, Nkese now struggled to understand how much of Brooklyn she wanted to leave behind and how much made her who she was. On this small New England campus far from home, she sensed a fixation on "Brooklyn" and what it seemed to represent. She felt frustrated with students who listened to hip-hop but didn't get the layers of irony and social critique in the lyrics of "conscious rappers" like Mos Def and Talib Kweli. From their comments, she gathered that her peers at Bates pictured where she came from as "the ghetto," where black people either lived in poverty or sold drugs and got rich. It was hard to know how to begin explaining that her Brooklyn contained people of all kinds. Yes, there was poverty and there were drugs. But "there are also a lot of people who don't sell drugs," and in other neighborhoods, "there are a lot of rich kids who do—they just don't get penalized as often for it."

In the Introduction to Women and Gender Studies class she took first semester, Nkese began delving into issues of race and class in ways that were both fascinating and disturbing to her. One day, her professor "brought this wonderful article about nail salons, basically saying that treatment differs depending on where you live in New York City." The article broke down the elements of the relationships between Korean immigrant workers and their clientele. It compared businesses in wealthy white neighborhoods with those in predominantly African American and Caribbean working-class sections of Brooklyn, like the neighborhood where Nkese grew up.[2]

As the class discussed why service in working-class neighborhoods was sometimes less courteous, Nkese felt increasingly upset. Some students commented that if "they don't pay as much, they don't really deserve to have that type of environment." That's problematic, Nkese said, "because you can use that kind of logic for anything. If you're not paying that much for health care, should you not expect good health care?" Nkese was also disturbed by the way her peers said, " 'these people do these things'—already the terminology was separating us and them." Though she was usually quiet in class, she spoke up and became emotional. "I was just like, 'You don't know what you're talking about.' "

In high school, Nkese had not thought much about the broad ethnic diversity at the Secondary School for Research, where her friends had included first- and second-generation immigrants with families from Eastern Europe, Latin America, the Caribbean, and Africa. Now, she found herself parsing identity categories for peers who seemed clueless. "I'm not African American, I'm actually Afro-Caribbean and Afro-Hispanic," she remembered telling a friend of her roommate in frustration. "You know, we're not all from the same place." "Oh, I didn't know that," the guy said.

Nkese also felt pressure to be involved with the multicultural center and to spend time with other students of color. "There weren't that many African American students my year," Nkese said, "but because it was more than Bates had ever seen, it was expected that we would all hang out."

Two friend groups emerged. "We were all from different places in the country, and you kind of congregate with people who are from your part of the country," Nkese remembered. In one friend group, all the girls had gone to private school and in the other, Nkese's group, "half of us were from private school, half from public." Each made assumptions about the other. "We assumed because all of them were from private school, all were from privileged backgrounds. This was not the case for any of them."

Tensions developed between the groups: "Somebody doesn't like someone, there's rumors. It was girl stuff, to be quite honest," Nkese said, "but it got blown out of proportion." Nkese found herself involved in drama reminiscent of high school. "I was trying to be peacemaker and one of my friends didn't want to hear it, and it just got really bad." One night, in a lounge area adjacent to the dining hall, the two groups confronted each other, yelling and cursing. "It got to physical, almost," Nkese said. "We all had to have a meeting."

The meeting was organized by Marylyn Scott and Carmita McCoy, the two deans who worked to recruit and support students from underrepresented populations at Bates. Both were clearly very upset. They reminded students that there was zero tolerance for violence on campus and spoke about how, as students of color, they had projected a negative image of themselves in a public space. The deans took the students to task for jeopardizing all they had accomplished in getting themselves to Bates and all that others had invested in them. They pushed them to figure out how, as minorities on campus, they could form a more unified community.

Nkese understood the motivation for the intervention and how easily the students' behavior could be perceived, in the larger campus community, as fulfilling negative stereotypes about race, gender, and class: "If the students of color are fighting, why would the college want to bring more students of color to campus? You know, there are assumptions." But as in high school, Nkese resented the involvement of administrators who thought they had a right to control students' lives. "I didn't feel I had to answer the administration's questions about why I didn't hang out with certain other students," she said. She spent time with her particular group "because they were good people, but also, we had a bond that kept us sane in this really crazy place."

Following this incident, Nkese said, "I had to withdraw myself, because I had to start paying attention to my academics. I was taking these really hard classes. I had maybe twenty papers my first semester in college, five-page papers, ten-page papers. I was taking psychology, African American studies, women and gender studies, things that I'd never thought in depth about. I was getting so confused about identity politics." Though she considered herself a social person, "it was hard to be in a social environment where you had to interact with people on an everyday basis. I had three roommates. It wasn't just like you saw them for eight hours then you were gone. It was a lot to do the first year."

Though several friends tried to get her involved in the life of the multicultural center, Nkese did not participate in many activities. Instead, she stuck with people who "were just not into that either, and we helped each other with our work. That was my way of escaping the madness that was Bates." When, in October, Bates held its recruitment weekend for first-generation college students and students of color, Nkese agreed to host a prospective student but did not accompany her guest to any events, saying she had to finish a paper that was due the next day.

Josh spoke to Marylyn Scott about Nkese around this time. Marylyn described Nkese's actions as uncooperative and antisocial, and Josh heard an accusatory note in Marylyn's tone: Nkese had clearly not become the "impact student" he had described in his letter of recommendation. At this time, Josh was advocating with Marylyn for other students from the Secondary School for Research who were applying to Bates. As during the previous spring, when Nkese had faltered in her college choice, Josh feared that his credibility with the college depended on what happened with this one student.

Josh also feared that Nkese's teachers may have been right in their skepticism about whether she could make it at the college. When he spoke with Nkese on the phone, she sounded tired and unhappy, telling him she was struggling with writing and failing biology. Josh assured Nkese that freshman year was always difficult. But he worried that instead of bringing her "closer to the life I desire," Bates would send Nkese back to Brooklyn, exhausted, discouraged, and ashamed that she didn't make it through.

As he pushed his second class of seniors through the college application process, it was difficult for Josh to know what conclusions, if any, he could draw from the freshman year experiences of Nkese's class, his first. It felt, at times, that there was more bad news than good. Ravell Robinson had to leave Hobart and William Smith even before the fall semester began: during the mandatory summer program for HEOP students, he had not completed any of his papers. Zhi Chao Zhou had started at St. Lawrence but continued to struggle with English and told Josh, in one of his frequent phone calls, that he might have to come back to Brooklyn before the year was over. Kirk Hillaire dropped out of City Tech before the end of his first semester there. Josh had helped him buy his course books on Amazon.com to save money, but the books, Kirk told him later, had never arrived: package-delivery was unreliable where he lived. Kirk didn't tell his professors that he didn't have the books, fell behind, and eventually stopped going to class.

Josh did not know how Dwight Martin was doing in North Carolina until December, when Josh was surprised in his office by a visit from Dwight's mother. She showed Josh a letter she had just received, in which Dwight was invited to be a marshal at the

Guilford Technical Community College graduation, an award for his outstanding performance in the field of aviation maintenance. Dwight, who had been a C and D student through high school and barely graduated, had finished his first semester of college with a 4.0.

Dwight recalled that he had not started college thinking, "I need to change." The decision to enroll at Guilford Tech had been part of the "crazy chain of events" following the fight at the end of his senior year. While recovering from his head injury, he had been living with his parents in Canarsie, and they argued incessantly. One night he felt as if he couldn't take it anymore. He left the house and walked all the way across Brooklyn, to the home of a friend. It was a three-hour walk that he knew he shouldn't be taking alone in the middle of the night. But Dwight felt most afraid of himself and what he might be capable of doing if someone confronted him.

A few days later, his father came to pick him up. Dwight got into the car and, as his father drove him to school, they spoke to each other in a way that felt new. Growing up, Dwight said, he felt as if his father was hardly ever around. When he was, he would just back up Dwight's mother in the conflicts that erupted. Dwight felt that, for the first time, his father was hearing him and getting some idea of what Dwight was going through.

The connection Dwight felt in this conversation was quickly followed by a new sense of powerlessness in the face of his parents' pressure. Dwight's grandmother had just moved to North Carolina, and one weekend before the end of the school year, his parents told him they were going to see her and to look at colleges. They brought him to see Guilford Tech, and he remembered an admissions counselor asking him, "What are you interested in?" When Dwight responded hesitantly, his dad interjected, "He's interested in the aviation program." In a single weekend, Dwight "got a driver's license, got a car, and enrolled in college."

Dwight resented that he "didn't get a chance to check out some of the colleges like I wanted to." If he was starting school, it was important that the decision be made carefully. "College, college . . . that's nerve-wracking," he said, describing his frame of mind. "You're paying for school, you don't have time to play around." He felt he needed time to think, to clear his head after all he had been through, and to identify a direction for himself.

After his graduation from the Secondary School for Research, Dwight moved in with his grandmother in North Carolina and got ready to begin the aviation program at Guilford Tech. When his parents returned to Brooklyn, he began to focus less on his resentment about the choices he felt they had forced on him and more on establishing his new life. "I kind of switched to the mentality, 'I'm grown now, and I have to do things on my own.' " Starting classes, he found himself one of the most capable students, the person others turned to for help. Though he still had uncertainty about aviation, he said, "I can't say I wasn't interested at all. As I got into it, I started learning more—I started learning a lot more." While other students fooled around, he focused on his work. "I was doing what I had to do, which was succeed. I just refused to not succeed, period."

Dwight later tried to explain the source of this motivation to Josh. "I think part of the reason why I excelled is because I wanted to make *you* proud. I said, man, I'm going to show Mr. Steckel that I can do this, because I was being such a damn knucklehead in high school." Though he hadn't always shown it, he said, Josh's message had reached him. "You told me I can't dwell in the past. You made me focus on what was in front of me, which was college, and improve myself from then on."

Dwight's 4.0 GPA his first semester signaled his new beginning. "I was loving it," he said. "I did like making everybody proud of me. I was just happy with progress. It was like this awakening. I don't know how to explain it. I just grew up so fast. I started realizing a lot of things. As you get older, things you wouldn't normally hear as a child you start to hear."

Dwight saw his awakening as part of a pattern in his life in which simultaneous extremes—the "really good and really bad at the same time"—could lead to progress. "Sometimes when things are falling apart, they may actually be falling into place," he posted on Facebook. He traced the beginning of his progress to Josh's influence in his senior year: "You being real with me and at the same time helping me at least try to make myself go forward."

Following his move to North Carolina, Dwight said, "it took a while for me not to be angry." A turning point came one evening while he was out with his cousin and her friend. His cousin, with whom he was very close, asked him to tell her about the fight, which she had only heard about from their grandmother. Dwight gave her the play-by-play and pointed to the egg-shaped indentation in his skull where the bat had hit him. His cousin and her friend were shocked at the story. "You almost died," they said.

Dwight remembered that it began to sink in then that he could be dead or brain damaged, and he felt blessed. He thought back to the moment when he lay bleeding on the pavement near his former middle school. This image linked up with Josh's message of belief in his future, and there was a spark. "The combination of that right there, and then you being one of the main positive influences in school, that really is what kick-started me," Dwight told Josh. "Without you, I'd probably be dead somewhere, to be honest with you, and that's just me being real about it."

In North Carolina, Dwight was able to imagine his future in a different way. He felt frustrated with his peers at Guilford Tech who "acted all hard" and got into trouble. "I tell people that they're privileged to live down here. First of all, you're not falling on top of each other. There's more space, and a more relaxed environment." Even the projects were "little houses." When he first arrived, he said, "I was almost jealous." He described a friend speaking about his childhood, saying, " 'I remember we used to climb trees and jump on the trampoline.' And 'Oh yeah, me and my dad set up this net connected to all the trees, and we used to jump off the top of the trees and land in the net'—all sorts of craziness. Everybody had pools, everybody had ATVs or dirt bikes." Dwight would tell his new friends stories about his Brooklyn childhood: "You know what we did for fun? We would go out and fuck with people. One of your crazy friends might have a problem with somebody at school, and they go pay him a visit. And hey, I got nothing else to do, so I'm gonna go with you."

In North Carolina, Dwight found more openness to crossing boundaries of race and class. At Guilford Tech, he made friends from a variety of backgrounds and let go of the veneer of hardness he had developed on the streets of Brooklyn. At the same time, he remained aware of the way his skin color defined him in the eyes of others and made him a constant target for police harassment. "It's just something we get used to, I mean, what are you going to do?" he told Josh. "I accept the fact that I'm going to be messed with, my entire life. Until the day I die, cops are probably going to screw with me."

Dwight described one incident from his first year in school. A friend had invited him to his house after the aviation class they were in together. His friend was white and lived in a wealthy area. "These homes were really big and nice."

After an hour, the two young men left the neighborhood to return to school for English class, Dwight driving behind his friend's car. When they turned into a gas station, Dwight noticed a cop parked there, watching him. Dwight drove up "to show that I wasn't scared or doing anything." Then, when they left the gas station, the cop followed him. On the highway, his friend started speeding ahead, and the cop got in front of Dwight, following his friend. Dwight kept inside the speed limit, about half a mile behind.

Then, as he approached the stoplight at the end of the highway, Dwight signaled, and switched lanes. The cop "slows all the way down, and then gets behind me at the stoplight. He pulls me over, pulls me out of the car, and says he's going to search the car. He's patting me down, and I'm in cuffs sitting on the trunk."

When Dwight asked why he had been pulled over, the cop told him it was because he didn't signal when he switched lanes. "I didn't want to be a smart ass," Dwight said, "but I'm like, you're half a mile ahead of me, following my friend, right on his bumper, and you're pulling me over because I didn't signal? And if I didn't signal for switching lanes, why do you need to search my car? I didn't realize you had to be in cuffs for that either. Do you do that to everybody? I mean, it's crazy, right? It's funny, right? But you can talk to almost any black person on the street and get the same information, so I should just stop talking about it."

Dwight described the way he learned to channel his anger into forward movement. "I'm one of those people who do believe in karma: what you put out is what you get back. Complaining isn't going to do anything. You have to take all that negative emotion and put it toward something positive. That's how I get by now."

Dwight earned a 4.0 GPA each semester in his first year at Guilford Technical Community College. In the fall and the spring, he was named to the president's list, the highest of three levels of recognition for academic accomplishment at the college. He was also selected as an ambassador, representing the school at special events, including breakfasts with government officials.

The first time Dwight returned to Brooklyn after his move to North Carolina was a shock. In gentrified Park Slope, everything was changing, with new restaurants opening, houses being renovated, "everything being taken care of." Then, he said, he rode through East New York, one of the neighborhoods where he used to hang out, "and it looks exactly the same. That same giant pothole is still there in the middle of the street. Some people have died, some are still there. Everybody's still a gangster, it's just as dangerous. I'm like, wow, this dude is still sitting on the stoop?"

The experience, Dwight said, was "like crossing the border. Everywhere else is improving, and the projects stay the same." He felt he had been transformed, and it was disorienting to encounter old friends and see the ways they hadn't. "Why is that? You can wake up and create change for yourself. But nobody's doing that, because either they just don't want to, or they're not getting help that they need." Dwight felt his life story was a powerful model: "If I'm doing it, you can definitely do it," he told a friend from high school. "You've seen how I was."

Dwight could see the negative turns his life could easily have taken. "Luckily," he said, "I decided to just stay a good person. Because I could have been really bad. It could have gone either way." Dwight said he wanted to help Josh understand the hopelessness that many of his students felt, "because you won't hear it from them, not until they might be about twenty-two. But it might be too late then. A lot of my friends got killed. All sorts of different ways. Some in car accidents, some shot. My best friend's brother got killed, right in your neighborhood. Someone put a shotgun to him, in Park Slope. I don't think it was even in the newspaper. It's kind of easy to see why you might not notice, because you're not caught up in stuff I'm caught up in. You don't see it from my perspective, you don't see the bad. You don't need to see it, I guess."

Though Dwight mostly avoided reconnecting with friends from Brooklyn, he stayed in touch with Nkese. Throughout their first year of college, they spoke frequently by phone, continuing to walk, but not cross, the line between friendship and romance. Periods of intense conversations alternated with times when Nkese refused to speak with him.

At the end of her second semester at Bates, Nkese did not return for "short term," the one-month session in late spring when students can choose to enroll in specialized seminars. "I wasn't sure how I felt about going back to Bates," she said. "I was like, 'I'm done.' I packed up my stuff and left. I just couldn't do it anymore."

4

Someone to Step Up and Pave the Way:
Ashley

Josh's first contact with Ashley Brown came the summer before he began at the Secondary School for Research. Like Nkese, Ashley had sent Josh an e-mail introducing herself. Going into her junior year, she was seeking information about applying to "early college" programs: "Some schools have told me that they offer early admissions to juniors for their senior year in which they can enter as a freshman."

Josh wrote back:

I need to know more from you in order to provide you with a decent answer. Why are you interested in leaving high school early? What advantages do you see in this over putting together a very strong junior year and then applying to colleges in the senior year?

In Ashley's response, she outlined what she hoped to achieve, the financial, educational, and personal obstacles she saw before her, and her plan to overcome them:

The reason why I asked about applying early is because of my career goals and personal life. My mother is a single mom of 3 kids, and I would like to become a physician in the obstetrics field.

84

My mom doesn't want me to work while going to school so
this year was my first and supposed to be last year to work. I
chose to work at NY Methodist Hospital this summer. I gave my
mom half of each check and saved the rest. While working there
I spoke to many physicians and residents, and they were happy
to give advice. I found out that I will need to spend a 4 year residency if wanting to pursue an Ob-gyn career, in addition to the
8 years in college. I wanted to get an early start before the pressures start kicking in. It already seems like it will take long and
I'm already starting to think lazy. Then since I won't be working
and my mom is going to have to take care of me, I wanted to at
least shed off one year of care. I'm a female, and at the hospital I didn't see anyone who was African American or who went
to school in America. Everyone was African, Middle Eastern,
Asian, and a few Caucasian.

Everyone is telling me all the scenarios of what could happen
and it's a scary thing. My grades are high, I'm focused, I don't
party, drink, smoke, etc. I feel that for my junior year, if I can get
all my work done, and apply for fall semester of college instead
of having my senior year, it might benefit me. So if I fail a class
or something of that nature I won't be a year behind, and at most
I'd be a year ahead. Everyone that made it and went to college
in my family never got to the 2nd year, except my aunt who is a
registered nurse, and my mom who is almost done with school
to become a registered nurse. I want to be the first person that
reaches high in my family and to help my mom.

From this first e-mail exchange with Ashley and throughout
his work with her, Josh knew that he wanted to play a role in helping her to reach her goals. Ashley had this effect on many of the
adults who came into her orbit. In her internship at New York
Methodist Hospital, busy doctors would take her aside to offer
advice. Her professors at the colleges where she took supplemen-
tary classes became her mentors. In her letter of recommendation,

principal Jill Bloomberg described Ashley as "a superbly dedicated and serious student," and concluded her letter, "I look forward to following her future."

At the Secondary School for Research, where students' capacity to realize their dreams often seemed uncertain, Ashley's determination was like a beam of light that helped teachers to see their own purpose. While so many students would miss appointments, fail to complete assignments, or resist help from well-intentioned adults, Ashley absorbed all she was offered. As her college counselor, Josh felt intensely his responsibility for doing what his work at Birch Wathen Lenox had best prepared him to do: help a superstar student find a place at a superstar college.

Josh met Ashley in person during his first week at the Secondary School for Research, the beginning of Ashley's junior year. She had a round face, a wide smile, and large brown eyes behind rimless glasses. Her words tumbled over each other, with a little laugh, or a pause for "okay," as she prepared to explain the "early college" requirements she had researched. Ashley had laid out options for herself with intense focus, but her manner in describing them was easygoing and warm.

As they spoke, Josh tried to get a handle on why Ashley seemed so anxious to get through her education and on track to a career. It wasn't that she felt unhappy or unchallenged at school. She loved the Secondary School for Research, where she had begun in sixth grade. "All the teachers care about us," she said. "They're not hands-off." In math, her teachers "actually took the time to break the subject down," and stayed late to give her extra help. In English, she enjoyed the challenge of expressing herself in essays and poetry and loved reading books that helped her "learn about other people and hear about their experiences." Even her take on the school's period of chaos was positive: after a year without a science teacher, the school's science coach, Amy O'Donnell, helped her prepare to retake a required New York State Regents exam, and the two developed a strong relationship. Ashley said that Jill Bloomberg was "a great principal" and that she had friends of many backgrounds.

Josh told Ashley that if she applied to college at the traditional time, her options would be much wider. He would love to be able to work with her, he said, to find the college that would be the best fit and to seek out scholarships. Ashley listened carefully and, soon after, told Josh she had decided against applying to college as a junior. She liked the idea of having more choices and, anticipating how hard she would have to work in college and medical school, she thought she should take Josh's advice to enjoy high school now.

Josh's intensive work with Ashley on her college application process began during the spring of her junior year. Her top choice at that time was the Sophie Davis School of Biomedical Education, which was founded at City College in 1973 "to recruit underrepresented minorities into medicine, increase medical services in historically underserved areas, and increase the availability of primary care physicians."[1] The program offers a five-year curriculum combining a bachelor's of science with the requirements of the first two years of medical school. If students pass their courses and licensing exam, they transfer to one of six medical schools for the final two years of clinical training. For Ashley, the program's accelerated pace made sense, as did the cost: the City College tuition would be offset by government grants and loans and by the scholarships she would qualify for with her high grades.

That spring, Ashley applied to the Queens Bridge to Medicine, a program run by Sophie Davis to prepare high school seniors for the rigors of premedical and medical studies. Students would take classes at their high schools in the mornings, then spend afternoons at York College in Jamaica, Queens, for intensive science and college preparatory work. Earning a B average in their Bridge to Medicine courses guaranteed students an interview at Sophie Davis, which accepted only 18 percent of applicants.

Josh was thrilled for Ashley when she was accepted into the

Queens Bridge to Medicine. "I am very proud of you, and it is just an outstanding opportunity for you. It sounds wonderful, and I think you deserve nothing less," he wrote in an e-mail. But Josh pushed Ashley not to focus too narrowly on Sophie Davis as her top college choice. He was concerned that the school's accelerated pace and commuter campus would make it difficult for Ashley to find the space for personal and intellectual growth cultivated at four-year residential colleges. Instead of trying to get to an MD as efficiently as possible, Josh encouraged Ashley to seek the right match between a college's character and her own. He wrote in an e-mail,

> While you're doing your research, keep an open mind, don't be so focused on the premed thing, try to imagine instead the qualities and "personality" of an institution that you would want to spend the next 4 yrs at. What are the students like? How involved are profs, what are classes like? Can you have a real relationship with your teachers, do they involve you in research opportunities? What do students do for fun? The answers to these questions, ultimately, are going to be the most important thing! Figure out which of the colleges you learn about seem to fit you well in these respects and how.

In guiding Ashley toward elite residential colleges, Josh tried to be self-aware about imposing his own priorities on a student whose experience he was only beginning to understand. Ashley did not express the desire to "get out," as Nkese had, and had no reservations about attending a school that was part of the City University of New York. But Josh also felt strongly that opening up what he saw as the best possible options for Ashley was the right thing to do. Ashley had made the choice to pursue her education at the Secondary School for Research, an underfunded, unknown public school that she had done so much to help. Now that he was the school's college counselor, Josh wanted her to benefit from the same kind of advocacy and connections that had helped his top students at Birch Wathen Lenox gain admission to Princeton, the University of Pennsylvania, and Columbia. Colleges like these would not only prepare her for medical school, he believed, but help her to grow into a leader on a larger stage.

Josh marshaled the knowledge he was beginning to build about the pipelines through which low-income public school students find their way into the country's most prestigious colleges. Though they express a desire to increase racial and economic diversity, most colleges do not effectively identify promising students from high schools outside their network of private schools or well-resourced public schools. For help, colleges turn to programs that create small pools of prescreened students through their own recruitment and application processes.

Questbridge, one of the best known of these programs, connects underrepresented students to the Ivy League, to highly selective research universities such as Emory and Vanderbilt, and to small liberal arts colleges such as Swarthmore and Williams. According to its website, Questbridge operates from the belief that, while top colleges strive to diversify, they "lack the reach to attract appropriate candidates from low-income populations" where talented, qualified students exist in large numbers but rarely apply to elite colleges. Though colleges may find it difficult to find them, every year "approximately 30,000 low-income students score over 1300 on the combined math and verbal SAT scores, and another 42,000 score over 1220. Moreover, over a third of top low-income performers don't take the SAT."[2]

Josh knew that Questbridge would be a stretch for Ashley. Ashley had scored 1100 on her SAT, well below the score of 1220 that Questbridge uses as a benchmark to identify promising candidates. That the program relied so heavily on SAT scores bothered Josh. He had no doubt that Ashley was one of the country's "best low-income students," and that like most students in her demographic, her SAT scores did not reflect her ability to be successful in college. Though Questbridge effectively helped many low-income students gain access to elite colleges, Josh saw it as supporting an admissions system that overvalues standardized testing.

Josh was more hopeful about Ashley's chances of winning a Posse scholarship. Posse seeks its scholars through an alternative admissions process that gives substantial weight to qualities it deems vital to success on campus and in the workplace, including intrinsic leadership ability, skill at working in a team setting, motivation, and desire to succeed. Posse scholars are awarded "four-year, full-tuition leadership scholarships" by the Posse Foundation's partner colleges and universities.[3]

Posse identifies applicants by asking public high schools and community-based organizations in major urban centers to nominate students. Nominees then proceed through stages of Posse's Dynamic Assessment Process. In the first round, Posse "trainers" observe candidates as they work through a variety of group challenges. As one example, a student described a task in which nominees were shown a robot made of Legos. Each group was then given a box of Legos and told to reconstruct the robot. The robot, however, had been moved to another room, and only one member of the group at a time was allowed to leave to look at the original model. In this kind of challenge, success depends on students' use of effective strategies for collaboration and communication.

Posse's structure is also based on the idea that students will thrive within communities of support. According to its mission statement, "Posse started in 1989 because of one student who said, 'I never would have dropped out of college if I had my posse with me.'"[4] In the third and final round of the Dynamic Assessment Process, each of Posse's partner colleges selects a group of students, a posse, from among the finalists, based in part on how they function together. When Ashley was a junior, students in the New York region were matched with colleges that included Babson, where Nkese's close friend Candace Jones had been awarded the scholarship; Brandeis; Trinity; Colby; and Franklin and Marshall.

Josh thought Ashley fit the profile of a Posse scholar: she was an excellent team player, and would benefit from the leadership training, academic guidance, and social support network. She was not economically eligible for HEOP, which provided similar services to participating students. But Josh also believed that Ashley had both the skills and the self-discipline to be successful in college outside the context of a comprehensive support program. In addition to encouraging Ashley apply to Questbridge and Posse in the fall, Josh began to think about colleges where he had strong relationships with admissions officers and could ensure Ashley's application was on their radar.

Josh and Ashley e-mailed back and forth throughout the summer after her junior year. In mid-July, when Ashley sent Josh her updated list, Josh responded with additions:

I would really like for you to take a good, hard look at Swarthmore. It's a seriously intellectual place, and I could see you really thriving there. I have to mention Haverford, too, which is right next door, and which is an amazingly tight-knit community of intellectuals and activists (and they have a really cool honor code). Both places are among the most selective small colleges in the country, and would surely help you to get to a great med school.

Did you look into Brandeis, or Trinity, as possible other Posses? I love the Posse program because they do so much to build leadership qualities and support their scholars, ensuring that they graduate successfully and get where they want to go after college.

And what happened with Dartmouth? You mentioned it to me, I wonder if you looked?

Finally, if you're going to consider Bates, you should look at Bowdoin, too. It's among the most elite small colleges, like Swarthmore, and also in Maine like Bates.

Remember, this summer it's GOOD to keep an open mind and let your list continue to be loose and open, even if it feels uncomfortable. Keep researching and keep looking at different

colleges. You want to really know about as many of the options
that are out there as possible before you make decisions about
where you are actually going to choose to apply. And because
you've done so well so far, there are a LOT of options out there
for you.

Many of the colleges Josh mentioned run "multicultural" recruitment weekends, when potential candidates are invited for
fully funded introductions to campus and academic life. Colleges
use applicant pools for these weekends to prescreen for competitive
candidates for admission. In August, Ashley received invitations to
apply to weekends at Cornell, Dartmouth, Colby, Bates, and the
University of Chicago, all of which would be held in September or
October. While he was spending time with family in Williamstown, Massachusetts, Josh thought of Williams College for Ashley.
The application deadline had passed for the Williams weekend, but
Josh was able to speak with Liliana Rodriguez, the director of diversity recruitment, who said that Ashley could still apply.

Along with working on applications for these programs, over the
summer Ashley began to draft her personal essay. It opened with
her great pride in her mother, Karleen Brown, who in June had
completed the coursework necessary to become a registered nurse
and graduated from the Borough of Manhattan Community College. Here is Ashley's final draft:

June 1, 2007. I'm sitting in Madison Square Garden and there are
seas of blue and orange marching to the rhythm of "Pomp and
Circumstance." Then I see my mom walking down the aisle of
the lower level. I still can't believe that I'm actually sitting here
at her college graduation cheering her on, the same way she has
done for me over the years.

My mom always said that her dream in life was to become
either a doctor or a registered nurse. When she was in Trinidad,

she started training with the Red Cross. But because of lack of finances and opportunities, she decided to come to the United States, where she had to start over from scratch. She worked long hours in a supermarket even while pregnant with me. Then when I was about two years old, she started a training program at New York Methodist Hospital to become a nurse technician. Although she got a better paying job, she still had to work long hours to afford the rent in a safe neighborhood and to take care of three children.

When I was in the ninth grade, my mom decided that she wanted to go back to school to become a registered nurse. It was a rough three years while my mom went through college. I had to balance housework, schoolwork, and extracurricular activities with helping my mom. But it was worth it to help my mom reach her goals. I volunteered to type the essays she wrote for class so that she could study. I helped her to make flash cards to memorize the names and uses of different drugs before her tests. There were many nights that we stayed up until 3 a.m. studying and doing homework together, to then have to wake up at 7 a.m. to do it all over again. We bonded during our late nights, and it gave us a lot of time to spend together within our busy schedules.

Seeing my mom so motivated and persistent through all of her obstacles helped to further motivate me. When she decided to become a nurse, people at work and others in our family told her that she was too old at thirty-seven to be just starting college and that she wouldn't get into the nursing program because there are younger aspiring nurses that don't. But my mom still pressed on, and is now an alumna of Borough of Manhattan Community College.

Just like my mom, the odds are against my dream of becoming a physician. Most of my family members have never gone to college, neither of my parents have a bachelor's degree, and my father and grandparents never graduated high school. I'm also a female "minority" living in a lower-middle-class household with one parent who isn't from this country. Since I'm the eldest and in the first generation of my family to go through my whole schooling in the United States, I didn't have anyone to teach me about the things I know about now, like the importance of the SAT.

I have also faced a lot of discouragement, even within my own extended family. My sister's father and his family look down on my father's side of the family for their lack of education and the many children with different fathers or mothers. They told my mother that I wouldn't make it in life, based on stereotypes within the African American community, even though I was getting good grades in school. Even as I apply to college, my sister's father told me that I shouldn't waste my time applying to selective schools because since my mother and I don't have any money, connections, or power, I won't get in.

For a long time I felt a lot of hurt and doubt about my future, even though my teachers always told me that I could do anything in life. But with my mom as a model, I have learned to let obstacles and discouragement make me stronger. When I hear that I can't do something, it only pushes me to do it more. There are many people who, because of fear or doubt, won't chase their dreams. If they want to be a lawyer, they settle for being a paralegal. If they want to be a doctor, they settle for being a nurse. Although there is nothing wrong with those jobs, they should go for their dreams. My dream is to get into a good college where I can grow and express myself, to go to medical school, and to become a mentor for others. I know that I'm going to achieve my dreams because I tell myself I am every day, and I believe it.

I'm not working hard only for myself. I'm working hard for all of those kids who people say will never succeed. Someone has to step up and try to pave the way for others.

As Ashley described in her essay, she and her mother pursued their education in partnership with each other, sitting together at their rectangular kitchen table late into the night. Karleen had been very strict with Ashley through elementary and middle school, and Ashley used to be "slightly rebellious." But as she entered her teenage years and Karleen began college, Ashley developed a strong sense that they were in this together. "I just said to myself, you have no choice; you can't be lazy. Your mother's in school and she needs more help." When Karleen worked nights, Ashley and her brother took turns washing and ironing their mother's uniform so it would be ready before she left for work in the evenings.

Karleen also began loosening up her rules for Ashley. "Bedtime started at eight, then it was ten, then twelve, one, or until you finish your work," Ashley said. With more flexibility, Ashley was also able to find ways to unwind from the stress of her busy life. She stayed away from parties where there was drinking, but spent time with friends, went to movies, and relaxed with a pint of Ben and Jerry's. Before bed in the evenings, she would read the Bible or books on spirituality. "I knew with the flexibility I still needed to be responsible."

Karleen held firm to one rule: that Ashley was not allowed to date until she finished all her education. Ashley understood why her mother felt so strongly that romance should wait. All the men in Karleen's life had brought trouble and heartache. And having seen her mother struggle to support three children without a college degree, Ashley knew she herself did not want kids until her career was set: "I don't want to have to work so hard and feel so stressed to take care of my family. I want to get a job I enjoy going to. I don't want to have to drag myself out of bed." But for an American teenager who anticipated twelve years of medical education following her high school graduation, it was hard to stick to the dating ban. Without her mother knowing, Ashley spoke with boys on the phone, and "once or twice, sneaked out."

Ashley began her senior year with a dense array of tasks and choices before her. She would need to complete the application for Questbridge by the end of September and select which one of its partner colleges would be her top choice. The Posse selection process also began in September. Some multicultural recruitment weekends were still accepting applications. Ashley would soon begin the Queens Bridge to Medicine program, where earning good grades would increase her chance of acceptance to the Sophie Davis School of Biomedical Education.

Sophie Davis was still at the top of Ashley's list, but she was beginning to have second thoughts. Living in Park Slope, she said, "a lot of my neighbors are doctors." One physician told her that "many minorities just want to go to Sophie," perceiving it, as Ashley did, as a fast track to medicine. Another doctor spoke about her own decision not to attend a similar accelerated program at Howard University: she discovered that what she needed wasn't less, but more time to work toward an MD, and ultimately completed her BA in five years. Ashley knew that many students at Sophie Davis did not make it through. "If you don't get the grades, you get kicked out, and then what are you going to do?" Ashley asked herself.

On Thursday, September 13, Ashley learned that she had been accepted to Windows on Williams (WoW), the recruitment weekend for which she had submitted an application in August. "Wow is right!" Josh wrote in an e-mail after she told him. Though neither Ashley nor anyone in her family had heard of Williams, Josh assured her it was one of the most prestigious colleges in the country. The event was just two weeks away.

The following Monday, Ashley began her Queens Bridge to Medicine classes. After taking physics, U.S. government, and physical education at the Secondary School for Research in the morning, she traveled more than an hour on the F train to York College in Jamaica, Queens. She joined a group of students who, like her, had an exceptional work ethic and had excelled in difficult circumstances. On Mondays, Wednesday, Thursdays, and Fridays she would take chemistry, English and calculus from 1:10 to 4:10 p.m., sometimes staying until 6 p.m. for tutoring. Tuesdays were for field trips, and Saturdays were reserved for SAT/ACT prep.

Ashley worried about how she would manage all of this along with her high school coursework, her role as the student representative on the School Leadership Team at the Secondary School for Research, her household responsibilities, the abnormal psychology course she was taking on Sundays at the Borough of Manhattan Community College, and the college visits Josh was encouraging her to make. Already, her commitment to the long weekend at Williams meant missing a day of Bridge to Medicine classes. Describing her first day in the program, she wrote to Josh, "They went a little easy on us today, but we're in for a lot of work."

In the third week of September, Ashley joined hundreds of nominees for her Posse group interview, the first stage of Posse's Dynamic Assessment Process. After the event, Ashley wrote a long e-mail to Josh describing her experience. She was sensitive to the way other students seemed to be jockeying for the attention of the trainers and feared that her quieter leadership skills had not stood out. For example, she said, "a girl started to talk and people started to talk over her. Then when I brought it to their attention, they let her get one word in and then cut her off again." But Ashley left feeling that if she were selected for the next round of Posse, she would persist in the process:

> Overall it was fun. I met some really cool and intellectual people and I got to see how it is to work under pressure. So you were right as usual lol it is something I'd be willing to explore.

The Friday after her Posse interview, Ashley traveled by bus to Williamstown, Massachusetts, for the Windows on Williams program. It was a beautiful weekend, the mountains around the campus just starting to turn orange for autumn. The spire of the Congregational church shone bright white against the blue sky. In the science quad, Ashley watched students in sweatshirts emerge from brick buildings with "Biology," "Chemistry," and "Physics" carved above the doorways. She tried to imagine what it would be like to study here, in a world far from her family and life in Brooklyn.

The three days were packed with activities. Ashley wrote to Josh that she had attended an art history class, played pool, and had dinner with faculty. She rode a horse for the first time. "Tonight," she reported, "we are going to a jamboree. They also have parties but I'm not a party person so I might go to the movies. If not I'll stay in and try to get some more work done."

Even as Ashley was soaking up the activities of the weekend, she was scrambling to finish her Questbridge application, which was due that Sunday. From her host's dorm room, she e-mailed back and forth with Josh, himself rushing to complete her letter of recommendation. It was in one of these e-mails that Ashley reported happy news: "My mom told me that Posse sent home a letter saying that I am moving on to the 2nd round. I'm shocked. Until I see the letter when I get home I still won't believe it."

As a Posse semifinalist, Ashley needed to rank her top three choices from among the Posse New York partner colleges. Her first choice was the Brandeis University Science Posse, for candidates who express strong interest in scientific research. Ashley decided on Franklin and Marshall College as her second choice and Colby College as her third, though she knew little about either school. In the next couple of weeks, she would participate in the next stage of the selection process: submitting her transcript, SAT scores, essays, and a writing sample and meeting for an individual interview with two Posse trainers.

Ashley also had to rank her choices for Questbridge. She decided to list Williams first. Her participation in Windows on Williams boosted her chances of acceptance there, and she had heard from another student at WoW that "there are so many Questbridge applicants that you'll only be considered for your first choice, because the other schools will be filled from first-choice applicants."

Though Josh knew Ashley was already managing a tremendous amount completing her Posse and Questbridge applications, he asked her if she would consider submitting an early decision application. "Tell me if your visit to Williams has changed your feelings about what colleges are most important on your list," he wrote in an e-mail. "Should we be thinking about applying early decision somewhere by November 1???"

Early decision requires students to commit to attending a college if they are accepted. As Josh told Ashley, many colleges are more willing to take a chance on and allocate resources to a student they know will attend. If Ashley did not move on to the next round in either Posse or Questbridge, early decision would be another way to improve her chances, if she felt strongly enough that a college was her first choice.

Ashley considered applying early to either Cornell or Williams. Cornell had been on her mind since the spring, when her mother spoke to a friend whose daughter had been accepted there. "Although it's not in NYC it's in New York State so my mom is willing to let me go since it's an Ivy League school," she had written to Josh. Karleen felt more wary about the idea of Ashley leaving home to attend Williams. But with her visit there still fresh in her mind, on October 13, Ashley wrote to Josh that she had decided to apply to Williams early decision. The deadline was November 10.

Ashley's application package was complete by the end of October. As a whole, it was a testament to Ashley's character as well as a record of her achievements. In his counselor letter, Josh described Ashley as "exceptionally intelligent and driven," as well as "humble, down-to-earth, and funny." Ashley, he continued, was

dedicated both to pursuing knowledge for its own sake and as a pathway to achieving her goals. She is mature and sophisticated in her analysis of behavior and situations, and endlessly curious about the world around her. I have never heard her say anything negative about another person. She is easy in conversation, her peers have the utmost respect for her, and she is friends with students from a huge range of ethnic backgrounds.

Ashley's science teacher Amy O'Donnell wrote,

Ashley has made bold steps to ready herself for a premed program in college, sometimes managing a solidly booked schedule without a hint of stress. She will surely be an excellent physician. In addition to her aptitude in science and collaborative nature, her respect and compassion for others are true predictors of a wonderful bedside manner.

Ashley's "meaningful activity" essay for the Common Application, about her experience as an intern at New York Methodist Hospital, made clear that her drive to become a doctor grew from compassion as well as ambition. Ashley knew the hospital well: her mother had worked there for as long as Ashley could remember, and it was just around the block from their home. Methodist was also right next door to the Secondary School for Research, and as a junior, Ashley had established an internship program there for other students from her school.

Starting her own internship, Ashley wrote, she had felt uncomfortable "seeing people naked and helping people with their private matters." But after a week, patients "began to open up to me, and I learned how to lower my guard and relate to them as human beings." Ashley grew to see how important this kind of connection could be:

I remember one day when I was picking up trays after lunch time, I saw a woman who had been there for two days. She was the only patient left in the room. I began to talk to her, and she began to complain about how tangled her hair was. I asked her if I could comb it and braid it, so that it wouldn't be a bother. While talking to her and doing her hair, I realized that she didn't know where she was, except for the fact that she was in a hospital, and although she knew that she was in a hospital, she didn't know how or when she got there. To me, not knowing where you are is a scary thing, and I was glad that she felt that she could trust me. I thought about my mom and how I do her hair at home, and I began to wonder where the patient's family was and if they were looking for her. My mom always tells me that I need to listen closely when people talk, because you can get clues about their intentions or how they are truly feeling inside if they don't want to express themselves. Although the patient never said anything about being scared, or about the surgery she had just learned she was going to have, by the soft way she spoke and the way she kept staring out of the window, I knew how nervous she was. But I think talking to me, and being able to start to piece together what had happened with someone she trusted made her feel less afraid. When the patient left for surgery she looked a little bit calmer, and although I wasn't able to go down with her in the elevator like she requested, I still knew in my heart that she'd be all right.

Josh felt satisfied that Ashley was in good shape with her applications. But by the end of October, Ashley had become anxious and despondent. She was in danger of failing both chemistry and calculus in the Queens Bridge to Medicine and was considering withdrawing from the program. On October 28, she called Josh to tell him that she had not been accepted as a finalist for Questbridge. In a follow up e-mail, she wrote,

I hope you got the voicemail message about Questbridge and about discontinuing Bridge to Medicine. I am awaiting your advice, so that if it is best for me not to continue I can alert the program as soon as possible.

It was new to Josh to see Ashley so full of self-doubt. He called the director of the Bridge to Medicine program to speak about

Ashley's situation. The director, who knew Ashley, was matter-of-fact: "Some students don't make it," she said. She suggested that Ashley spend more time in the tutoring sessions that the program offered and devote more hours to studying.

Josh felt defensive at the suggestion that Ashley could work any harder or that she might not have what it would take to make it through. He felt even more strongly that Ashley's potential would be better recognized and cultivated at a liberal arts college than at Sophie Davis. Liliana Rodriguez, the Williams admissions counselor who had read Ashley's application to Windows on Williams and met her during the weekend, told Josh, "She's golden."

Josh told Ashley he would support a decision to withdraw from Bridge to Medicine. She was already doing too much, and with her early applications in, he didn't think withdrawing would harm her college prospects. But Ashley knew that quitting Bridge to Medicine would mean giving up on the idea of Sophie Davis, which, if none of the early options worked out, was still among her top choices. She decided to stick with the program, meeting with the math teacher from the Secondary School for Research early in the mornings for extra help in calculus.

In the first week of November, Ashley received the news that she was a finalist for Posse, one of approximately 300 chosen from the 3,500 students who began the process as nominees. She was one of twenty students matched with Colby College, her third choice. Just before Thanksgiving, she would need to complete the Common Application with the Colby College supplement and drop it off at the Posse offices. Then, in December, the twenty finalists for the Colby Posse would come together for stage three of the Dynamic Assessment Process: another set of group challenges, with university officials present. During this final round, Colby would select the ten students who would comprise its Posse.

Because Posse requires students to make an early decision commitment if they win the scholarship, Ashley could not simultaneously apply early decision to Williams and accept her position as a

Posse finalist at Colby. She would need to decide which application to withdraw.

The principal, Jill, felt strongly that Ashley should continue with Posse. Jill was a huge fan of the program, which she saw as vital not only for providing students like Ashley with a pathway to highly selective colleges but for challenging injustice within the system. She saw Posse's assessment process as more accurate and more democratic than traditional admissions criteria. She also admired the way Posse trained its scholars to become agents of change in their campus communities.

Josh shared Jill's view of Posse, but was very excited at the idea that Ashley might attend Williams. He tried to assess the degree to which this feeling came from his own desire for a triumphant outcome to the long process they had been through together. Would the difference in level of prestige between Williams and Colby be significant for Ashley? Ashley had never visited Colby, but Josh agreed with Jill that Ashley could not go wrong with Posse, where her chances of being accepted at this point were probably higher. Posse would offer her a full-tuition scholarship, leadership training, a powerful support structure during college, and a network of professional connections after graduation. If Ashley were not selected as a Posse scholar, she could still apply to Williams in the regular decision pool. But withdrawing her early application to Williams would significantly lower her chances of admission there.

Josh felt he could not advise Ashley to drop out of Posse without having some measure of confidence that admission to Williams was likely. He called his admissions contact, Liliana Rodriguez, and explained Ashley's situation. He knew that an admissions officer would never give him a straight yes or no answer before a decision was made, but that in a relationship of trust he could get some indication of how things stood. Josh learned that Lili had reviewed Ashley's application and run it by the director of admissions and that it looked strong. Without telling Ashley about this conversation, Josh told her that he thought she had a high likeli-hood of getting into Williams.

Ashley remembered weighing her options. She feared the iso-lation she would face in leaving her mother, who was uncertain about letting her go, though she would ultimately respect Ashley's decision. Posse was attractive as a way to get to know a group of people who would ease her way into the school. "I have a lot of friends, but I have problems warming up," she said. But Colby was even more remote than Williams, and Ashley had never visited the campus. "The problem with Colby was the distance," she said. "How was I going to get my stuff there?"

Ashley made a pros and cons list. "Since I actually went to Williams, I wrote down all the things I wanted to do there," she remembered. "I loved the classes, the professors." She imagined continuing conversations she'd had with faculty and joining them in research in their labs. At Williams, it seemed, the stress of studying would be offset by the thrill of riding horses or the ease of attending a movie in a college theater. She had missed an archery event during the weekend and imagined another chance to try her hand at a bow and arrow. She withdrew her Posse application.

5

Away from the Madness:
Mike and Abby

Michael Forbes and Abigail Benavente, who were in the same class as Ashley, received their admissions results in late March and early April 2008. Abby, who longed to leave home, was accepted to Muhlenberg, Hobart and William Smith, Union, and St. Lawrence, all private residential colleges where she would be fully funded, as well as to Hunter College in Manhattan. She was placed on the waitlist at Skidmore.

Mike, still conflicted about whether to leave his family while they were in desperate circumstances, was accepted to Brooklyn College, as well as to Skidmore, Alfred, Hobart and William Smith, Union, and St. Lawrence. He was also admitted to Morehouse and Clark-Atlanta, both historically black colleges in Georgia.

Mike told Josh that he had decided to go to Brooklyn College. He did not even want to visit the other colleges to which he had been accepted. Since he had decided that staying in New York City was the right thing to do, he would be better off not knowing what he was missing.

Josh had a lot of trouble accepting this decision from Mike. As he had been doing since the fall, Josh continued to speak with Mike about all he might gain from a residential college experience. But Josh finally began to see that his advice was only increasing

Mike's stress. Mike was hearing him, but Josh hadn't really been listening to Mike. The more time Josh spent with Mike, the more Josh realized he needed to let Mike come to the decision himself. It was Mike's sense of how badly his mother needed him that had tipped the scales toward Brooklyn. Mike didn't need to worry instead about disappointing Josh, whom he had begun to call his "white dad" as a joke.

Josh was also losing his sense of certainty that the choice to leave home was the right one for Mike. Like Abby, Mike would be fully funded through HEOP at the New York State liberal arts colleges where he had been accepted. But maybe declining a full scholarship to a selective residential college was not as crazy as it first seemed, even for a student who was homeless. Perhaps the best option for Mike was to attend CUNY, the application that had taken him twenty minutes to fill out. He would be able to continue to help his family and to move forward with his education without launching into a world that would distance him, physically and psychologically, from the people he loved.

Still, Josh knew how impersonal the CUNY college experience could be. Even the most highly motivated students could get lost in the system's bureaucracies, their plans derailed by administrative errors or misunderstandings. And, as in high school, Mike would need to study with the daily stress of holding his family together. If he went away, he could focus on learning and pursuing extracurricular activities, as he had when he was younger in Georgia. Brooklyn College had excellent professors and was among the best of the CUNY schools, but the experience didn't have the same potential to open new doors. In speaking to Mike, it was hard for Josh not to push him to at least visit the residential colleges, so that Mike could understand more fully what they offered.

Mike at first resisted. But eventually his own curiosity and desire "to have things laid out in my mind" won over, and he agreed to make the visits. Mike ruled out Morehouse and Clark-Atlanta because of their weaker financial aid packages, but agreed to attend "accepted student weekends" at the colleges in upstate New York.

Known among admissions officers as "yield" events, these visits are intended to give admitted kids a flavor of life at the college and convince them to come. The weekends are fueled by students' excitement to finally be wooed by the colleges they have worked so hard to impress. College life is concentrated into several days of classes, parties, presentations, and sleepless nights hanging out in dorms with the students who host them. HEOP offices often run their own events and provide transportation to bring students to campus from New York City. In April, Mike and Abby both signed up for weekends at Union, Hobart and William Smith, and St. Lawrence. Mike would also attend the weekend at Skidmore.

Abby's father was reluctant to let her make these visits. He was afraid of the drinking and parties he associated with dorms and didn't like Abby staying out late. Abby was not attracted to partying. What appealed to her in campus life was the space and time to pursue her own development. At Union College, she stayed with Emilia Strzalkowska, who had graduated from the Secondary School for Research the year before. "Everything was in her hands," Abby remembered observing during the visit. "She had time to study, time to do activities, time to have fun." At home, Abby said, "I was just so limited. We had no money. We were tight on space. The house was crazy. I wanted to be able to control my own life. And I wanted to be able to be by myself, and to be able to say, 'I'm doing it on my own.'" Her favorite visit was to Hobart and William Smith, a beautiful and remote campus on Seneca Lake in upstate New York.

Mike tried to imagine himself at each of the colleges he visited. He asked his student hosts questions: What are the girls like? How are the professors? He found himself at ease at the parties, despite the fact that in Brooklyn he rarely socialized with anyone outside of school. The stress and anxiety that had consumed him for months seemed to evaporate. "I wasn't really much worried about anything," he said.

On the bus ride back from Union and Skidmore, which he had visited over the same weekend, the weight of the decision bore back down on him. Thinking over the experiences, he asked himself, "Is this something worth leaving my family for or would it be okay if I didn't go?" Like Abby, Mike was attracted to the independence of college life: the chance to manage his own time, to select his own classes, to live in a dorm where he could come and go as he chose. Brooklyn College would be "thirteenth grade," an extension of high school, where he would attend classes, perhaps participate in an after-school activity, and then return to his family responsibilities. As the bus approached New York City, he decided he wanted to go away.

Which college? Mike analyzed his impressions from the visits. He had enjoyed his experience at Union, in Schenectady, New York, where he was impressed by tours of academic buildings and science labs and noticed more students of color than at the other two colleges, though he didn't know the numbers. He had also observed that "every girl he saw was holding hands with some guy," and he had less contact with HEOP staff than at the other colleges. Hobart and William Smith seemed large and spread out, and black and Latino students "had their own parties," and didn't seem integrated with the larger population.

He had most consistently enjoyed his visit to Skidmore. His host waited for him outside the bus with Mike's name on an oversize index card. The dorm room where he stayed was a triple, with a fridge full of Keystone beer. Two out of the three roommates were athletes. Mike's host explained how the student ID worked—that you could swipe it to get into the residence hall, to check out library books, or to pay for meals. He told Mike about the dorm's quiet hours and that each dorm was supervised by a head resident as well as a resident assistant on each floor; this sense of order and respect appealed to Mike, who was still living with the daily humiliation and squalor of life at the shelter. The floor Mike stayed on was gender-neutral, meaning that guys and girls might share a suite. This also appealed to him, though he disliked the openness of the hallway bathroom, where he wouldn't be able to control its cleanliness.

Mike was struck by the friendliness of the students. His host left one of his classes fifteen minutes early to meet Mike and had collected fliers listing campus events. Once, while he was walking across campus, a student noticed Mike was lost and stopped, asking, "Are you a freshman?" When he told her he was on a college visit, she walked him all the way to class, chatting the whole time. Mike liked being mistaken for a student. It made him feel that he was wanted and could fit in. And during a panel on student life, a student observed that for guys, the "female-to-male ratio is in your favor." Mike decided to skip the upcoming visit to St. Lawrence, a seven-hour-drive away, and settled on Skidmore.

When Mike got off the bus at New York's Port Authority, he felt a mixture of elation and anxiety. He wondered, "What could possibly happen in my future at college? What would it be like being the guy sitting on the grass outside reading a book?" At the same time, it was nerve-wracking to imagine announcing his decision to his mother, his brothers, and his girlfriend. He played out the conversations in his head: "My mom would say, 'Okay, yeah, that's good, go upstate to school,' but really be thinking in the back of her mind, 'What am I going to do now, with two kids and a job and no help?'" He imagined having to explain to his brothers that he was going away. He knew that "the conversation would make me feel worse, because I'd be telling these kids, nine and ten years old, that they have to take care of themselves, and they're still so young."

At the end of April, Abby was notified she had been accepted off the waitlist at Skidmore. While she had been excited about Hobart and William Smith, Josh encouraged her to take the spot.

The Skidmore HEOP program was reputed to be the best in the state, the college had the rich extracurricular life Abby would love, and if Mike decided to go, they would be there together.

Mike made a list of the pros and cons of going away. He put a big star next to some items, a little star next to others. His mother and brothers needed him. But he wouldn't be gone all the time and would only be a phone call away. If he went away, he would be happy. If he wasn't happy, he decided, he wouldn't be successful.

Two days after their graduation from the Secondary School for Research, Mike and Abby arrived in Saratoga Springs to begin Skidmore's Summer Academic Institute, the bridge program required for students in the college's Opportunity Programs.

Mike drove to Skidmore with his mother, Ebony. The two had been companions on many long car rides. The first was when Mike was in kindergarten, when Ebony first got him out of Brooklyn. This move had been spurred by an event still vivid in Ebony's mind. One morning, she had left Mike at his school bus stop with other parents while she ran back to her apartment to go to the bathroom. From her doorway, she had heard gunshots and a woman screaming, "A boy has been shot." Lying on the sidewalk was a boy Mike's age, dressed in the same jeans and Timberland boots Mike had been wearing, struck by a stray bullet from the shooting.

Ebony had moved first to Virginia, then to Georgia, supplementing her work as a dialysis technician with sideline businesses, saving money, and seeking houses in districts with good schools. She remembered, with humor, the anxiety she provoked among her mostly white neighbors. The day after she moved into their house in Lithia Springs, Georgia, she was stopped by a state trooper. He had seen her out-of-state commercial license plate—she had previously used her car as a taxi—and wanted to know what she was doing in the neighborhood. The state trooper harassed her for days, she remembered, until he began to show up at her yard sales, buying her bootleg DVDs.

Ebony called Mike her "ambassador" because his natural friendliness endeared him to everyone. The couple who lived next door had initially seemed uncomfortable when Mike's family moved in, but Mike helped make a neighborly connection. When Ebony had to go away for a few days, she received a call on her cell phone: there were intruders in her house. The neighbors felt bad, Ebony said, when she explained that these two black men were relatives.

As a gesture of apology when Ebony returned, the husband brought over a freshly killed deer. Ebony hesitated—she didn't know what to do with it, she said. Her neighbor popped a piece of raw meat in her mouth. "Delicious, right?" he said. The couple taught her to garden, and she enjoyed fresh lettuce and greens, until she realized her next-door neighbors were shooting and eating the rabbits the plants attracted. Despite their differences, Ebony grew close to the couple next door, who let her younger sons, Anthony and Justin, spend long afternoons catching crawfish in the creek behind their house.

Ebony's last long drive with Mike at her side had been their journey from Georgia back to Brooklyn. During her year in Lithia Springs, the stomach troubles Ebony had experienced since childhood had intensified, with abdominal and back pain that was often debilitating. When she saw doctors, she was repeatedly told that they didn't know the cause and that there was nothing they could do.

Ebony believed her chronic stomach problems were exacerbated by her work as a dialysis technician, where she was surrounded by people who were sick. She found a new position selling cars: the best job she ever had, she said. She made twelve thousand dollars in the first month, selling Toyotas on commission. Benefits would begin after she had worked a certain period of time, and Ebony did not purchase insurance independently, instead paying out of pocket for continued doctor's visits.

It was during this time that she was referred to a specialist, who diagnosed her immediately with a stage two abdominal cancer. Soon, she became too sick to work regularly. She applied for Medicaid, but was not eligible because she owned her own home. To pay for her chemotherapy treatments, she depleted her entire IRA and sold her house. She received disability for a short period of time but was unable to renew it. The problem, Ebony realized, was that to qualify for disability you have to be out of work for a year, and she kept returning to work when she could.

When Ebony ran out of money, the hospital told her she could no longer receive treatments there. She called Grady, the large public hospital in Atlanta, and was told she could be scheduled for an appointment in three months' time. They would need to do the whole diagnostic process again, because they could not provide services for an illness they had not documented themselves. Ebony didn't think she had three months to live. She decided to move back to New York City. She now qualified for Medicaid and would not have to wait for treatment at Kings County Hospital.

Her return to Brooklyn kept Ebony alive, but the city seemed to her a place of grayness and death. Driving Mike to Skidmore now, the hope and pride she felt as she brought her eldest child to this plush, green upstate college was mixed with her fear of going back to Brooklyn and a life without him.

Abby's parents, Jaime and Angie, both came along to drop off their daughter, who sat among suitcases in the backseat of their crowded car. The last few days had been filled with excitement. At graduation, Abby posed for photos with the teachers and friends she loved, dimpled and beaming in her wire-rimmed glasses and large hoop earrings. Abby's friends played with Valerie, her two-year-old niece, who made everyone laugh with her chatter and mischief, her diaper sticking out beneath her flowered dress.

Both of Abby's parents, however, felt intense ambivalence about her leaving home. Her father worried about how he would send her the money she needed, and how their household would function in her absence. It was hard to imagine the family's resources stretched more thinly, and they depended on Abby to care for Valerie while her sister Ruth worked. Jaime also felt misgivings about the permissive atmosphere he associated with college campuses. In Peru, by his own account, he had sinned deeply: drinking, using drugs, fighting, and being abusive to those he loved. His religious conversion, inspired by an encounter with an old man who read him a verse from the Bible, transformed his life. Jaime knew that on campus, boys and girls lived together in dorms and social life centered on parties and drinking. He worried how Abby would fare among these temptations without her parents and her church to guide her.

Abby's mother understood her daughter's desire to start somewhere new. Their home was crowded and chaotic, and financial stress sometimes set off screaming fights between her and her husband. Angie was often frustrated with what she saw as Jaime's willingness to accept life in survival mode, to be content with sleeping in the car he drove or on a rented couch. "Always give your kids what you didn't have," she would tell Abby.

But Angie was very worried about her daughter's lupus. So much was unknown and unpredictable about the disease. Symptoms could be set off by environmental triggers, including an infection, exhaustion, and emotional upheaval. It was worrisome to think of Abby making a stressful move to a new place.

The two families drove toward campus along Saratoga Springs' wide tree-lined boulevards, past the large Victorian houses preserved from the town's history as a destination for its hot springs and spas. Summer visitors to the racetrack and performing arts center strolled through the well-heeled downtown, men in pastel shirts and khaki shorts, women in broad-brimmed hats.

Skidmore's campus, adjacent to downtown Saratoga Springs, was expansive and modern. The buildings were red brick and gleaming glass, the green lawns brightened by summer flowers. Mike and Abby were greeted by Skidmore staff, and at their dorm rooms they unloaded their bags and said their good-byes. While their parents returned to Brooklyn, Mike and Abby found each other and headed outside for an orientation and kick-off barbecue.

Mike and Abby's peers in the Class of 2012 Opportunity Programs were mostly students of color and came from New York State and around the country. All were considered "economically and educationally disadvantaged" and would not have qualified for admission in the college's general application pool. At Skidmore, as at most selective colleges with comparable programs, this meant that they had scored well below the mean for admitted students on the SAT and that they lacked access to educational resources like AP classes, SAT tutoring, and extracurricular activities.

Skidmore's Opportunity Programs commit to providing students with the support they need to earn high grades and graduate in four years. Unlike at many elite schools, Skidmore's support programs for low-income students maintain data on students' academic outcomes. While mean SAT scores for participants coming in to Skidmore's Opportunity Programs are approximately 300 points lower than those for Skidmore's general population, their mean grade point average earned at the college is comparable,[1] and their graduation rate is significantly higher—reported at 94 percent the year before Abby and Mike's arrival on campus. A paper authored by members of the program's staff attributes this success to students' "motivation to succeed and the support they have available to them at Skidmore."[2] A central element of this support is the Summer Academic Institute, the four-and-a half-week summer bridge program that Abby and Mike were just beginning.

Classes started the morning after students arrived. Along with a study skills class and testing to determine their summer placements in writing and math, all students attended a course called

Pre–Liberal Studies. This class, the cornerstone of the summer bridge program, introduced the critical and interdisciplinary thinking integral to Skidmore's curriculum. It was taught by Sheldon Solomon, a self-described "egghead experimental psychologist" known for his research on the psychological effects of terror. He had devoted his summers to the Opportunity Programs for more than twenty years.

Sheldon Solomon had a long ponytail, played music before class began, and inflected every sentence with cursing, yelling, and gesticulating. He told the class, "I'm going to get all biblical on you now: Know thy shit."

Abby remembered thinking, "I'm definitely in college now."

Sheldon, as the students called him, introduced writing by Alfred North Whitehead and Allan Bloom on the idea of a liberal education. He described Whitehead's belief that to cultivate their imaginations students require "some leisure, freedom from restraint, freedom from harassing worry," and "the stimulation of other minds diverse in opinion."[3] The texts by Bloom argued that the university should create an atmosphere of free inquiry where, within a frenetically busy society, students can recognize their own capacities and contemplate life. At its best, a college formed a community of "true common good," dedicated to reason, freedom, and equality.[4]

Abby found the texts difficult to absorb, overcome as she was with the pressure of the program's "academic boot camp" mentality. She was still processing the emotional intensity of high school graduation and good-byes from the week before. The professors' expectations were clearly high at Skidmore, and she worried about whether she would be able to make it through.

But Abby was excited for the challenge. As she honed in on the readings, she thought about the ways they described the college experience she had dreamed of: a space away from the work and worry of home, where she could satisfy her curiosity about the world. She looked forward to making friends and could see how her peers in the Opportunity Programs would form a strong community. She welcomed the involvement of professors and tutors, who made it clear that they would be a constant presence throughout the summer program and would offer continued support during the school year.

Mike, however, was already chafing at the program's restrictiveness. On the first day, the tutors took away his laptop, telling him that it was too much of a distraction. Why were they treating him like he couldn't be trusted to manage his own education? He had been through so much to graduate high school and get to college. Now, the structures meant to support him seemed like another kind of entrapment. "I felt like they were punishing us," he remembered, using language that echoed his description of the homeless shelter. During the mandatory study hours, when Mike was tired but not allowed to sleep, he napped under his bed to avoid the tutors who came to check on him.

The schedule for every week was highly structured and full. Students would attend classes from 8:15 a.m. to 4:30 p.m., with a short break for lunch. From 4:45 to 5:30 p.m., they were encouraged to attend Sheldon Solomon's office hours, to read, or to work out at the gym or pool. Dinner was from 5:30 to 6:45 p.m. From 7:00 to 10:00 p.m., Sunday through Thursday, there were mandatory study hours in the dorms, supervised by tutors.

During lunch on the third day of the program, Abby suddenly felt like she needed to throw up. "You're not pregnant, are you?" she remembered Mike asking. "No!" she replied. Her stomach continued to hurt during class, and she shivered with cold despite the summer heat. Mike saw immediately how sick she was. Normally rosy cheeked and buoyant, she was pale and inarticulate. Abby went with Mike to his dorm room during their free time at 4:45. He gave her his Skidmore sweatshirt to wear, and Abby lay down in his bed.

Abby remembered speaking to a nurse on the phone, who told her that they could take her to the emergency room. Abby said that she needed to see her own doctor. The nurse, she remembered, asked her if she was stressed or homesick—maybe she didn't want to be there? Abby was hurt and angry at the suggestion. She wanted to be at Skidmore more than anything. But she felt sick and confused, unprepared to try to explain her symptoms to a doctor who didn't know about her lupus. Mike looked on as Abby called her parents. When Abby hung up the phone, she told Mike that her mother was driving to campus to get her. Mike sat with Abby for a while, put on the television show *Friends* for her, and then went out to play basketball.

Mike had a sinking feeling that he would be left at Skidmore alone. Like the program staff, he didn't know that Abby had lupus. But he knew how hard it had been for her parents to let her go, and how often students from backgrounds like his and Abby's dropped out. Now Abby, who had been the main cheerleader in the college process at the Secondary School for Research, who had spoken to him about all the reasons to leave Brooklyn, was going home after the third day. How long would he last himself?

During the mandatory study time after dinner, Abby returned to her own room because Mike needed to work. She looked at her assigned readings, but felt too sick to focus and got into bed. "You need to read," her roommate urged her, upset that Abby was breaking the rules. When a tutor checked on them and saw Abby on her bed, the tutor warned her that she would fall behind in her courses.

Monica Minor, the director of Skidmore's Opportunity Programs, came in to speak to Abby. Monica warned Abby that she couldn't enroll at Skidmore in the fall without successfully completing the summer program. If she missed more than a day or two of the Summer Academic Institute, she would have to withdraw, Abby remembered Monica telling her. Abby fell into her mother's arms when she arrived. She would go home for a checkup, Abby decided, and then return.

Abby called Josh to tell him what had happened, and Josh spoke to Monica that evening. He could hear Monica's frustration. The college had taken Abby off the waitlist in part because of Josh's advocacy. He had raved about Abby to Monica, describing her incredible curiosity, tenacity, ability, and desire to be at Skidmore. Now, after three days, Abby was going home with what looked like the flu and cold feet, and it was too late to find another student to fill her spot.

Monica's tone changed completely when Josh told her that Abby had lupus. Abby had mentioned it in her application essay, but the information must have gotten lost in the college's race to pull applications from the waitlist before students committed themselves to other schools. Josh blamed himself. Why hadn't he thought to connect Abby's family with medical resources at Skidmore and ensure that the college was fully informed about her condition? Why hadn't he realized that a family who lived so close to the edge would require advocacy in matters related to access to health care? He had worked so intensively with Abby on all aspects of her application, but missed what he now realized was the most crucial factor in ensuring that Abby had the chance at the education she longed for and deserved.

Abby remembered ignoring the disease herself. "I never really talked to anybody about it," she said. "I didn't feel like it would stop me from anything." She was used to living with lupus, and through her senior year of high school had few symptoms. "I had so many other things to worry about in getting to college," she said, "especially Skidmore because they put me on the waitlist." When she was finally accepted, she didn't want to focus on her illness or anything that might jeopardize her acceptance. "I wanted to be able to know that I had my place set, that I had a place to go after I graduate."

Abby was hospitalized for a week. Her illness was caused by the effect of stress and a new climate on her immune system, she remembered hearing from doctors. She was told that there was a problem with her liver and that she was dehydrated.

Abby felt vindicated by the severity of her symptoms. But she was still stung by the nurse's suggestion that her sickness was a self-generated excuse to leave school and upset that she was not able to return. "I thought it was unfair. It wasn't my fault I got sick." Now she would lose the opportunity for the kind of expansive education Sheldon Solomon had described and return to the limited world she knew. "It's a whole lifestyle that's been changed," she said.

Monica told Abby that she could defer her offer of admission from Skidmore and begin the Summer Academic Institute again the following year. But she would have to take a year off, instead of enrolling at another college and then transferring back to Skidmore. Abby would not consider this choice. "I couldn't miss the whole year of school," she said. "I have to go to school."

Josh was just beginning to understand this attitude. For students from the Secondary School for Research, the idea of a year off had a very different meaning than it had had for his private school students. He used to tell some families at Birch Wathen Lenox that deferring college could provide a crucial time for growth, exploration, and identity formation. It was a way for students to avoid the crush and pressure of the traditional admissions pathway, and understand what it meant to live or work independently. Ultimately, this could make their college experiences richer.

For Secondary School for Research students and their families, it was a truism that it was hard to get back on track once you left school: life would intervene. The end of high school was a crossroads. It was the time when even a student like Dwight, who did not see himself as college-bound, could find himself traveling in a new direction. Returning to school once this moment of opportunity had passed required extraordinary momentum. In starting at Skidmore, Abby had started down a kind of educational path she had not previously thought possible. Now that this pathway had been cut off three days after it began, she feared the consequences of leaving school entirely. As Ashley had articulated in her first e-mail to Josh, there were many "scenarios of what could happen" to a female student of color with limited resources.

Before meeting Josh, Abby had dreamed of going to Hunter, which she knew as the most prestigious of the City University of New York schools, and where she had been accepted that spring. Josh helped her to secure a spot at the college and enroll in Hunter's SEEK program. SEEK, which stands for Search for Education, Elevation, and Knowledge, is CUNY's version of the New York State Opportunity Programs. The oldest of these programs, SEEK provides academic support for low-income students, though in a less intensive, individualized way than through HEOP at most New York State private colleges. Abby's tuition would be covered by funds from the federal government's Pell Grant program and New York State's Tuition Assistance Program (TAP), and SEEK would provide an additional stipend for out-of-pocket costs like transportation and books. As a SEEK student, she would have an adviser with a smaller caseload than those working with the general student population and additional orientation and advising days during the summer.

Abby told herself she should be happy with Hunter, and that the issues with her health meant staying home was the only choice. It was too late for her to enroll in SEEK's summer bridge courses, so Abby spent July and August taking care of her niece and hanging out with friends.

One sunny day, she and her cousin Shirley took the subway to Coney Island. They rode the clacking wooden Cyclone and wandered along the boardwalk, past the dusty game booths and the bright signs advertising fresh clams, cold beer, hot corn, and Italian ice. They stopped at Shoot the Freak, where, in a vacant lot between two graffiti-covered brick walls, you could pay five dollars to shoot a paintball gun at a teenage boy who ducked ineffectively behind rusty metal barrels and broken furniture.

As Abby and Shirley peered over the wall, a tall young man started chatting with them. He had an ironically courtly manner and charming awkwardness that made the girls laugh. He told them his name, Quentin, and that he worked at the Astroland amusement park. Mayor Michael Bloomberg had sought developers to overhaul and revitalize Coney Island, but thanks to a popular outcry the old park was open for one last summer. Quentin asked for both Abby and Shirley's numbers, though it was clear that he was most interested in Abby. Quentin also entered his instant messaging screen name into Abby's Sidekick phone, without her realizing it.

When, the next week, Abby noticed the new contact in her phone, she messaged, "Who's this?" though she figured it was Quentin. He asked if she wanted to go out and chill with him. Abby was nervous. She was still with her high school boyfriend, though they had planned to break up when she went away to college. She had never dated anyone else and wasn't used to flirting. She told Quentin she would go out with him, but only if Shirley came, too.

Quentin met the cousins one evening outside Abby's house in Sunset Park. They walked around the neighborhood, past the small brick row houses, the Catholic school and convent, the ices stand with brightly colored syrup in glass jars. Quentin took Shirley aside to tell her he liked Abby. "You can go for it," Shirley said, "but she has a boyfriend and she's not going to pay attention." After about an hour Abby told Quentin she had to go home. She didn't have a curfew, but her father didn't like her to stay out late.

Abby broke up with her boyfriend soon after, and Quentin called again. He said he wanted to hang out alone with her and asked if she would meet him at Coney Island when he was finished with work. He had never been on the Wonder Wheel, he told her, though she knew it was a lie. From the top of the Ferris wheel, Abby looked down at the edge of sand and sea, the red and white circle of the merry-go-round roof, the rectangular towers of the housing projects. "That's where he gives me the first kiss," she remembered. They spent the afternoon "just talking, sitting on the side of the boardwalk where there aren't so many people." That same day, Quentin took her to meet his family, who lived close by on Stillwell Avenue.

Quentin had dropped out of high school and worked at Coney Island until Astroland closed, in September 2008. With Abby's encouragement, he enrolled at Manhattan Day and Night, a "transfer school" serving students who were behind in their high school requirements and older than their classmates. The school held classes in the evenings and on weekends to accommodate students who worked. Quentin also enrolled in a program in culinary arts through Co-op Tech, also a New York City public school, which offered vocational education for students completing their academic requirements elsewhere.

Abby began at Hunter that September, and Quentin would often meet her there during the hours between his morning classes at Co-op Tech and his evening classes at Manhattan Day and Night. Quentin would nap in Central Park while Abby was in class, and during her two-hour break between classes, they would sit on the steps of a Hunter building, eat lunch, then walk in the park together.

This time with Quentin eased the loneliness Abby felt as a new student at Hunter. The classes seemed impersonal, the professors distant. "It was hard because the teachers were not as there for you as they were at the Secondary School for Research," she said. At the Secondary School for Research, "I was so used to staying after school with the teachers. I was one of the geeky ones." At Hunter, "teachers would just teach you and then leave."

She was also frustrated with CUNY's bureaucracy. In her second semester, she completed her course registration feeling excited about her schedule, with classes at times that enabled her to balance study, work, and home commitments. But due to an administrative error that affected many students, federal money that was part of her financial aid package did not come through. The bursar notified Abby that because she had an outstanding balance, her registration was no longer valid and all the courses she had signed up for had been dropped.

After multiple visits to the financial aid office, hours with a semi-helpful SEEK counselor, and several calls to Josh, Abby was able to get her application for federal aid processed and ensure that Hunter's bursar had the funds on record. But Abby needed to register again, and at that late date, this meant enrolling in courses she felt less excited about, at times that made her schedule more difficult to balance. "It lasted about two, three weeks. I was going crazy. I was like, 'I hate it, I hate it here.' And everyone was like, 'Oh, the system sucks.'"

Abby thought about applying to transfer to Barnard College, an elite residential college where she could still be close to home. But it was daunting to think about another application process, and she gradually got used to Hunter. She joined a service-oriented co-ed fraternity, Alpha Phi Omega, where she organized walks for the March of Dimes, volunteered with children and the elderly, and made new friends. Her relationship with Quentin became more serious, and she invested herself in helping him pursue his education.

But college was not the new beginning she had imagined. "It sucks, because I've always felt limited at home, so tight on space and money, but now I feel limited at school, too." She knew that if she had stayed at Skidmore, the independence she longed for would have come with risk. "It's crazy, because it was so different, the type of life over there. I think it would have been hard for me, because you're really on your own. Everything was going to be my responsibility. I didn't have my mom, I didn't have my dad. The only one I knew was Mike." Skidmore would have pushed her to greater heights and raised the stakes of failure. "If I fell, I would have fallen harder than if I were to fall here," she said.

But at Skidmore, "I probably would have been smarter—well, not smarter, but with better classes and more experience."

While Abby imagined the independence she might have found at Skidmore, Mike began at the college frustrated by the limits it placed on him. After completing the Summer Academic Institute, he had very little choice in his classes for the fall. For his freshman seminar, he was assigned to Human Dilemmas, the follow-up to Sheldon Solomon's Pre–Liberal Studies class. He had decided to pursue a premed track, which meant that he had to take calculus and chemistry. He found his classes difficult and dull. "The way the classes were going shaped everything else that was going on freshman year," Mike said. "I remember a lot of times I would choose not to sit down and study hard, because I knew it would be really boring. Studying chemistry was like pulling teeth." His performance was tracked by HEOP staff, who contacted Mike to offer tutoring. But Mike found this even more demoralizing. "I didn't like to have to have someone to hold my hand, just to do coursework," he said.

Mike got along easily with his peers at Skidmore and was surprised to find himself at the center of freshman social life. One weekend night at the beginning of the year, he received text messages from eight different people who thought he would know what parties were happening. This was a big change from the Secondary School for Research, where he had hung back socially, thinking people would look at him differently because he was from the South. At Skidmore, he said, "since everyone was from different places," he "wanted to believe it was like a fresh start," where nobody would make assumptions about who he was based on where he came from.

It was just a few weeks before he "realized this wasn't necessarily true." People knew that students in the Opportunity Programs came from "disadvantaged" backgrounds, and Mike felt that other students looked down on him. He was constantly being asked,

"Oh, where are you from? Are you from the city?" Like the sections for family and demographics on the Common Application, these questions seemed a way of "putting you in a box." During his childhood in Virginia and Georgia, he had grown used to being the only black student in a class, and he tried to let comments that betrayed bias roll off him. But, he said, "I'm not a very patient person when it comes to ignorance." He remembered, in a discussion in his sociology class, when an affluent white student argued that "if an African American person or other minority were to try really hard in school and go to college, then they could get any job they wanted." Someone brought up the fact that not everyone can afford college. "Then their parents should have tried harder," the girl countered.

Mike constantly weighed the value of what he was experiencing at Skidmore against what he could contribute at home. He felt this tension especially after speaking with his mother about her financial troubles. She told him that she had asked for help from his brothers' father and from his uncles, but that none of them came through. "She's saying nobody's helping, but I'm also not helping. And then when I say I'm doing work-study and I can send something, she says, 'No, you need that to buy your own stuff.'" Mike knew his mom was not sharing everything that was going on for her and the boys and that she was protecting him from the realities of their life in Brooklyn.

Mike tried, in his first semester, "to have one foot at Skidmore, and one foot back at home with my family." He talked to Anthony and Justin every other day and bought software through which he could track their computer usage at home. "I could monitor what they were looking at online, and how much they were on X-Box." Mike traveled back to Brooklyn "by train, bus, friends, however I could." He held on to the possibility of transferring to CUNY. "It was always in the back of my mind, if something serious happened at home."

In his second semester, Mike dropped his calculus class and quit the premed track. He started to think about a business major and realized he could complete the college's math requirement with a course in economics, which was something he actually wanted to take. This was when "things began to turn around." Mike started to work harder and his grades improved. Monica, reporting to Josh on how Mike was doing, said with affection that Mike was learning that "he couldn't just get by on his good looks."

Mike also began to feel more connected to campus life. He got involved with the school senate, attended weekly meetings of the African American and Hispanic culture clubs, played intramural sports, and worked out at the gym. He joined SkidTV, the college's television station, and quickly learned how to use new technologies and to manage the creative, collaborative process of making videos. He was thrilled to have the chance to interview hip-hop artist Talib Kweli, who had performed on campus. He decided to add a minor in film to his business major.

That spring, Mike began dating Jamie, a junior from Long Island. They quickly became a serious couple. Jamie was an ambitious, outgoing psychology major who earned high grades and pushed Mike to work hard. She also recognized his tendency to block off his feelings and encouraged him to open up. "Over the years I've learned to deal with bad situations in a way that I don't get too emotional," Mike said. "I get in trouble sometimes in relationships." Mike provided Jamie with nurture and stability, helping her manage stress. He convinced her to go with him to Shabbat dinners and services at the campus Jewish center. "I wanted her to embrace her Jewish roots, and she didn't object," he said. "I find Jewish culture very interesting."

The summer after his first year, Mike returned to Brooklyn and found a job at the Gap. His mother was working, and the family was living in a three-bedroom apartment that Ebony had been able to rent through the federal Section 8 program. But his mother was still sick and barely holding it together. "She won't ever be the same as she was in Georgia," Mike said. "Working all those hours over the years takes a toll."

Mike couldn't feel at home in his family's apartment, despite his efforts to keep it clean. Though there was nothing "specifically wrong with it," he was uncomfortable in the space and hated the neighborhood. "I didn't like anything about where we were," he said. His distance from his mother had grown wider during his year away. When he was younger, he said, "she was my rock. I didn't agree with her views on interracial dating but other than that, I would tell her everything." That summer it was "you stay out of my way, I'll stay out of yours. When we did talk, I just heard about all the problems. It didn't feel like we were on the same page as each other."

Mike saw that his brothers already were not "steering toward the completely right path." They spent their time sitting around playing video games, and he had to push them to do their chores. "If you don't stay on my brothers they'll pretend like they don't hear you," he said. His mother returned home from work too physically and emotionally depleted to give them the attention they needed, and he worried about the negative influence of the streets. Mike thought about how, for the next summer, he would try to get them to overnight camp. "Nobody's showing them the right way," he said. "I want to be successful in my life, but I hope it's not too late for them to have a good childhood. I had a decent childhood, even though toward the end of it, my teen years weren't too great."

In going away, Mike had begun to see all he could gain at Skidmore. But he also saw the effect of his absence on his family. "I'm the only one benefiting right now, because I get to get away from the madness," he said. "No disrespect to my mother, but I know she can't do it on her own."

6

Do You Know What It's Like to Live My Life?
Kennetta, Angie, and Rafael

During the summer before his second year at the Secondary School for Research, Josh began a series of conversations with Christopher Hooker-Haring, dean of admissions and financial aid at Muhlenberg College, about the college's desire to recruit urban public school students. Josh had worked with Muhlenberg while at Birch Wathen Lenox, and his new school caught Chris's attention. Chris told Josh that he recognized that traditional means of evaluating applications did not appropriately value the struggles low-income students have to overcome in their everyday lives. He wanted to develop a relationship with a high school to help identify compelling "under the radar" students and ensure that they would "get credit for what they deserved credit for."

Chris proposed a partnership between Muhlenberg and the Secondary School for Research in which Muhlenberg would commit to admitting a group of Secondary School for Research students every year, offering them extensive academic and personal support and generous financial aid. Josh would work closely with the admissions staff to help them get to know the strengths of individual students and judge who would be the best fit. The proposal was based on the notion that thoughtful and well-resourced collaborations between individual high schools and colleges could help to ensure college access and persistence for low-income students. The idea for the partnership also drew on the model of Posse, in that students who already knew one another would be admitted as a group. Chris hoped that, as with Posse, this group would offer mutual support and opportunities for leadership development on campus.

The partnership began with a campus visit for students participating in Let's Get Ready, the SAT preparation and mentoring program that the Secondary School for Research had begun work with that summer. On a sunny August day, the students rode for two hours on a coach bus to Muhlenberg's campus near Allentown, Pennsylvania. They walked down Academic Row, the tree-lined walkway along the expansive green quad, facing the Gothic façade of the Hass College center, where a bell chimed the hour.

"What do you think?" Josh said to Kennetta Christian, a student with a passionate, stubborn determination and a grace Josh saw in her dancing in school talent shows. Kennetta walked alongside Frederick D'Anjou, her close friend, with a bounce in her step. "I love it here. I want to come here," she said. Many students commented how big the campus seemed, though Josh knew that with about two thousand students, Muhlenberg was a small school—an enclosed, mostly white world insulated from Allentown's struggling economy.

The student tour guide, a young woman with a wide smile and long brown hair, led the group around the campus. In the New Science Building, students admired the long lab tables outfitted with shining equipment, the flat-screen monitor that showed a nature video. The boys posed for photos with a taxidermy polar bear in a tall glass case, rearing up on its hind legs with its teeth bared.

At the information session, students met with Christopher Hooker-Haring and with Cynthia Amaya, the admissions officer who would be Josh's main contact for the partnership. Josh knew Cindy from his work at Birch Wathen Lenox. She handled all applications from New York City and was also director of multicultural recruitment. Cindy was a Muhlenberg graduate and told Josh that she had herself been the first in her family to go to college. She felt she understood the challenges the students faced in crossing worlds, and wanted to do what she could to support and encourage them.

After the information session, Daina Spencer, an intense, reserved girl who had come to the United States from Jamaica just a few months before, tapped Josh on the shoulder. Chris had mentioned students could return for an overnight, and she wanted to know if he really meant it. "Ask him," Josh said. Daina hung back through the rest of the visit, whispering her indecision to friends. At the end she approached Chris with her unsmiling poise. Chris responded enthusiastically and committed to planning a specially designed overnight visit for Secondary School for Research seniors in November.

Following the trip, Josh considered which students he would promote for a Muhlenberg "posse." The clearest choice was Kennetta, who had fallen in love with the college. Kennetta fit the profile Chris described of a promising student who would usually be off the radar for a college like Muhlenberg, and who, without support, would never have considered it a possibility. Kennetta had a B average, along with intelligence, work ethic, and leadership qualities recognized by all her teachers, but she was by no means certain she would go to college at all. It was exciting for Josh to see, from this one visit, how a positive connection with a college could reshape her sense of possibility.

Kennetta's responsiveness to this kind of connection had first struck Josh the previous spring, when he brought a group of juniors to SUNY Albany. In planning the visit, Josh kept in mind the experience of Nkese and Dwight's class at SUNY Albany, which they had visited before Josh's arrival at the Secondary School for Research. During Nkese and Dwight's visit, some students' horsing around meant that all the seniors were made to feel that they didn't belong. Josh brought a smaller group and prepped them in advance about how to represent themselves and their school. He also arranged for class visits and a meal in the dining hall with current students in the college's Educational Opportunity Program.

Kennetta and her friend Brittany Gardner didn't eat much at lunch and, just as everyone was heading to the bus, they told Josh, grumpily, that they were really hungry. Josh reluctantly let the two girls stop at the food court. When he came to rush them out, he found them leaving the building doing a little dance. "I'm a college student, I'm a college student," Kennetta sang as they walked back to the bus. Kennetta told Josh that the person serving them had asked for their meal cards, thinking they were enrolled at the university. The interaction had transformed their entire experience of the visit.

Josh knew that Kennetta and her family lived close to the edge economically. That summer, Kennetta and her friend Chiquita Hamblin had approached him to ask if subway fare could be provided for travel to Let's Get Ready, the SAT prep program at the school. The student Metrocards they received for travel to and from school only worked during the academic year. Their families had trouble coming up with the extra four dollars each day, they told him, and they knew this was the case for others as well. Josh was able to secure free Metrocards for all the students, and was grateful to Kennetta and Chiquita for their courage in making the request, helping their peers overcome an obstacle he hadn't anticipated.

The extent of the struggles his second class of seniors faced became even clearer that fall, when Josh began working with students on their personal essays in English class. After graduation the previous spring, the twelfth-grade English teacher, Menucha Stubenhaus, had been hit by a car on Coney Island Avenue, and her leg was seriously injured. Until she was able to return to school, Josh had agreed to cover her classes together with Leah Grossman, the school's literacy coach.

Josh and Leah began the class by introducing the personal essay and distributing examples written by seniors from the year before. Leah read the class a brief definition she and Josh had put together: "A personal essay is an essay you write about your experiences. Typically, personal essays show how a memory of the past significantly affects the present or the future. They weave together the story with the explanation for why this memory is significant in your life now. Try telling the story of an important memory and why it is important to you."

Midway through one of the first in-class writing assignments, Kennetta put her head on her desk. Josh walked over and asked, "Why aren't you writing?" Kennetta didn't answer. She pushed her spiral notebook toward him. Kennetta had written, in her large, rounded handwriting,

Do you know what it's like to live my life?

Sharing one room with three siblings, living in a two-bedroom apartment with seven people. Hearing and seeing fights, gunshots all night, yelling and screaming every day. Scared to walk anywhere by myself, not eating for a day or two because we don't have any money, almost being homeless a couple of times. Going to school trying to keep a smile on my face so my struggles at home don't show. Having to listen to my friends tell me about their problems and having to encourage them while yet, I'm hurting inside myself. Running to almost everyone I see just for attention to make my pain go away.

That's my life.

Josh looked back at Kennetta, but her head was still down. He stared at her notebook again, unsure what to say. For a moment he felt removed from the noise and movement of the classroom. Kennetta's writing pushed back against the future-focused momentum of the college process, asking him, it seemed, to stop, and to try to stand inside her experience.

Josh knew from his first year at the Secondary School for Research how wrenching his students' essays could be. But Mike,

Abby, Kennetta, and others in Josh's second class of students told stories that revealed with even greater rawness the poverty, trauma, and instability they experienced at home. Chiquita wrote about the day, the year before, when she came home to find her mother with suitcases packed, saying, "Let's go, C.J.! We're leaving! Get your things." Chiquita stopped, paralyzed. Her mother screamed and cursed at her stepfather, then went into the bathroom and attempted suicide. Chiquita described her own psychological reaction:

> All that year, I was so focused on my mother, I forgot how to be a kid, I forgot about Chiquita, how the simplest things in life make me smile. Seeing my mother's pain affected me physically. I didn't take care of myself, and I blocked out what mattered most to me: my social life, and, most importantly, my schoolwork. I felt like I was trapped in a glass bottle, like no one could be going through what I was going through, like no one could hear me because no one could understand.

Many students resisted writing about painful memories. "Why would anyone be interested in this?" some said, or "I don't want people feeling sorry for me." For most students, maintaining their poise meant blocking out the images that reminded them of their vulnerability. Angelica Moore, who Josh knew as high-achieving and charismatic, active in the Senior Committee, and earning mostly A's, described how in high school her self-possession "was all a front. I can't even say how insecure I was." She explained, "I was always told since I was younger not to show my weakness because people will take advantage of it. It's better to walk around with my head high and make it seem like I have it together."

Angie described how the effort to maintain her "front" in school could be debilitating. During her freshman and sophomore years, she had experienced the sudden deaths of many people she loved. "I turn my head to the left and in a blink of an eye somebody else has died," she wrote in her personal essay. When Josh had first seen Angie's transcript, he was shocked to see that during her first two years of high school she had earned C's and D's. Trying to explain why this happened, Angie speculated that "with stuff taking place at home, and then me coming to school and trying to pretend that everything is normal and realizing it's not—that, I guess, took a toll on me." Angie remembered with stinging embarrassment when, during her freshman year, she broke down in uncontrollable tears in the lunchroom. "I knew that I never wanted to do that again; I didn't want to actually break down like that."

Among their peers in class, reading the personal essays out loud seemed to bring responses of empathy, rather than pity or shame. Janet Wu, the daughter of Chinese immigrants, described how in her first two years at the Secondary School for Research, she had only "hung out with Chinese people." Janet had been the target of incessant bullying, and when she went home to her parents, they would reinforce her fears and stereotypes about the kids who picked on her. To comfort herself, she would mentally repeat what her parents told her, "They are not going to graduate," or "They'll be out in the world dealing drugs." Janet's circles of friendship had widened as a junior, and now, beginning her senior year, Janet was moved by the essays she heard read and by the responses to her own. She began to see the kids who used to tease her as people with complex lives, and she felt they began to understand her as well. "You could see change, after the essays," she said. "They would stop picking on me. They started respecting me."

Josh saw how hard it was for students to tell the stories that emerged in their personal essays. But he believed that confronting what was difficult in their lives would help them shift from the challenge of simply getting through a day to the process of envisioning a future. As they recalled painful moments, students were putting together pieces of lives that felt fragmented, recognizing, at least on paper, their achievements and their inner strength. "I am that trail of scattered glass," Chiquita had written in a poem.

Angie concluded her essay with her desire to become a child psychologist: "I want to help children overcome their fears. I want to give children something I never had. Safety." Kennetta ended hers with the resolve, "I think to myself that if I was able to get through all of those struggles and still survive, I can accomplish going to college and making something of myself."

Kennetta decided to apply early decision to Muhlenberg, which meant she would commit to going there if she were accepted. She came to Josh's office every day, demanding his attention and expressing frustration when she couldn't get it. "Forget it, I'm not going to apply to college," she would say loudly if he were busy with another student. But during the last period, when she did not have class, she would sit down in the corner with her lunch and lean over her homework, application work, or, most often, a book or Sudoku puzzle. Josh described this shift in his letter of recommendation:

> It's wonderful when she's there because she's a little bit unlike the Kennetta I'm accustomed to. Usually, she's such a presence in a room, moving, talking, dancing, joking, laughing. But when she's in the office, nose in a book or chewing a pencil with a puzzle on her lap, she gets tiny and quiet, totally absorbed and inward. At the beginning of the year, when I asked her why she always comes to the office, she told me that it was just a kind of break or stopover, a little mental and physical rest before she went off to work. Then she'd leave the office every day at ten minutes to three and return a few minutes later wearing her uniform for Chuck E. Cheese's, where she'd spend the next several hours.

Kennetta remembered making this daily transition. Josh's office was a quiet place where she could imagine that "in spite of all the things I had to manage, anything was possible," where her future seemed open. Going to her job was a plunge back into her high-adrenaline, chaotic, unstable present. She'd cross the speeding lanes of traffic on Flatbush Avenue and enter the Atlantic Mall's branch of Chuck E. Cheese's, "where a kid can be a kid." She ran pizzas to parents and children, wiped down tables, and traded the paper coils of tickets the games spit out for plastic prizes. On weekends she usually worked with Chiquita, who was birthday party manager. Together, they soothed anxious parents, corralled wild children, and performed in the dance show with Chuck E., the oversized mouse.

At the end of her shift, sweaty and exhausted, Kennetta returned to the apartment in East New York where she lived with her parents, grandmother, and three younger siblings: Kent (called "Doobie"), David, and Danielle. Most nights, her boss would allow her to take home extra pizzas for her family, which meant that her mother, grandmother, and siblings would have enough to eat. On other nights, her mother and grandmother would eat less so the younger children didn't go hungry, and Kennetta would usually skip dinner herself. "Most of the time my biggest meal was at school because my friends would buy me food. When I got home I didn't want to be another burden on my parents."

Kennetta's father worked a late shift as a patient care technician at Cabrini Medical Center. When he returned at night, "fighting would sometimes start off between my parents." Kennetta would come to her mother's defense by confronting her father, "most of the time rudely and with an attitude." Then, Kennetta said, "my mom would start yelling at me," saying, "You need to be respectful to your dad." As Kennetta tried to fall asleep she would hear her mother crying.

Nighttime in East New York meant gunshots from the gang warfare in the neighborhood. Kennetta feared for her own safety when she walked outside, and even more for Doobie, a year younger, who was beginning to be "caught up" in gang life. In elementary school he had been a quiet student, recognized by everyone as "really smart" and placed, as was Kennetta, in a program for gifted students. Even during difficult times, Doobie used to be the most positive and hopeful in the family: "When he prayed, he was like, 'Things are going to get better.'" Doobie's academic focus, and his faith, were eroded by the incessant assaults he suffered at the hands of other boys. "He used to get jumped every day. He got sick and tired of it. They used to tell him stuff like, 'If you don't join us, we'll kill your family.'"

For Kennetta, her faith was her source of strength, and her church was a central part of her life. When she was eleven or twelve, she received a "prophetic word," recognized in Pentecostal Christianity as an utterance by an individual who feels inspired by the Holy Spirit. A lady "came up to me and said, 'Do you like science?'" When Kennetta responded that it wasn't her favorite subject, the lady said, "I'm sorry to tell you, but you're going to make a cure for disease."

This encounter was transformative for Kennetta. Within the church, her place of hope and belonging, she could see, for a moment, the future her fellow worshipper had seen for her. "Ever since that day, I excelled in all my classes. I got all A's and B's, and I fell in love with the sciences," she said.

Kennetta believed in this vision of herself as a medical researcher. But the gulf between the present and future seemed impossible to bridge. She knew, of course, that becoming a scientist meant going to college, but she didn't see how she would get there. Before Josh came, she said, "I knew about college, I obviously had heard of it, but I wasn't planning on going. I didn't think I would qualify—academically or financially. My mom was in debt. How was she going to pay? There was no way."

Kennetta's mother, Annette, who was a teacher at a parochial school, carried a crippling $96,000 in debt from her own college degree. She was raised in Brooklyn by her grandparents, who had adopted her, and attended a Christian college in Spencer, Oklahoma. When her adoptive father had a stroke during her freshman year, he had to retire and could no longer pay her tuition. Annette took out loans, which rapidly accumulated interest since she had little money to repay them.

Annette met Kennetta's father in Oklahoma, and during her college years, the couple married and had Kennetta. Kent had been a star baseball player in high school and believed he could have played in college. But when he was sixteen, his father got sick, and Kent took on three jobs to support his family. Of the college degree and baseball career that never happened, Kennetta's father would say, "I probably would have been rich now, but I never would have met your mom."

When Annette finished her bachelor's degree, she and Kent moved to Brooklyn. Kent found a job at Cabrini Medical Center, and the family moved to an apartment in Brownsville, where Kennetta's brother Doobie was born. They left that apartment because of a rat infestation. Kennetta's grandfather helped the family move into "a nice apartment in Bensonhurst," on the second floor of a house. Of those early years, Kennetta remembered, "everything was big. It was a beautiful house, huge." There was a backyard, and she and Doobie shared a room. Their cousins lived on the first floor, in a room just below them.

When Kennetta and Doobie were five and six, her cousins were smoking downstairs, and when their mother walked in, they hid their cigarettes, forgetting to put them out. The curtain caught fire first, and then the house. "We lost everything," Kennetta said. "Me and Doobie's toys, everything. That's when we were homeless."

The family of four moved in with Kennetta's grandparents, sharing what had been her mother's childhood bedroom. "Me, Doobie, my mom, and my dad had to share one bed. My dad always came home late. My mom and dad would switch off sleeping." After some time, her grandparents rented the apartment above them for Kennetta's family.

When Kennetta was eight years old, her grandfather died of

a massive heart attack. Kennetta had been very close with her grandfather, who would send her to school every morning with "a stick of Juicy Fruit gum and a dollar" and have cold-cut sandwiches ready for her and her brother after he picked them up. As she grieved his loss she began to understand how close to the edge her family was living, and this was "hard to deal with, especially at a young age." Her grandfather had helped support the family financially, and with his death, food became scarce. Some days, her father would call on his lunch break to ask her mother if the family had eaten anything that day. "My mom would lie to my dad and tell him yes, so that he could stay focused at work and not worry about us."

Her grandfather's death, Kennetta remembered, "also caused my father to lose it. He began to drink very heavily." She described her father coming home at night "drunk and on edge." If there was even a spoon left in the sink, he would wake up her mother, "yelling and cursing at her, saying that the house is a mess." Then, he would come to Kennetta and Doobie's room, "and start beating us to get out of the bed to clean up." They knew he was drunk, "and that he had no clue what he was doing."

The fall of her senior year, her father's job situation became unstable. Kennetta was haunted by the prospect of complete destitution. In her college essay she described "the nights and days my father said he wanted to leave us because he couldn't take not being able to provide for us." She remembered feeling that if "I wasn't ever born my parents would have more money for my younger siblings and themselves."

Though Kennetta sometimes felt like no more than a mouth to feed, at other times, she felt the power of the prophetic word she had received and saw herself as a scientist saving lives. As she did what she could to help her family survive, she held on to the image of herself strolling along Muhlenberg's quiet green quad. She remembered what the dean of admissions had told his disbelieving audience in the information session: that they had something important to contribute to life on this campus and that the college was looking for students just like them.

As promised, an overnight visit to Muhlenberg for Secondary School for Research students was scheduled for November. The college would pay for the students' bus tickets, arrange for a van to transport them from the station to campus, and cover their food expenses. Kennetta and seventeen others signed up. With Chris and Cindy's encouragement, Josh had made the trip open to everyone, even students he thought were unlikely to be admitted. The college wanted to send the message that its goal was to help the Secondary School for Research build a college-bound culture. While Josh didn't want to create false expectations, he felt that the visit would offer students a picture of campus life, create community in the class, and inspire seniors to pursue their education after high school, even if it wasn't at Muhlenberg.

One student who signed up was Rafael Padilla. This was a surprise to Josh. Josh had first met Rafael the year before, in the college seminar he led for juniors. When Josh asked students to write a response to the question "Why college?" Rafael had tersely explained that college was not an option for him. Even if he wanted to go—which he didn't—family and personal issues would make it impossible. Since the beginning of high school, Rafael had barely maintained a C average, and throughout the college seminar he cultivated an air of active disengagement. Outside of class, though, Josh saw Rafael as unusually mature. He worked forty hours every week as a manager at a drugstore and earned the respect of his peers as a kid with money in his pocket and adult responsibilities.

Josh knew it was unlikely that Rafael would be admitted to Muhlenberg—his grades were just too low—but he was very pleased to see Rafael show an interest in college. "What made you decide to go?" he asked Rafael. "My friends convinced me," Rafael said with a shrug.

Rafael remembered, from his junior year, that he understood Josh's pitch for college, but considered the seminar a waste of time. Josh had to pull kids out of physical education to attend every other week, and like many other boys, Rafael resented this. "I shouldn't even be here," he would think. "I should just be back in the gym."

At that point, Rafael remembered, "I had no expectations of going to college." His main priority was independence and financial stability. "The minute I turned fourteen I started working at Health Max, twenty-five hours per week. They were just waiting for me to graduate high school to make me manager of a new store."

In the activity essay he would write the following year Rafael described his entrance into the world of work:

> I remember how excited I was the day I started my first job. I was nervous, too, about messing up on the first day of training. It felt like a big step in my life. I had gotten the job through my cousin, who was working security in a local pharmacy. I started as a stock guy. I filled in the shelves with the overstocked items we kept in the back room and basement. I worked hard, I always came in on short notice when they called me, I was accurate and efficient with deliveries, and I always came in on time.

Within his first nine months at the pharmacy, Rafael was trained to be a floor supervisor. He "had access to the main computer, where items needed for the store stock were ordered" and was in charge of "making sure that the stock and cashier crew on the shift were staying on assignment," supervising people who were much older than he was. "There were times when they felt they did not have to respect my orders, and while this was frustrating, I learned how to speak with and manage the other employees," he wrote. During his sophomore year, Rafael was offered a position with "more money and more authority" at another branch, in

Queens. "I felt it was a great opportunity, even though the store was located about two hours from my home."

Starting work from such a young age, Rafael wrote, "helped me understand early what it is to earn your own money, and it also taught me the value of a dollar. As I got older, I began to help pay for groceries, for the cable bill, and for rent for my family. I felt like this was too much to ask of a teenager, but it also helped me to understand how hard it is to live day to day without a lot of money."

Rafael's family depended on his support. His mother was constantly in and out of the hospital due to chronic asthma and kidney failure, and as a result could not maintain full-time work. When Rafael was in elementary school, he and his siblings used to help her in her job as a superintendent for a group of apartment buildings. "She would take care of all five buildings: mopping, sweeping, utilities." Rafael's mother studied to become a certified occupational therapist assistant and found part-time work in the field, "in nursing homes, here and there." But because of her health issues, this work was never regular. Rafael's father was "never really around." He was "either out working, or out drinking." If the family saw any of the money he earned "it would be groceries, very little."

Rafael was in charge of his mother's care and helped her keep track of "an enormous amount of medications." He also managed the household when she was in the hospital. "Cooking, cleaning, clothes, taking out trash, going to work, making sure my mom had food in the hospital, that my sister and my younger brother were going to school." For himself, Rafael said, "School was never a priority. I would take care of everything else, and if I had time, go to school."

Though Rafael held his family together, his role was a conflicted one and had come after years of rebellion. Rafael, like Kennetta, began his college essay with the death of a grandparent, a loss that for him brought family upheaval and the end of childhood.

Rafael remembered his grandmother as the only person he could really talk to. Even though she spoke little English and Rafael's Spanish was weak at that time, he wrote that he "would find a way to tell her everything and she would do the same, even if she didn't know the right word or how to pronounce the words." Rafael described how as a young child he loved being with her. "Even when she was sleeping, I would sit there and just wait for her to wake up."

Rafael's grandmother went into a coma and died when he was seven. He remembered how her death changed him. "My grandmother always told me to talk about how I feel and not to hold it in, because that will make it worse. Now that she was gone, I just exploded on whoever made me mad at the time." He resented his family for not recognizing his grief and for saddling him with household responsibilities. His father, he wrote, showed him he was not wanted. "I would get hit and beat whenever he either felt I did something wrong, when someone else did something wrong, or when he was upset."

Rafael began spending more time with his cousins, who lived close by. They were involved with the gang life of Sunset Park, where, Rafael told Josh, things were "getting worse as far as Mexican gangs, MS-13, Latin Kings, Crips, new gangs forming." His cousins' gang connections made Rafael feel safer in the neighborhood. "Something was always going to occur, you just didn't know when," he said. "It made you uncomfortable just walking to the store. They did everything—shooting, knives." Sometimes the violence was connected with drugs, "other times, it was families taking vengeance on other families on the block."

By the age of ten or eleven, Rafael said, whether or not to join a gang seemed like a choice he had to make. "Sometimes I thought of doing the whole process: that would have become my life." Many other family members were involved, and "some have passed because of it." Rafael knew he "had to make a decision," and his inner battle continued until he was thirteen or fourteen, when he also started working. At that time, his cousins were just extricating themselves. "They made the mistake, and managed to get out."

Rafael did not affiliate with a gang, but as he transitioned into high school, he was still living on the edge of a world of trouble. As he wrote in an early draft of his personal essay, he released the anger he felt by "fighting, drinking, and smoking." Though Rafael was successful and respected in his job at Health Max, in his family, he wrote, "I was continuously called a failure. I had been arrested, I sometimes came home drunk, and I never wanted to go to school. I was always told I was going to end up a drop out and not going to make it anywhere in life."

When he was about sixteen, Rafael wrote, "I started to change my act and get myself together." He attributed this shift to "being so busy, taking care of my mom. Because I had to work, and take care of everything else, I wasn't always in the street." But jail and violence were always close by. His younger brother was in and out of juvenile detention centers, constantly skipping school and getting into trouble. Rafael described how his brother "would try and pick fights with me," baiting Rafael to "hit him, so he could call the cops," and taunting Rafael that he would "send your ass back to jail."

One day, his brother "caught me on a day I was already upset." Rafael's mother had to stop the fight, and his brother filed a report, accusing Rafael of causing the bruises on his body. Rafael's future seemed to turn on who arrived from the child welfare system, where his brother had been assigned a caseworker after his repeated absences from school. "Luckily," Rafael wrote in his essay, "I did not start the fight and the social worker was a person who listened to the story." The social worker spoke with both Rafael and his mother before reporting the incident to the police. She understood, Rafael said, that his brother's bruises had been caused by sports and saved Rafael from going to jail for assault. After that incident, Rafael and his brother did not speak.

Rafael concluded his personal essay by saying, "All of these situations in my life opened my eyes to let me know I am alone in this world. I have learned how to depend on myself, not to expect others to feel bad for me." At this same time, his friendships at school were taking a new turn. He had begun to speak more personally with Kennetta, Frederick, Chiquita, and others, who, like Rafael, usually kept their troubles to themselves. Rafael attributed this new attitude among his friends to their work with Josh in the college process. When you were around," he told Josh, "we opened up in our own groups of friends. We had conversations: Things aren't going well, how can we change it? College may be the way."

For the November overnight, Muhlenberg created a "visit plan" for every student from the Secondary School for Research. Each was given an individualized itinerary that included classes in their areas of interest, and each met for an interview, over lunch, with a member of the admissions staff. Working from the idea that Secondary School for Research students would be accepted and support each other as a group, they were separated in the dorms they stayed in and in the classes they attended, but brought together to talk about their experiences. The Secondary School for Research students spent the evening at the multicultural center, where they were met by a group of Muhlenberg students who were also students of color.

For Rafael, the most powerful part of the visit was the connection he felt with his peers from the Secondary School for Research and with the students he met at the college: "That bond was what got me. It seemed like a place where I could hang out with friends and feel like I'm at home." His experience of Muhlenberg as a quiet, supportive community was a stark contrast to the embattled independence he maintained at home. "It was peaceful, relaxing. The campus seemed huge. Everyone was nice: students, staff, admissions officers." He appreciated the honesty with which current students spoke about life as a racial minority on campus: "They were going to just tell us the truth." He asked questions about "employment, and how would I be able to get around," trying to imagine how he might support himself as a Muhlenberg student, and how he would get home to Brooklyn if there was a family emergency. He expressed interest in the college's business program and began to imagine himself taking management courses like the one he sat in on, learning the skills he would need to become an entrepreneur.

Describing their interviews, students reported their surprise that admissions officers did not focus on academics, but just seemed to be trying to get to know them. Angie met with Cindy. "It wasn't much of an interview for me," she said. "Me and Cindy just spoke about family and culture. I told her that my father was Hondurian, and she said she was Hispanic, too. We were making jokes, laughing, telling each other about our experiences of family: a big family, a protective family, a not-so-protective family. I told her I love kids, that I want to do child psychology. I walked in so nervous, but it was so calm, a relaxing conversation. I didn't even want to leave."

Kennetta's interview was with admissions counselor Amy Morse. Josh had sent a draft of Kennetta's personal essay to Chris and Cindy, and Amy had read it. "As soon as I walked in she started crying," Kennetta said. "She said, 'Your personal essay, it touched me, oh my God.' "

Kennetta remembered her mixed reaction to this display of emotion: "I was shocked, I was touched. I was like, this is so weird. She's supposed to be interviewing me and she's crying. Is she going to look at me in a certain way? I don't want her to think, I'm sorry for you." Kennetta remembered staying calm and just having a conversation. "I don't remember talking about anything dealing with academics. She told me about her family."

After the overnight, Amy sent an e-mail to Kennetta with the subject line, "Hello from Muhlenberg College." She expressed how much she had enjoyed meeting Kennetta, and offered her help in the application process. Kennetta wrote back,

Dear Ms. Amy Morse,

I would like to thank you for taking the time out of your busy schedule to interview me. I had such a great time speaking with you. You made me feel very comfortable talking to you about some personal things about my life that I don't usually talk to anyone about.

I really hope to get accepted to Muhlenberg because I love the environment and the people. Filling out these college applications is very hard and a lot of work but thanks to Mr. Steckel I am getting them done. Well I hope to talk to you real soon. I wish you and your family a HAPPY THANKSGIVING!!!!!!!!

Thanks again,
KENNETTA

In the e-mails that followed, each described their Thanksgiving dinners. Amy wrote,

As it turned out, we had a quiet Thanksgiving dinner here because my husband, Rich, had to work for part of the day and my relatives and friends all had invitations for dinners out of town. However, I gotta say, sitting here at the dinner table with Rich, Emily (she's a sophomore at Muhlenberg), and Kenny (our tenth grader), it was really special. We had a chance to talk to each other and laugh and feel very thankful for our blessings of good health and love. I felt really happy deep in my heart.

I'm glad that you felt that you could talk to me during our interview. Your honesty and openness reinforced my feelings that you have a beautiful soul and that you are such an amazing young woman. Be proud of everything you told me and everything about your life. You are more special and incredible than you realize. And I'm pretty good at spotting that stuff !! :)

Kennetta responded,

> I am happy to hear that you and your family had a good time. My Thanksgiving this year was actually one of the best Thanksgivings we have ever had. There was plenty of food and a lot of my friends were there at my house with my family and me. We ate a whole lot and actually sat down with one another and spent time with each other. After that we played games. It was sort of funny looking around the room at every one partnered up playing all types of board games.

She concluded her e-mail, "I can't wait to visit you again."

Rafael remembered how, following the visit to Muhlenberg, he and his friends offered one another motivation and support as they completed their applications. At this time, he said, "my mom was in the hospital and I was always working overtime." When he was down, "because all of a sudden the stress came again, and there was college paperwork I hadn't even looked at," he would call one of his friends, saying, "I don't know if I want to do this anymore. I don't have time to worry about my family as well as worrying about college." His friends, he said, would "push me, literally force me to fill out my info. Kennetta would say, 'Bring it over to my house.' Chiquita always yelled at me. She would see I hadn't done paperwork, say, 'We're filling it out,' and pull me into our social studies teacher's classroom. If something was bothering her, we would talk. Kennetta would say, 'The sooner we hand this in, the sooner we can leave and start off fresh.' Muhlenberg seemed like the place to start off new."

Before Christmas, Secondary School for Research seniors ran an event to raise money for the College Fund spearheaded that fall by Abby, who was also a leader in the class. At the Barnes and Noble down the block from the school, the students wrapped gifts and solicited donations from holiday shoppers. When one customer asked the group about their postsecondary plans, Kennetta answered, immediately and matter-of-factly, "I'm going to be a biochemist. I'll study diseases and find ways to treat them." She told all who asked that she wanted to go to Muhlenberg. When a woman responded that she was a Muhlenberg alumna herself, the two spoke for a while, breaking the boundaries of mutual distrust that usually separated the students from neighborhood residents.

Josh scrambled to make sure all Muhlenberg applications were complete by the end of January. Kennetta, Frederick, and Rafael were applying as early decision candidates. Muhlenberg accepted early decision applications as late as February, and students knew that committing to attend the college would increase their chances of admission. Fourteen others applied in the regular decision pool. Cindy and Chris had hoped for more early decision applicants: like Posse, in order to select students as a group, they needed to be able to count on accepted students to attend. Josh explained that students' unstable family and financial circumstances had made it difficult for them to make an early decision commitment. He listed the students he thought were likely to attend Muhlenberg if admitted, highlighting Daina, Chiquita, and Angie.

Chris responded that he was encouraged to hear this: he had feared the plan would not come to fruition. In an e-mail, he reiterated his commitment to the idea of accepting students as a group:

> I certainly believe it would be great to have an actual posse from the Secondary School for Research so that the kids have their own support system here for each of them, and so that we can get our arms around them as a group, both to support them and to encourage them to be agents of positive change here as they grow into the place.

The strongest candidates among the applicants, Josh believed, were Kennetta, Daina, Chiquita, Abby, and Janet: all had solid A and B averages and had written powerful essays. Josh knew that there were other students who had very little chance of getting in, including Rafael and Frederick. Rafael's grades through junior year were almost all C's. Frederick's were worse: he had an overall average of 70, and was turning twenty that year. Josh had great respect for Frederick, who was kind, sensitive, and thoughtful, and who, along with his friends, had come into the college process with a new sense of possibility. But Josh had felt very conflicted about encouraging Frederick's interest in Muhlenberg, as the college would almost certainly not be a real choice for him.

Josh was most uncertain how Muhlenberg would read Angie's application. Though as a senior Angie was earning mostly A's, her overall average through the end of junior year was a 76, and Josh feared that her low grades during the first two years of high school would hurt her chances. He hoped that Muhlenberg would recognize that Angie's improvement was in itself an achievement and see the ways Angie's growth as a student had helped her to become a leader and inspire others.

As Angie later described, the shift in her academic performance between sophomore and junior years had come with her resolution to go to college. She had been earning "sixties, seventies . . . and then one day it flipped to eighties." Angie had been supported, throughout high school, by Groundwork for Success, a community-based organization working to promote college access for youth from East New York. Angie's junior year "success coach" at Groundwork was a recent college graduate who had herself grown up in Brooklyn. Her coach helped her to realize, Angie said, that despite all of the tragedy she had lived through, and the challenge that defined her day-to-day experience outside of school, "I had to do better in school in order for me to go to college, to get a better life for me and my family."

With help from Groundwork, Angie connected with College Summit, another college access program for low-income students, which each summer runs workshops for upcoming seniors on college campuses across the country. Angie spent a week at

Tufts University, where she engaged in intensive group leadership training and worked on developing material for her college applications. By the end of January, Angie had applied to thirty-two colleges, including several historically black colleges and universities, which held strong appeal for her.

On February 28, Chris wrote to Josh with his impressions after reading the students' application files:

> At this point, I have read Kennetta's app cover to cover, and I support her for admission ED. What a story! Also, whether ED or Regular, Daina Spencer looks like a clear AC for us. I think Rafael is very risky academically, but still possible. I understand from Cindy that you support him strongly, and he sounds like a great person. Fred D'Anjou may not work out, at least as I read him so far. I like him tremendously as a person (I interviewed him when he was here), but I think he may just be too great a stretch academically.

Muhlenberg sent its acceptance letters to both early and regular decision candidates from the Secondary School for Research in early March. To Josh's astonishment, Rafael was the first to receive a letter, and Angie the second. Both were thrilled. Angie remembered that she saw the letter as a recognition of all she was capable of accomplishing. "It proved I could be successful. I wasn't concerned with anyone being proud of me, it was just me being proud of myself."

Daina, Abby, Janet, and Chiquita were also admitted. Frederick did not get in. He accepted the disappointment with resignation, and Josh helped him to enroll at the Borough of Manhattan Community College.

Kennetta remembered the anxiety she felt when she learned that Angie and Rafael had been accepted but had not heard anything herself. Several days later, Josh called Kennetta into his office. Over the phone, Cindy told her she had gotten in. "I was excited," Kennetta said, "but I was like, 'I need to see this in writing.' " When her letter finally arrived the next week, the dream of going to Muhlenberg seemed possible.

After sending out decision letters in March, Muhlenberg waited to see if an actual "posse" would materialize. Up through the May 1 General Reply deadline, by which all students were required to commit to one of the colleges where they had been made an offer of admission, the seven Secondary School for Research students accepted to Muhlenberg struggled to make their own decisions. As Josh had seen previously, this involved complex negotiations between their desires, their families' needs, and their belief in their own capabilities.

Rafael seemed transfigured by the acceptance. He was excelling in all his classes, and his grades during second semester senior year were the highest he had ever received. Rafael became an enthusiastic leader of the Senior Committee, running the yearbook and planning bake sales and parties. As though on a mission, he took on the role of mentor to younger students he saw struggling, inspiring them with his message: "If I did this, so can you." One of these students, a sophomore with a 66 average, astonished her teachers with a dramatic turnaround.

In addition to his schoolwork, Rafael was turning his attention to planning a business he had conceived that January with his cousin, formerly a gang member, and his sister Rosy, then a student at Brooklyn College. The business, called Past, Present, Future, would help people who had been in prison make the transition to work. On his block, Rafael could only think of five people between the ages of seventeen and thirty-two who had attended college. Sixty to 70 percent had been in the prison system at least once. The business would offer them new opportunities. "Some wanted to change, but didn't have the proper education, didn't know how to use computers, or didn't have skills to gain jobs. Everyone wanted a chance."

That spring, to find the time for homework and to build this new venture, Rafael changed his priorities and reduced his family responsibilities. "I finally put my foot down. I made sure I paid bills, but I didn't take care of my younger brother. It was me saying, 'I'm not here to babysit, I have to take care of my own needs. Everyone else has to take responsibility for cleaning, etc.' "

A couple of days after Rafael made this announcement, his brother sent an e-mail to all the members of his family. He told them he was planning to commit suicide. He recounted how each family member had let him down, focusing on Rafael and the way their distance since the fight the year before had taken a toll on him.

While his brother did not act on his threat, Rafael worried and blamed himself. In planning to go to Muhlenberg, he was doing what he believed was best for himself, but "at the same time, I was going to be abandoning my family at the time when they needed me most."

For Chiquita, who unlike Rafael had always been a strong student, getting into college catalyzed a crisis of self-esteem. In addition to Muhlenberg, she had been accepted to Union College as an HEOP scholar, and Josh thought his main role would be to help her decide between the two. Instead, Chiquita returned to an earlier conviction that Josh thought she had put behind her: that she wasn't college material and that it would be a safer bet to enlist in the army, as her father urged. She had to work so hard to succeed in high school, she said, how could she make it through college courses?

In addition, Chiquita's father believed that the financial aid packages offered by both colleges would not see her through. She had been awarded $45,000 in grants and scholarships, but he felt that the $1,500 both Union and Muhlenberg were asking as a family contribution was too much of a burden and that taking out a student loan for this amount would be a big mistake. Chiquita feared going against her father's wishes. She also feared the consequences of leaving her mother. Her father had been abusive in the past, and Chiquita didn't see how her mother could make it on her own.

Chiquita's uncertainty lasted until the deadline for her to make a deposit, which she finally did at Union. She had enjoyed her visit there, and as Josh explained to Chris and Cindy, her family was concerned about whether her New York State health coverage, Child Health Plus, would travel to Pennsylvania.

Janet decided to attend Queens College, part of the City University of New York. While she had been accepted to several upstate New York colleges as well as to Muhlenberg, her family responsibilities overrode her desire to go away. Muhlenberg had been Daina's first choice throughout the process, but when she went to Hobart and William Smith for its accepted students' weekend, she changed her mind.

Angie had been admitted to two historically black colleges, Virginia State University and Morgan State University, but neither college had offered enough financial aid to make it possible for her to attend. Along with Muhlenberg, her other real choice was Hobart and William Smith, where, like Mike and Abby, she had been accepted as an HEOP scholar. Angie returned from the accepted students' weekend there wearing the college's sweatshirt. During the visit, she "had a lot of fun," and felt a stronger sense of community among the students of color than she had at Muhlenberg. At Muhlenberg, she said, "the community had seemed forced. Like, let's put all the minorities together and see how it works out."

Angie "waited until the last date" to decide. On May 1, Cindy called, and Angie told her she would go to Muhlenberg. Distance was ultimately the most important factor. Hobart and William Smith was five hours away and, if anything happened to her family, it would be hard to go home to help.

In June, Angie won the Broad Prize for Urban Education, awarded in selected public school districts to students whose academic performance improved dramatically from ninth through twelfth grades. In an e-mail to the Secondary School for Research faculty, Josh wrote that Angie "is extremely proud, and rightfully so." Out of the thousands of nominees in the New York City public school system, about six hundred students were selected as finalists and asked to write essays about their academic, extracurricular, and personal development. Angie was one of 250 students selected to receive a $10,000 scholarship, $2,500 for each of her four years of college. Angie, Josh wrote, "will be able to attend Muhlenberg College ($44,000/yr) for FREE (with $1,000/yr coming back to her for expenses like books and transportation!) for all four years."

Soon after Kennetta's acceptance to Muhlenberg in early March, the Cabrini Medical Center closed, and Kennetta's father lost his job. Kennetta suffered intensely from doubts about whether leaving home was the right thing to do. "I knew that if I left, I would be one less mouth for them to feed, but they'd still struggle. Working at Chuck E. Cheese's, I was at least able to bring home food for them."

Kennetta remembered how hard it was to hold herself together at this time. One day she walked into one of her classes and put her head down on the desk. Kennetta had a close but conflicted relationship with this teacher, a former war correspondent with a stubborn streak like Kennetta's. In the letter of recommendation she wrote for Kennetta, she described her as "a young woman who battles back; a young woman who is deeply devoted to her family and her faith; a young woman determined to succeed."

When her teacher told her that no sleeping was allowed in class, Kennetta responded, "I just really need to rest my head for like five minutes, there's a lot on my mind." Kennetta then asked to leave the room to use the bathroom. She remembers her teacher refusing, and telling her, "You're not the only one with problems."

Then, Kennetta remembered, "I stood up. I threw the desk." Rafael and another friend held her back. "I was like, 'Do you have to worry about what you're going to eat tonight, where you're going to live?' "

The teacher called the assistant principal, who knew Kennetta well. "That doesn't sound like my Kennetta," she said. Kennetta sat in the assistant principal's office "and just got my mind right for the remainder of the period."

Later, Alissa, the school's guidance counselor, brought Kennetta and her teacher together. Kennetta remembered saying, "I already know you don't like me. I don't care because I don't like you either." The teacher responded, "I do like you, a lot. I feel like we're so alike, we bump heads."

In Josh's office that spring, Kennetta's moods alternated between explosive and withdrawn. One morning in late April, she sat down in her usual spot in his office and began writing in her notebook. Josh came over and asked to see what she had written. It was a suicide note.

Josh closed the door and sat with her. Kennetta spoke about feeling paralyzed by the crises her family faced. She felt tremendous guilt about her intention to leave them to go away to college. It was hard for her to imagine getting through to the end of the year. Josh shared the content of the note with the school guidance counselor and told Kennetta she could stay in his office for the entire day. Before the day ended, Kennetta told Josh she was not actually planning to take her own life. She gave him the letter she'd written and asked him to throw it away.

As Kennetta moved forward in her plans to go to Muhlenberg, Josh worried about how she would get by there. Would the support the college promised to offer, along with the support of Rafael and Angie, be enough to help her make it through? Were these students prepared for Muhlenberg? Was Muhlenberg prepared for them?

7

Finding the Best Fit:
Ashley

In December 2007, a month after turning down her position as a finalist for the Posse scholarship, Ashley Brown was accepted to Williams College as an early decision applicant. During the summer after she graduated high school, she successfully completed the Williams College Summer Science Program, aimed at "highly motivated and hardworking individuals who are interested in studying science and who come from underrepresented minority groups or from families with little or no college experience."[1] She spent the following fall and spring semesters as a premed student at Williams. Her bill for her first year at the top-ranked liberal arts college in the country was $253.

In June 2009, Ashley wrote to Josh that she had decided to take a leave of absence from Williams. That fall, she wrote in an e-mail, she would enroll in pre-nursing classes at the Borough of Manhattan Community College.

This news did not come as a complete surprise to Josh. He had been in touch with Ashley since the beginning of the school year about her dissatisfaction with Williams. In early September, she had told him she felt homesick and out of her element on campus. Like all her peers from the Secondary School for Research who attended selective liberal arts colleges, she described the ways she stuck out as a low-income student of color. Williams, with

its prestige and large endowment, had a greater capacity for multicultural recruitment and funding than a lower profile college
like Muhlenberg. But as Ashley observed, many students of color
came from higher-income families and well-known high schools.
"There were other people from New York, but they weren't from
the same background as me," she said. She told Josh about a time
when, in the course of a playful argument, an African American
student from a well-to-do suburb said, "Are you going to cut me?"
as though Ashley were some kind of thug because she came from
Brooklyn. "You knew it was a joke, but it still was coming from
preconceived stereotypes."

Throughout the semester, Ashley also expressed extreme frustration that despite her hard work and discipline, she was not earning the top grades that she knew she needed in order to be accepted
to medical school. Ashley had chosen Williams as part of her path
to a career as an ob/gyn, which she had been mapping out since
her sophomore year of high school. What was the point of making
the personal and family sacrifices that being at Williams entailed
if the education she received there would not help her become a
doctor?

Josh had written to Phil Smith, dean emeritus of admissions
and a family friend, to say he was concerned about Ashley. Phil
had helped connect Josh with Lili Rodriguez and the Windows on
Williams program, and had followed Ashley's admissions process
the previous year. Phil met with Ashley and reported his impressions to Josh in an e-mail:

> I have just come back from having lunch with Ashley. She's off to
> the lab for the first part of the afternoon.
>
> It seems to me that Ashley is okay. She misses NYC a lot and
> she'll go home over fall break in a couple of weeks, which may
> help on that front. I asked her what she did when she was home,
> and it was movies, friends, and trips to the library—all of them
> things she can do here.

She seems to have some friends from the summer as well as from her entry.

She's finding the work much more complex than in high school, especially the chemistry. She'd just had a session with Professor Thoman, so she took the initiative to talk with him and he gave her some suggestions. Ashley indicated that as a pre-med she was concerned with getting all A's and doing very well. I urged her to take one semester at a time and told her about my first paper at Williams ("D–, see me after class!")

She doesn't seem to have financial problems and seemed happy with the financial aid situation.

I thought she looked fine and that her uncertainties were the normal ones and tried to reassure her that lots of people were feeling the same way, but not showing it.

Hopefully you will get a chance to see her when she comes home.

I asked her if she was learning anything, and she readily said yes. I told her to keep learning and not to worry about the grades for now. It doesn't seem as if she is behind in any subject and she seemed perfectly happy with all of her courses and not overwhelmed.

As a way of contrast, we just sent a Botswanan senior back home after she encountered a severe bout of depression. Her voice sounded terrible and she couldn't make any decisions. Ashley was just the opposite.

My guess is that she will be fine with some time.

At the end of October, Ashley told Josh that she was submitting a transfer application to Sophie Davis, the City University of New York program that combined a BS and an MD and the pathway Josh had helped convinced her to abandon. Ashley expressed ambivalence about the idea of leaving Williams. "The only other school I would consider transferring to is Sophie and this is the only opportunity," she wrote. "Things are getting better here, but

I still feel that I may be needed at home, I am still missing NY and not liking the boondocks, etc."

At the end of December Ashley received her first semester grades. When she found out that she had received a C in chemistry, her sense of frustration with Williams came to a head. She wrote to Josh,

> I am through. I stay up all hours in the night studying. I stay focused, never went to a party, etc., so I don't understand how I could be getting these grades. I even started going to a psychologist at the school once a week so that I can stay on track and learn how to focus and manage my time better. I am transferring closer to home and hopefully I get into Sophie Davis.

As he heard from Ashley throughout the year, Josh felt confusion, guilt, and anxiety about whether he had steered her in the wrong direction. He replayed the decisions they had made together in her senior year. Would she have been happier and more successful at Colby as a Posse scholar, where she would have had a stronger network of social and academic support? Should he not have guided her away from her original focus on Sophie Davis? Maybe he should have worked on New York University, where she would have benefited from the prestige and resources of a private college while living at home.

At the same time, it was hard for Josh to give up on the vision of Ashley, the top student in her class at the Secondary School for Research, as a Williams graduate, and he felt certain she could be successful there. Ashley had received an A– in her one humanities course, and though she was upset by her final grade in chemistry, she knew herself that she was improving: she had earned an 84 on the midterm, and a 98 on her final quiz. She had sought out leadership roles on campus, and instead of withdrawing from a social life she saw as centered on parties, athletics, and a cappella singing groups, she took steps to organize movie nights. She was one of three students selected to meet with members of the Congressional

Black Caucus when they came to campus. She had developed a strong relationship with her biology professor and had been hired as a research assistant in a lab.

Ashley's main struggle, as Josh saw it, was with, or because of, the stress of the premed pathway. He had been premed himself, at Duke, and remembered the well-known freshman year phenomenon in which many students who began as premed changed their minds after one or two semesters of introductory biology and chemistry. Half of the remaining class was weeded out the following year during organic chemistry, which was notoriously difficult. For Ashley, sticking with the premed pathway at Williams would mean continuing to struggle through classes she did not enjoy. If she opened her mind to other fields, she could enjoy college and graduate with a credential that would open many doors.

But it was hard for Josh to know whether he should push Ashley to give up her goal of becoming a doctor, particularly in the face of his uncertainty about the role he had already played in guiding her. When Ashley told Josh she had not been admitted to Sophie Davis and was hating organic chemistry, which she took as a second semester freshman, he wrote an e-mail to Jill, the Secondary School for Research's principal, reflecting on Ashley's situation:

> I know that if Ashley were to let go of med school she would be able to engage in a new kind of academic self-discovery, and that she would have the time to explore college life in exciting ways. But the amazing, stubborn, iron drive that got her where she is is also what keeps her from allowing herself to even imagine this.

Ashley told Josh that at Williams, her adviser had suggested that she complete premed requirements in a postbaccalaureate program, offered by some colleges as a bridge to medical school after students complete their undergraduate degree. This route did not make any sense to Ashley. It would not only extend an educational pathway that felt perilously long, but would require her to go into significant debt.

Already, Ashley faced a bill for her upcoming sophomore year at Williams that had jumped to $6,000. Ashley's mother, Karleen, had earned more income that year as a result of her new degree, and the financial aid office's calculation of the amount the family was able to contribute had increased significantly. Paying this tuition in full would be impossible for Karleen that year. If staying at Williams seemed right, Ashley and her mother decided, they would take out a loan. But Ashley felt that the burden of debt would not be worth the risk if she could not say where her education at Williams would lead.

The report from Ashley that she had decided to leave Williams for the Borough of Manhattan Community College (BMCC) saddened Josh. The community college, and the nursing program, seemed so narrow in comparison to the opportunities Williams offered. But backing off was clearly the right thing to do. "It sounds like these months have been full of big decisions for you!" he wrote in his e-mail response. "I trust your decision-making process completely."

Josh met with Ashley two years later, when she was in her second year of BMCC's associate's degree program in nursing, a 65-credit sequence that she anticipated would take her three years to complete. "Can you tell me about where you're at now?" he asked her. "Ooh," Ashley said with a laugh. That fall, Ashley had begun the clinical portion of the nursing program, which combined classes, lab work, and hospital rotations. Though she was very busy, she seemed energized by her responsibilities. "I love everything I learn, and it's amazing how I'm able to apply it. It's one thing to learn it, then you go to the hospital, and you're like, wait, I'm really doing this. I really am making a difference."

Ashley detailed her packed schedule. She had classes all day Mondays and Tuesdays, and would return home to study for the exams that were given every two weeks. On Wednesdays she prepared for clinical work on Thursdays, when "we're in the hospital from 8:00 a.m. to 4:00 p.m., with a one-hour lunch break." Student nurses were evaluated based on how well they accomplished specific tasks, which in the obstetrics rotation included assessing the health of new mothers and giving injections to newborns. On Fridays, Ashley would study for the microbiology lab class that met on Saturdays. Currently, she said, "we're figuring out how bacteria respond to antibiotics and disinfectants, and what antigens and antibodies go together during the reactions." Saturday nights were her free nights. "That's when I watch movies, relax with family, dance."

Josh asked Ashley about her study habits. She described the same routine she had written about in her college essay, in which she and her mother spent evenings together at the kitchen table helping each other with their coursework. Her mother, who had herself earned her associate's degree in nursing at BMCC, was now pursuing her bachelor's degree online through Chamberlain University. "We'll kind of go back and forth," Ashley said. Karleen would pretend to be a patient awaiting catheterization, quiz Ashley about antipsychotic drugs, and bring needles and gauze from her job at New York Methodist Hospital so Ashley could practice injections on oranges. Ashley would ask her mother questions about her readings and brainstorm ideas for her mother's papers.

When Ashley spoke about what went wrong for her at Williams, she focused on the sense of loss and guilt that had come with leaving these routines behind. "Abandonment: that is the word," she said. It was hard for her mother to balance work, school, family, and household responsibilities without her help: "When my mom had to come home, and then cook, and do all the chores, it seemed like she had less time for her studies." Things seemed to be falling apart in Ashley's absence. Her mother dropped the class she was taking at Long Island University because "it just got to be too much for her." Her sister struggled with high school math and science. Ashley's brother was having behavioral problems at school, and on the phone, Ashley said, "I couldn't get into the core of the problem, because he didn't really want to talk about it."

Now that she was home, Ashley told Josh, the family support structure was back in order. Ashley was preparing her sister for her Regents exams, helping her brother with his college applications, and talking out ideas for papers with her mother. In her family, Ashley said, "we feel like we should work together, so everyone in the family can move closer to our goals." After she finished her nursing degree, she said, "we're considering putting money together and getting a house. Together."

Seeing Ashley so happy made it hard for Josh to think she should have stayed away. The tension Ashley experienced between self-advancement and family responsibility was similar in some ways to Mike's, but with significant differences. Mike's intense guilt at leaving his family came, in part, from his sense that it was the distance from their troubles that gave him the space to grow and explore. Ashley, whose economic circumstances were far more stable than Mike's, seemed to feel most herself when she was home and helping.

In speaking about why she left Williams, Ashley also described a new idea that had begun to take shape in January of the year she spent there. Williams offers a Winter Study semester: a month when students choose courses in a wide variety of topics outside of traditional academic categories. Ashley had enrolled in a course called Women's Work, taught by her psychology professor's wife, a midwife. The class visited a hospital, listened to mothers speak about their birth experiences, and watched *The Business of Being Born*, a documentary produced by Ricki Lake, which critiques the American health care system as overreliant on medical interventions in childbirth.

Ashley remembered experiencing a "lightbulb." The class, she said, "exposed me to the world of possibilities" that came with being a midwife. "My main goal from when I was younger was to find a job I would be happy going to every day," she said. "I know a lot of people are not satisfied with their jobs. I don't want to be that person." She had had an interest since early in high school in pregnancy and birth. Though she was aware of midwifery, she had not considered it because of the "stigma attached to it," and because she wanted the autonomy that came with being an ob/gyn.

Now, she said, a New York State law enables midwives to write prescriptions and do much of the same work as an ob/gyn, excluding cesarean sections. This in itself was a draw for Ashley. When she saw C-sections while volunteering, she said, "I felt a little hot." Surgery was not appealing to her: "Even though I know it's important to have that option available, it's hard for me to see myself cutting someone and pulling. I'm more of a soft person. I like just regular, vaginal birth."

Midwifery requires a degree in nursing, and during her second semester at Williams, as she worked hard to pull her grades up in premed courses she disliked, changing her path made increasing sense to Ashley. She understood that in leaving Williams she was giving up an opportunity coveted by many and felt the magnitude of her decision.

But once she returned home and began at BMCC, Ashley said, "I was like, okay, this is nice." She felt this sense of satisfaction even more strongly when she began the clinical program. "Nursing, that's me," she discovered. "I like the holistic approach, I love that caring is a focus. Also letting people know that they have a choice in making their health care decisions—that I love. Some people like a lot of diagnosing. If that's your focus, then medicine's good for you."

This sense of certainty helped her keep at bay any regret about leaving Williams. Ashley kept in touch with a friend who, like her, came from an urban public school and had a difficult freshman year. "What motivated him to stay was that he wanted to be politician, and he knew Williams would be the way to help him. Then over time, he grew to love it there, because his passions were being fulfilled." But for her, Ashley said, "since I love nursing, even if I stayed at Williams, I don't think it would have gotten better.

If Williams had nursing, it would have been something else. I tell everybody every day, if Williams had nursing, I would have stayed, period."

Ashley also refused to express regret at having chosen Williams in the first place. "From my point of view as a Christian," she said, "everything happens for a reason." Not only had the college introduced her to midwifery, but her Williams experience, she told Josh, helped her to be a successful student at BMCC. "If I didn't go to Williams first, I don't know what would have happened to me in this nursing program," she said.

Ashley described the ways she saw other students in the program fail or withdraw at various points. To progress from pre-nursing liberal arts requirements into the clinical program, students needed to earn at least a 3.8 GPA in four prerequisites: an introductory English course, a math course, anatomy and physiology, and general psychology. They also needed to pass a nursing pre-entrance exam. Once admitted to the program, students had to maintain a C in each class, and receive a score of 80 or above on a math exam.

The program was very competitive, Ashley said, and "a lot of people are struggling. That's the one thing they tell you once you start nursing. If you got A's before, and you don't get A's now, don't beat yourself up over it, because it's so much work, and it's so demanding." Ashley, who at Williams had already experienced the frustration of seeing her straight-A average drop, was now once again a top student. She attributed this success at BMCC in part to the writing and critical thinking skills she had honed at Williams, where test questions were open-ended, and "you had to really think about what the question is asking you."

The BMCC program also required the self-discipline and focus Ashley had always possessed, but which she felt she had further developed during her time away from home. "The other students who are doing as well as I'm doing have another degree in something else," Ashley said. "All of us have some experience in another school." Many of the more successful nursing students were in their forties or fifties, coming, like her mother, from years of work.

The idea that Ashley's Williams education functioned as preparation for an associate's degree from BMCC took Josh some time to assimilate. But the explanation, delivered in Ashley's upbeat, matter-of-fact tone, made sense. That community colleges have notoriously low graduation rates can be attributed, in part, to the unstable economic situations of many students who attend, and the inadequate preparation many receive in high school. But these colleges also lack the support structures that at liberal arts colleges cushion the path to graduation. "What I did like with Williams," Ashley said, "was that the professors are there to help you. They see you're struggling, and they will tutor you: they will really make sure that you at least have a chance." At BMCC, "the professors are there to go over your exams, and if you have questions. But it's not like they would take out an hour of their time, after class, and sit down and go through everything with you." The attitude she perceived at BMCC was sink or swim, with the expectation that many would not make it through.

The BMCC associate's degree, Ashley explained, was a desirable choice because at comparatively low cost, students could earn the credential they needed to become registered nurses. "The only difference between an associate's degree in nursing and a bachelor's is theory. No more clinical work is necessary: we're ready to practice once we finish," she said. Bachelor's programs had a saner pace and less stringent GPA requirements, but were significantly more expensive: "That's why everyone's running to the associate's degree schools." But students often left the college in debt and without a degree, unprepared for the bureaucratic and academic hurdles they would encounter at BMCC and lacking guidance about how to overcome them.

Ashley took it upon herself to fill this gap. She was prepared not only by her year at Williams, but by her mother's experience going through the same degree program at BMCC. "Not everyone has someone to tell them, 'This is how you navigate throughout the school,' " she said. "I was blessed to have that, so if I see anyone who needs help, I try to talk to them."

Ashley recognized that for many students, in-person guidance made the difference between success and failure in the nursing program. Though each student was given the name of an adviser, most did not take the trouble to meet with that person before registration. "Nobody's going to say, I'm going to go up to the school so I can wait on a line for hours to see an adviser, to pick out three or four classes." Instead, they would follow the often misleading guidance of the online system. Ashley spoke with students who had been taking prerequisite classes for two years, and "sometimes they don't even have all the classes that they need, and it's a waste of time and money."

The only way to find the correct prerequisites for nursing was to see the academic adviser for the nursing department, who "gives you the paper, which says, first semester take this, second semester take that. But that's if you even know to go to his office." Then, simply knowing the requirements was not enough to help students balance a full schedule of classes with clinical work. Ashley advised new students about which courses to take when, what grades they needed to earn, and when entrance exams were scheduled. "It's stuff that I learned from trial and error and from other students. I tell them so they can have an easier journey."

Ashley was confident she would make it through herself and had her educational path carefully mapped out. Once she finished her associate's degree, she would take the exam to earn her license and begin work as a registered nurse. At the same time, she would pursue a bachelor's degree online at Chamberlain University, as her mother was doing now. The online program was less expensive than a traditional college and much more convenient while working full-time. Since most courses were based on reading, Ashley saw no need for in-person classes. "Last semester, I found myself teaching myself anyway, because my professors didn't really teach," she said. Following her bachelor's, Ashley planned to begin a doctorate in nursing practice (DNP) with a focus on midwifery. For this degree, it was important to "go to actual school."

In speaking with Ashley, Josh began to see why a BMCC associate's degree could be a strong option for a student of her caliber and why making it through might actually require her exceptional maturity and drive. Teachers and counselors often recommend hands-on, technical programs for students who seem bored or impatient at school, who are anxious to get into the world of work. Ashley was not this student: it was her intellectual excitement, her openness to getting to know many different people, that made her seem so well-suited to the experience of a four-year liberal arts college. Ashley had given Williams a chance, but had refused to stay simply for the sake of the cachet the degree would bring. Instead, she crafted the educational path that felt right for her, selecting among the vast, shifting, landscape of American higher education the stepping stones to a stable and fulfilling career. That she was able to do this independently reflected a level of self-knowledge, skill, and persistence that set her apart from many of her peers.

The path Ashley had chosen seemed to leave little space for the kind of intellectual and personal exploration Josh had hoped Ashley would encounter in college. But here, again, Ashley would surprise Josh and everyone who knew her. During her time at BMCC, Ashley's preprofessional path became a voyage of self-discovery that, as Ashley told Josh when they spoke during the summer after her third year at BMCC, "was long and it's still going. It's never going to end, until death."

Ashley located the beginning of this voyage in the English course she took in her second semester at BMCC. The class was reading Sophocles, and, in small groups, discussing the concept of predestination. Ashley's group included a Jewish student, two Muslim students, an atheist, and herself, a Christian. "We were all putting our own spin on it, in terms of our religious background," she remembered. Ashley found speaking with the Muslim students particularly interesting. "I know you guys don't believe in Jesus," she told them, and was shocked when they responded, "Whoa, we don't believe in Jesus? Jesus is a prophet in Islam."

Starting from this conversation, Ashley developed a close friendship with the two Muslim students and was spurred to explore her own religious beliefs. "I gave them some Bible scriptures to read, and they were telling me, read this in the Q'uran. Everything I was reading sounded pretty much the same. I started thinking, if I could accept the Old Testament, and if I could accept the New Testament, why don't I accept the Q'uran? I felt I wasn't sure why I was Christian: Why wasn't I Jewish? Why wasn't I Muslim?"

Ashley embarked on an intensive, self-driven study of world religions. "I found myself all of a sudden really reading everything, reading, reading, reading. Even though I'm not polytheistic, I looked at Jainism, Sikhism, Hinduism, Buddhism, so at least I know about them. I read about Scientology, and Jehovah's Witnesses. I read the whole Bible, and at the same time I was reading the Q'uran. I'm comparing, I'm taking notes, I'm writing questions."

Ashley's investigations echoed her approach to finding her professional vocation, combining systematic research and self-examination. "I wanted to make sure and prove to myself that there's no better religion for me. In terms of the connection between me and my creator, I wanted the best fit. Whatever it was going to be, I would move there." Ashley opened herself to hearing the convictions of others and to imagining how, when she decided on her path, she would be able to explain it to her family and friends. "Everyone has a brain, everyone thinks. It's not just, 'you went to Harvard.' If you want to persuade someone, you have to have evidence."

This religious quest continued through Ashley's third year at BMCC, when she also began her first serious relationship. Up until then, she had stood by her mother's rule that romance had to wait until her education was finished. "Going into the semester, I said I was not going to date," she told Josh. "I didn't want to be distracted." But in her fall semester, "there was a guy in the same clinical group, and we ended up liking each other." Their friendship turned into "dates, dates, dates. We jelled, laughed together, we would go to movies all the time, we had the same interests."

The only problem they had initially, Ashley said, was religion. He was Muslim, and she was Christian. He was surprised when she told him she was reading the Q'uran along with the Bible and knew about Islam. "He started asking me questions and he was like, 'you really do.' He knew stuff from the Bible, and we started exchanging verses."

Ashley's boyfriend had grown up in a Muslim community in Africa, though he was now experimenting with a more permissive American lifestyle. He encouraged Ashley's interest in Islam, and their discussions of religion, she said, "enriched the relationship." He got to know Karleen, Ashley's mother, and when he was dismissed from the nursing program after failing a third-year class twice, Karleen helped him to look for jobs. Ashley spoke with his mother on the phone in Africa, and he put Ashley's photo up on his Facebook profile.

Then one night Ashley saw a flurry of missed calls on her phone. She assumed they were friends calling for advice: "I'm the advice guru," she said. But instead, "everyone's calling me because there's a girl on Facebook, under my picture, saying, "Is this my rival?" The girl's profile referred to Ashley's boyfriend as "my man."

Ashley sent a playful message to her boyfriend, saying, "Oh, I have to fight girls now?" She made a joke out of it, she said, but also demanded some reassurance, which he refused to give. The girl was in Africa, and he didn't feel he had to offer any explanation.

The girl posted more messages, asking again, "Is she my rival or not?" Ashley's boyfriend responded, "She ain't." Ashley had enough. "I don't need stress right now," she said. "That's why I didn't want to date in the first place." She told him their relationship was over.

Trying to woo her back, her boyfriend sent Ashley's mother a message saying, "I love your daughter." Karleen, who had herself suffered intensely because of infidelity, felt fiercely protective. "He doesn't get it," she told Ashley. "Until he gets it, no." As Ashley recovered from her anger and disappointment, she felt even more strongly that her mother was the only person she could count on.

Following the breakup, Ashley said, she delved even more deeply into investigations of Islam, which had begun to hold increasing appeal for her. Her main problem with her church was that "I don't put Jesus and God on the same level." In Islam, she found a more open, God-centered view of the world, which seemed more inclusive than the Christianity she had grown up with. "It says specifically in the Q'uran that anyone from any religion can be a kind person. Anyone can go to heaven." Ashley said that she prayed to find her direction and promised, "Wherever You put me, I will go there." Slowly, she started leaning toward Islam.

In a way, being single gave her more confidence as she pursued her quest. "I didn't want people to think I changed religions from being in a relationship. Relationships come and go." Two weeks after breaking up with her boyfriend, she decided to become Muslim. Her greatest anxiety was over how to tell her mother.

Karleen was not a devout Christian, but Ashley knew her conversion would be hard for her mother to accept. Karleen did not have negative associations with Islam, Ashley said, but found its rules, like those of Orthodox Judaism, too extreme. "Too much focus on modesty, too many restrictions on food, and too much praying," Ashley said. "She just feels like it's too much work." When Ashley told her mother about her decision, they agreed that Ashley would wait until she finished school to convert.

Ashley told a Muslim friend what she had decided. "Why would you wait?" her friend asked. "What if you die tomorrow? Wouldn't you want to do things that please God?" Her friend told her that all she needed to do to convert was to recite the Shihada, a testimony of faith, in front of two witnesses.

With her friend's guidance, Ashley learned the Shihada from a YouTube video. She repeated it over the phone to two other friends, and later at the prayer room at BMCC. "That's all you have to do," she told Josh. "It's an easy process. When you go to church to become Christian, you have to plan it a month in advance. You have to have the baptism, the white outfit. Ask Kennetta, she'll tell you about it."

When Ashley told her mother what she had done, Karleen simply responded, "Oh, okay." The next day it hit her: "Wait, that means you're Muslim now? So you're going to start praying?"

Ashley had the times for daily prayers on her phone. In the family's living room, she put her laptop on a chair and found YouTube instructions for the words and motions. Then she rolled out her yoga mat and began to bow down. "My mother was like, 'Oh, no, no. This is too much for me, you're really praying.' "

Each change Ashley brought into her life after converting required an adjustment for her mother. "After a month, I started covering my hair," Ashley said. She began by wrapping her head in a scarf with a bun in the back. "That looks nice," her mother said. "I can work with that." Then one day, Ashley wrapped the scarf like a hijab. Her mother didn't like it, but accepted it.

Ashley's "reversion"—the term preferred by many Muslims—had taken place in January, just as the semester that she thought would be her last was beginning. Her plans to graduate that spring were disrupted by a cheating scandal at BMCC, which involved allegations that a student paid a staff member to provide answers to an end-of-semester exam in a required third-year course. In response, professors made the test harder. Some students continued to cheat, and did well, but all the others, including Ashley, received low scores.

In the uproar that followed in the nursing department, some students decided to sue. Ashley did not participate in the litigation or contest her grades on the exams. She knew from past experience at BMCC that this kind of fight burned up time and energy and decided instead that she would use the opportunity to learn more. "I was like, forget it. What happened, happened. Let me just take another semester to make sure I really understand the material before I go on the hospital floor, because these are people's lives at stake."

That spring, Ashley began an externship, a short experiential learning opportunity, at New York Methodist Hospital in Brooklyn, a place she already knew well. One day, in June 2012, she was approached by the Muslim chaplain, who saw her head scarf and asked if she knew that there was a prayer room in the building across the street. Ashley responded that she usually went home to pray, since she lived so close, but that she would check it out.

Ashley began to use the prayer room and became better acquainted with the chaplain, Ibrahim. When, in July, Ashley asked him questions about Ramadan, they decided to continue their conversation over lunch at a Thai restaurant on Seventh Avenue, a block away from Methodist.

After lunch, Ashley and Ibrahim agreed they had a lot more to talk about. They arranged to meet again the following afternoon, when Ashley did not have work and Ibrahim was on call. They stayed on Seventh Avenue, where students leaving the Secondary School for Research at the end of the day rubbed shoulders with Park Slope families and hospital employees. They browsed at the Barnes and Noble next door to Methodist, then returned to the same Thai restaurant for dinner.

Through the afternoon and evening, they talked and talked. Ibrahim, Ashley learned, was twenty-nine and ordained as an imam. He was completing his residency at Methodist, where chaplains make rounds to provide psychological as well as spiritual counseling to patients of all religions. Ibrahim grew up in Guinea, within a Fulani-speaking Muslim community. He played an active role as a youth leader for the Guinean immigrant community in the Bronx, delivering weekly radio addresses and organizing trips to Six Flags for kids. Ashley peppered Ibrahim with questions about Islam, culture, and family. They spoke about choices families make to stay together, and different approaches to parenting. At 10 p.m., Ibrahim proposed to Ashley, and she accepted.

Josh spoke with Ashley at the beginning of August, before her wedding. Her engagement had not changed her plans for education and work. She would complete her final semester at BMCC that fall, take her licensing exam, then look for a full-time job as a registered nurse. Where she looked would depend on Ibrahim's plans. He had received a job offer from Greystone Park Psychiatric Hospital in Morris Plains, New Jersey, and though neither wanted to leave Brooklyn, the position was attractive. Bellevue Hospital, where Ibrahim did per diem work, had also offered him a position in their prison ward, where he had previously worked as a resident.

The top choice for both Ibrahim and Ashley was to stay at Methodist, where they had come to feel part of an extended family. Ibrahim's colleagues "all love him," Ashley said, and "they're really pushing for him to get a full-time position." This would depend on how much funding the hospital was prepared to commit: as a resident, Ibrahim earned thirty-two thousand dollars a year, a salary that would jump to sixty thousand for a full-time chaplaincy.

Ashley's own desire to work at Methodist had become even stronger. "The externship gave me the opportunity to see if Methodist would be a good fit for me after I graduate, and I could definitely say yes."

During her externship, Ashley had deepened her understanding of the ways nursing could change lives. "There are a lot of people, especially in New York, who live by themselves, and don't have a lot of family. Or they have children, but they're in other states. So what happens if they fall in the bathroom, and they're there for hours, and they don't have a relationship with their neighbors?" Ashley's training, she said, enabled her to offer both physical and emotional support. She described an elderly patient from Park Slope she had seen the day before. "Her son brought her into the hospital. He said that he decided to call the ambulance after she was lying in the bed for ten hours without moving."

Speaking later with the woman, Ashley discovered that she was distressed by her son's plans to move her to a nursing home. When Ashley asked the woman what she wanted for herself, she asked Ashley, "Can *you* come to my house and take care of me?" Ashley had heard this request many times before. Patients would tell her, "You know what you're doing, but you're kindhearted at the same time."

Ashley told the patient she couldn't move in with her, but came in to see her again at the end of her shift, accompanying a nurse. When the nurse tried to give the woman her medication, she refused to take it.

Ashley, who as an extern was not allowed to administer medication herself, asked why. "I'm done with everything," the woman responded. "Everyone's aggravating me, I'm too much of a burden. Just give me a pill so I can sleep permanently."

The nurse left Ashley to talk to the patient on her own. Ashley eventually convinced her to take her medication. "But still," Ashley said, "she was asking, 'why should I keep going on?'" Ashley thought about how alone the woman must feel: "It's just her and her son. That's where spirituality comes in, and counseling. People really need other people to talk to." Ashley was glad that, as a nurse, "there's a counseling role, a caregiver role, a teacher role, everything."

On the morning of August 17, Josh attended Ashley and Ibrahim's civil marriage at City Hall. Ashley was dressed in an abaya, an overgarment worn by traditional Muslim women, with a long embroidered lavender panel in front. Ibrahim, very tall and slim, wore a Fulani outfit: a shin-length striped shirt of African *bazin riche* fabric, with matching trousers.

Ibrahim had a confident, soft-spoken friendliness, and he and Ashley were full of smiles. Karleen greeted Josh, apologetic for being tired after just finishing a night shift. She had become close with Ibrahim, who often visited her on her floor at Methodist. Ashley's sixteen-year-old sister, Stephanie, had also gotten to know Ibrahim well and had served as chaperone whenever Ashley and Ibrahim spent time together after their engagement: traditional Muslim couples are not permitted to be alone together until they are married. Ibrahim, Ashley said, wanted "a relationship where there's a real joining of families." His mother was still in Guinea, and his father had passed away. Ashley had spent time with Ibrahim's uncle, brother, and sister, who helped communicate with Ibrahim's mother and offer support for the marriage in the face of her doubts about his marrying a non-Fulani American.

Two days after the civil ceremony, the couple had a Muslim wedding at Ibrahim's mosque. Ashley wore a sparkly white dress made of African lace, and her mother, visiting the mosque for the first time, a red outfit embroidered with gold, her head covered in a white scarf. Though everyone sat on the floor on prayer mats, Karleen requested and was brought a chair. Also breaking with tradition, Karleen said, many people took pictures, even the imam. Following the ceremony, the couple gathered with family and friends for a celebratory dinner at the Thai restaurant where their courtship took place.

Soon after her wedding, Ashley became pregnant. That fall, she completed her final semester at BMCC. She was offered a position at Methodist for the spring as a nurse extern. Once she passed her licensing exam, her status would change to registered nurse.

At the end of the semester, Ashley posted a message on Facebook expressing her gratitude for all that had happened in the past year:

There is no amount of praise or worship that can be equivalent to the gratitude that I have for all that Allah has blessed me with. First I reverted in January, then in August I married the most loving and responsible man that I know. In September I became pregnant with my son. Now in December I passed my class and I am officially done with nursing school, and a college graduate.

8

Forward Movement:
Nkese and Dwight

Two years after his first class of students graduated from the Secondary School for Research, Josh received an invitation from Boris Komarovskiy, whose high school dream had been to own the New York Knicks, to join him for a baseball game at the new CitiField in Queens. Boris secured tickets through his summer internship with the New York Mets organization and also invited Candace Jones and Nkese Rankine, who were still his good friends. All three had completed their sophomore years of college. Boris was an accounting major at St. John's University in Queens. Candace was studying business as a Posse scholar at Babson College and interning that summer with Travelers Insurance. At Bates College, Nkese was double-majoring in politics and in women and gender studies, with a minor in German. She was an intern at the Eleanor Roosevelt Legacy Committee, which aims to build "a new generation of pro-choice Democratic women candidates," and to increase women's participation in New York State Democratic politics.[1] Nkese looked like a New England college student, dressed in a blue cardigan and gray slacks.

Nkese told Josh she felt she would be unrecognizable to her high school self: "I would probably be like, who is that young lady?" The significant change, she said, was not in the way she dressed or spoke, but in her outlook. "I didn't know that I would be the person I am today. I have the same core personality, but the goals and the drive, everything about me now is totally different."

At the end of her first year at Bates, Nkese said, she had considered transferring to another college but rejected the idea because she had not passed biology. She had otherwise done well as a freshman, receiving A's in three classes, but she "didn't want to apply somewhere with an F on my transcript." She decided she would give Bates a chance in the fall. "I was like, all right, I'll come back first semester, see how it is, and find ways to cope with the culture."

During sophomore year, Nkese began to adjust. She formed a close relationship with her women and gender studies professor, Rebecca Herzig. She fell in love with German, which she described as a "very strong language," and enjoyed learning about German culture and literature. She began attending meetings of the Women of Color group. She traveled with the Bates admissions office to reservations in the region in order to educate Native American students about the college admission process—an activity she had begun as a freshman—and volunteered with the Somali community in and around Lewiston.

Nkese had begun, that year, to enjoy campus life. "I was more social, hung out with more people, got a more diverse group of friends. I was just more into campus." In making this shift, Nkese said, she "mainstreamed," as students of color described the process of adjusting to the majority culture. "Even my clothing style—I toned it down. In order to evolve, you have to cope, but I don't think I forgot who I was and what I was about, and some of the struggles I had before."

As Josh caught up with Nkese, Candace, and Boris, they talked about news from other students from their class. Aundre Walker, who had been the DJ for the Halloween dance their senior year of high school, had completed his second year at Utica College. He had e-mailed Josh an invitation to a party he was hosting, as "DJ Vybz," to "bring a taste of the islands to upstate New York." He also wrote that he was "taking up a new responsibility in fathering

Kirk." After leaving City Tech, Kirk Hillaire had followed Aundre to Utica. He was now living in the same dorm as Aundre, and using his car to attend classes at Herkimer Community College, located nearby.

Nkese had tried to keep in touch with Krystle Guejuste, who in high school had led the protest against the cell phone ban, but whose unstable living situation meant that she was often absent from school. Though Krystle had been accepted to several colleges, she had joined the U.S. Army after high school graduation and was now serving in Afghanistan.

Erica Silvestri had finished her second year at SUNY Binghamton. In a phone conversation, she told Josh about a time when a professor in a huge lecture class reprimanded her for wearing headphones. Erica laughed when she recalled being yelled at for sucking her thumb in AP English. This felt different: she didn't fault her professor for calling her out, and reflected on how much she had grown intellectually and personally since high school.

Kory Fleurima, who had told Josh he wished he had always known college would be possible, had spent a year at York College in the SEEK program, but was dismissed for academic reasons. He was readmitted after working with Josh on an appeal letter in which Kory expressed his resolution to focus and improve his performance. Kory also explained the difficulties he had faced managing his schoolwork and part-time job during a time of family and financial instability. By the end of the year, however, he had to withdraw again.

Struggles like Kory's were not unusual. But the majority of students from Josh's first class were still in school, and many described their experiences as transformational. Some whose college pathways had initially been a disappointment had made new beginnings. Roshney Licorish, whom Josh had hoped would be able to attend St. Lawrence University after high school, had finished her associate's degree at Kingsborough Community College with high grades. In the fall, she would continue toward a bachelor's in psychology and neuroscience at Queens College. Ravell Robinson, who had not successfully completed the HEOP summer bridge program at Hobart and William Smith Colleges, had taken a year to manage his physical and emotional health before making a fresh start at Kingsborough. His first year at the college had gone well, and he felt a renewed sense of excitement about his education. It had been hard for Josh to know, when he met this class at the end of their high school careers, what the college experience would bring them. It was gratifying to see how many were doing well.

Josh caught up with Dwight Martin around this time, too. Dwight had completed two years at Guilford Technical Community College. He had continued his remarkable success, earning a 4.0 GPA and the college's highest honors every semester. He had also earned two technical certificates in aviation maintenance and passed the Federal Aviation Authority certification exam, a long, difficult test that had required many hours of study. Comair, a subsidiary of Delta, had recently opened a maintenance facility in Greensboro, North Carolina. The company had close connections with Dwight's program at Guilford Tech, and Dwight, one of the college's star students, was offered a job there.

Though he still needed four more courses to complete his associate's degree, Dwight jumped at the opportunity to begin working. He remained uncertain that aviation maintenance was the field he wanted to pursue and figured it made sense to try it out then complete his degree later, when he had a greater sense of clarity that the money he was spending on school was taking him in the right direction. Dwight was also anxious to increase his independence and to help his grandmother, with whom he still lived.

Dwight began work in Comair's huge hangar, a 41,000-square-foot facility hung with international flags, where each night about four planes came through for maintenance. Dwight began with an entry-level job, but was often asked to do complex technical work by supervisors who recognized his skill: when brakes needed to be set before a flight could leave, for example, Dwight would be asked to take care of it.

Dwight told Josh that he found his job challenging and exciting and enjoyed the camaraderie he felt with colleagues: "It's a great group of people there, I love them," he said. After working hard, "seven days a week," for two or three months, he was promoted to another department and saw further opportunities for advancement. "I'm just trying to build up my résumé," he said.

During the first semester of her junior year, Nkese left Bates to study abroad. Sixty percent of Bates's junior class participates in international study, sometimes offered through Bates, sometimes through other colleges and universities. Nkese had identified an Antioch University program that combined her interests in gender studies, politics, African American studies, and German, called Comparative Women's and Gender Studies in Europe. Over the course of three months, the group would attend seminars and conduct independent research in Berlin, Krakow, Utrecht, Amsterdam, Prague, and Istanbul. The students in the program came from other East Coast liberal arts colleges including Williams, Skidmore, and Hampshire, and for the first two weeks of the program, the group participated in a seminar with graduate students from across Europe.

From the beginning, Nkese felt inspired by her interactions with her peers. She described one of the first discussions she remembered, just after the program began in August. At the time, President Barack Obama's health care reform plan was hitting roadblocks in Congress, and students in the group talked about their countries' differing health care systems. The conversation started simply, "How much do you pay to go to the doctor?" then expanded to larger questions of how government policy affected access to quality health care. Nkese spoke about her views on the flaws in America's system: for example, she knew that when low-income women could not afford basic services like birth control and cancer-screenings, lives could quickly unravel. "All these things are just very interlinked, and if you don't have access to them, there are things that can happen to turn your life for the worse."

Nkese found it fascinating to engage in this discussion with people who were "well-seasoned in activism and gender studies" and whose insights she found so eye-opening. Her peers were mostly white women, though the group included one other black student and one man. All of the students had chosen to delve into issues of race and class and shared a commitment to deeper understanding and reflection. There was no need to explain, as Nkese felt she had had to do in her freshman year at Bates, what was okay and not okay to say about black people. "We were moving forward from those types of things. I had never been around a group of people who just got it."

Within a few weeks of the program's beginning, Nkese felt driven by a new sense of purpose. "I was reading a lot of Foucault and Freud, and they're saying such important things." She posted on Facebook, "Had one of the best lectures on the intersectionality of race, sex, as well as gender. These lectures keep motivating me to want to help people including myself to create a world where no oppression of any kind exists." She heard about the ways her friends were involved on their campuses and began to think about changes she could make at Bates. "I saw all these great things going on, all these women's movements, race movements. I would talk to my friends who were on the program with me, and they're involved in queer stuff, and I'm like, I want to be involved, too."

Despite being a women and gender studies major, during her freshman and sophomore years at Bates, Nkese said she had never attended a meeting of the Women's Resource Center. She did not join OUTfront, which focused on gender and sexuality on campus, "because I was scared that people would think I was queer." The African American studies group "was just too much. I didn't know how active you needed to be, and a lot of the people were very political."

This all changed the second semester of her junior year. "I came back from abroad with a new battery on my back, powered up to change the campus and change politics." Her first opportunity for leadership came through a friend, a year behind her, who was involved in OUTfront. He said, "I really want to change the face of this group." "I'm down for it," was Nkese's response. Nkese and her friend attended a conference and connected with student activists at Williams, Skidmore, Middlebury, and Bowdoin. Though she had only just become involved, Nkese was chosen to lead OUT-front. Then her friend said, "If you're going to do this, you should also do the Women's Resource Center." Her initial response was "whoa!" but Nkese jumped in.

With her suddenly packed schedule came a sharp improvement in academic performance. "What's funny is that's when my grades were 3.5 and higher. Sometimes I wonder—do I need a lot on my plate to pass? I don't think it's just that. I think the passion has to be there." This passion animated Nkese's academic work. When she spoke in class, her professors told her, "You came back from abroad so much different. You've grown so much. You seem on fire." In three months she had made leaps in her writing: "I was acing my papers like there was no tomorrow."

Nkese's first-year seminar professor and tutors at the writing center had helped her to correct her grammar and organize her thoughts. But it was her experience abroad that enabled Nkese to grasp the power and purpose of analytical writing. "I came back with a little more depth in my thinking, a little bit clearer, and not worried about what other people were saying or thinking."

Nkese laughed as she remembered the first paper she wrote as a freshman at Bates, answering the question "What is a woman?" for Introduction to Women and Gender Studies. "I wrote that 'a woman is someone who is free from all societal pressures,' which is obviously not true. 'A woman is someone who can give birth to a child'—obviously not true. 'A woman is someone who wears certain types of clothes'—that is not true. 'Some women aren't free, but that's because they live in Muslim societies'—that's obviously not true. 'There are trans-gender people, but they're not really women'—that's obviously not true either."

Her first paper was worlds away from the project she began while abroad and which would become her senior thesis: an analysis of German cultural identity through the lens of Afro-German feminism. With an undergraduate's struggle to master the dense theoretical language of contemporary scholarship, Nkese unpacked categories of race, culture, and nationality, including white majority culture. "Analyzing whiteness is a growing scholarship that works to explain how the racial group 'white' acts as a neutral racial category. White people often separate themselves from the racial discourse as if race is exclusively a non-white person's problem," she wrote.

When Nkese began at Bates, she had struggled to find her voice on a campus that seemed a bastion of white privilege. Now, she began to see her presence at the college as part of a history still in the making. She connected what she was learning in her classes with Bates's origins, the changing political culture of its student body, and the recent focus on diversity. When she began to see herself as an agent of change, "I began to understand Bates, what works and what doesn't work. That's when I started to enjoy Bates."

Nkese began her senior year as co-leader of the Women's Resource Center, OUTfront, and the Caribbean Students Association, which she had founded the previous summer. For the first two organizations, "What I did first was clean out the offices, and say we're doing everything different this year." Nkese "changed the look," created Facebook pages, and focused on advertising. Attendance at Women's Resource Center meetings grew from several students to twenty-five. "It's not about bragging," Nkese said. "You just have to know how to market to the people you want to market to. First, go to your friends. Say, we have conversations about these same things—let's go to the meeting." She began throwing events, and reaching out to other organizations, like Planned Parenthood, to co-sponsor them. "I started promoting their events, they promoted ours."

In March of that year, Nkese's activism took shape with a new force. "What happened," she said, "was that there was a hate crime." A friend of Nkese's was attacked at an off-campus party and called anti-gay slurs. Nkese was very upset, horrified both by what her friend had been through and by the vacuum he found when he looked to the college for support. "The only structure to deal with it was me. I'm a student, writing a thesis. This is not okay."

Nkese spoke to friends and fellow leaders at the Women's Resource Center "to figure out what we could do to address it, and change the atmosphere on campus." It was common, she said, to walk into the dining hall and hear students casually tease each other by saying, "you're a faggot," or "you're a dyke." The Women's Resource Center decided to hold a forum, which was organized for March 18, 2011. "We put it together in two days. We did a lot of promoting on Facebook, Twitter, e-mails, our friends, posters. We had over two hundred people show up, which was amazing—usually, no one shows up to anything, because our campus is really passive now. We had administration, students, coaches. This was exciting. This had never happened. I didn't know what to do with how many people showed up."

Standing in front of the audience, Nkese and her fellow organizers described the incident that motivated the forum, and opened a discussion about hate violence and discrimination of all kinds. People in the audience voiced concerns. "They called out some of the structures on campus," Nkese said. None of the rape hotlines were working. Muslim students described their anger at the anti-Islamic slant of a recent talk on campus by Rick Santorum. Some students felt that the new Office of Intercultural Education, which had replaced the Multicultural Center, wasn't addressing the real concerns of students of color.

The forum caught the attention of the Bates administration, and Nkese and fellow leaders began a series of meetings and exchanges with university officials and members of the board of trustees. Nkese described the interactions as driven by mutual respect. "They were receptive toward change. They understood we were not trying to say Bates is a terrible place. We love Bates. That's why we're doing this."

The meetings brought results. Students helped create a website for campus safety, which established working hotlines and listed resources for support. The university also added a Web page "celebrating queer diversity on campus." Nkese described efforts to hire a full-time staff member to counsel students on issues of gender and sexuality and to change the way the college treated these issues at freshman orientation.

Alongside these triumphs, Nkese found herself embroiled in new conflicts with her fellow students of color. "A lot of the men of color weren't happy with some of the work that the anti-discrimination movement was doing. They felt that it was too gender-oriented and that there weren't enough men in the group." Nkese also faced negative responses from friends in the Women of Color group, whose meetings she now rarely attended. They "painted the Women's Resource Center as a white women's group, which is weird, because there are a lot of women of color in the group." She added with a laugh that she herself, the co-president, "was not a white woman" and that before that moment she "had never been branded as one." During her senior spring, she said, "I kind of had to stop hanging out with my friends of color, because I was so in the mainstream culture for that moment. That was a really tense time."

Nkese ended her senior year with a great sense of pride in her accomplishments. It had taken her a long time to get accustomed to Bates, but she had figured out how to function effectively and how to be successful. She had cried when she made the dean's list for the first time, and she would make it again that semester. "I really love this school," she told Josh. The college had given her so many opportunities to grow, and her professors and fellow students had helped her to see and describe the world in new ways. It was hard to believe how much she had learned.

In the four years since Nkese began, diversity at Bates had significantly increased. Nkese's class had been the first product of new multicultural recruitment efforts: for the class of 2011, Bates reported that 17 percent of domestic students were from "underrepresented minority groups," as compared to 10 percent for the previous year. Six percent of the class were international students. The college also increased the overall percentage of students who were first-generation college students. These higher percentages stayed constant in the three classes that followed Nkese's.[2]

During Nkese's four years, Bates also developed structures to support incoming multicultural students. These included the "swing dean" system, in which the admissions dean in charge of recruitment for one year—for Nkese this was Marylyn Scott—moved to the dean of students office the following year, enabling incoming students to develop a relationship that would be a source of continuing support through their freshman year. When Nkese was a sophomore, Marylyn Scott had invited her to be a mentor at the "swing dean retreat," a day when incoming freshmen gathered at a country house with Marylyn and with older students to speak openly about some of the challenges they might face at Bates. Nkese spoke about her own first-year experience, describing her academic and social struggles and expressing how meaningful it was to her that she could now help advise younger students.

Nkese observed that while the college had focused its efforts on helping students of color adjust to Bates, she saw a crucial next step as finding ways to help the majority population understand what it means to live and learn with people from different backgrounds.

"Half of the students of color are from other countries, and half are from urban schools, and then you've got all the other kids on campus who don't have any experience with people who aren't like them." She wanted to see more structured ways to help everyone understand how to engage with difference.

Josh went to Bates for Nkese's graduation. It was a cool morning, the sky light gray. Chairs were set up on the leafy quad. Josh saved several seats and waited for Nkese's family who, Nkese told him over the phone, were running late. The bus they had taken from Brooklyn the day before had broken down, and the trip took twelve hours. They were staying forty-five minutes away from Bates: all the lodging closer by had been booked since January.

Josh spotted Nkese's mother, Peggy, whom he recognized from Nkese's high school graduation. With her was Nkese's younger brother Rasheed, who had graduated from the Secondary School for Law and was now a junior at Skidmore, and Nkese's thirteen year-old sister Risa. Peggy greeted Josh, and the family sat down. A bell began to clang in the copula, and the graduates filed in to the music of a horn ensemble.

Everyone stood up and peered forward. "There she is," Josh said to Peggy. "Nik!" Peggy called. Nkese gave a small wave. Like many of the graduates, she wore a green armband on her robe. Rasheed told Josh that this was in solidarity with the antidiscrimination movement in which Nkese had been a leader.

After the ceremony was finished, Josh, Peggy, Rasheed, and Risa found Nkese standing on the lawn surrounded by friends. She was wearing a brown and white patterned dress and sandals, and looked a bit flustered. She and her friends were talking about how the reader had mispronounced everybody's name: "Colón" as "Colin," Nkese as "Nkesé." "Always criticizing," Josh teased Nkese, reminding her of her many objections to the graduation ceremony at the Secondary School for Research.

Josh asked Peggy if she would have imagined Nkese and

Rasheed like this, at Bates and Skidmore. "Not so far away," she said, echoing the anxiety about distance she had expressed during Nkese's application process. Peggy used to call Nkese every day on her cell phone, and if Nkese did not pick up, she would call the phone in her dorm room. If there was no answer there, she would call security. Peggy was beside herself with worry when Nkese told her about plans to go to Europe. "The first thing I did was go get a passport," Peggy said.

When Josh asked Peggy how she thought college had been valuable for Nkese, Peggy spoke about how Nkese had learned to interact with many different kinds of people. This would help her in the workplace, especially in the kind of leadership position Nkese hoped to attain. Even within her own family, Peggy said, there were significant differences: Peggy had "many Republican values and some liberal, Rasheed was mostly liberal, and Nkese was *very* liberal." You don't have to agree with everyone's ideology, she explained, "but you can at least listen and think about it." It was so important, Peggy said, to try to "understand where people are coming from."

In August 2012, a year after Nkese's graduation, Josh went to visit Dwight in North Carolina. In phone conversations leading up to the visit, Josh learned that Dwight had been unemployed since early that summer, when Delta shut down Comair. This had not come as a complete surprise to Dwight: the destiny of the company had been uncertain for several months. But losing his job intensified an already emotionally difficult time. That spring, his long-term girlfriend had become pregnant, then had a miscarriage. His relationship with his girlfriend ended, and Dwight grieved a double loss.

Dwight had been working hard at Comair, often through the weekend. Now, he figured, he would try to enjoy his life. Since losing his job, Dwight told Josh he spent his time partying "five out of seven days a week," working out at his gym, and riding the motorcycle he had bought in April, the fulfillment of a longtime dream.

Dwight and Josh made plans to meet at the Southpoint Mall in Durham. Dwight, coming by motorcycle, covered the sixty-mile distance from Browns Summit, where he lived, in well under an hour. He met Josh in one of the mall's plazas, next to a fountain with bronze sculptures of children in raincoats. Dwight had his leather biker gloves in the back pocket of his jeans and wore boots made of bulging black and red plastic. His Brooklyn Nets T-shirt fit snugly around his heavily muscled shoulders and arms. Dwight greeted Josh with a big smile and handshake. Josh told him he looked great and "much bigger!"

Dwight and Josh walked up and down the mall's "street," past Pottery Barn Kids, Barnes and Noble, an Apple Store, a stage set up for musicians. It was tax-free weekend in North Carolina, and the mall was packed. Josh noticed the way Dwight moved with practiced, careful politeness, holding doors and stepping aside to allow people to pass.

Dwight pointed to the stretch marks on his biceps as evidence of how fast he had built up muscle. At his gym, he often worked out with a Marine Corps trainer who had been one of his colleagues at Comair. Dwight showed Josh his friend's picture on his phone: a six-foot-four-inch white guy with a short hair cut, the huge space of the Comair hangar behind him. With his friend's help, Dwight had honed his skills. He had rehabilitated his own shoulder and knee and helped friends and family recover after injuries. Dwight was well-known at his gym and had been offered a job in sales there. Sales was "not his thing," Dwight said, but he told the manager that he would be interested in any trainer positions that opened.

Josh reminded Dwight that during the three days they spent together during Regents week five years before, Dwight had written an essay about personal training for the Common Application. Maybe now he was finding his way back to this passion. Josh mentioned other job pathways he thought might interest Dwight, like exercise science, kinesiology, or physical therapy. But talking about careers clearly made Dwight anxious. Dwight described the pressure he felt to make a decision about what he wanted to do with his life: "Adults don't understand how hard it is," he said. He had been meaning to enroll in fall semester classes to finally finish his associate's degree, but he felt like he needed to know where his coursework was leading before paying for the credits.

Dwight was considering several directions. He had enjoyed the courses he had taken at Guilford Tech in network engineering, and others had encouraged him to follow this path. He had also thought seriously about joining the military. Dwight liked the physical training that was part of military life and was comfortable with guns: his father had always taught him how to be safe around them. He had spoken with friends, who, returning from service, had found exciting professional opportunities. But he had also heard "terrible stories" about life in the military, and none of his loved ones wanted him to enlist.

Dwight's parents had moved back to North Carolina, and now they treated him as an adult, which, Dwight said, was both good and bad. It was his grandmother who kept him sane and stable, and he couldn't imagine making it to this point in his life without her. His grandmother was retired, but was always busy, gardening and fixing things around the house. She was a real powerhouse, he said, and growing up, had been the disciplinarian who tried to keep him on track. Around her, he could let his guard down and be himself.

After lunch, Dwight took Josh out to the lot to see his "baby": a Suzuki GSX-R motorcycle, big and sleek, painted with red flames. The most important development in his life, Dwight said, was becoming a biker. He was learning how to fix his motorcycle, and how to control his body so he could ride fast and stay in control. Dwight showed Josh a scrape mark on his boot: he made a turn at such a low angle that the peg scraped the ground.

Dwight talked about the community of bikers, which included all kinds of people. There was a place in Raleigh where they all met, with rows and rows of motorcycles lined up. People shared information about the best roads for riding fast, and everyone respected one another. Once, a policeman who stopped him for speeding saw he was a serious biker and let him go without a ticket.

Among the biker community there were some guys who got into trouble, but others, like Dwight, connected the sport with a search for meaning. Dwight found in biking a way to escape his anxiety about where he was going in life and to be in the moment. Faith and spirituality also helped him find this sense of peace. He was "not a Bible person," he said, but he spent time with certain passages of scripture. He felt that he had some purpose in the world but didn't yet know what that was. He spoke about a desire to give, to sacrifice in order to support others.

Dwight told Josh he could take his motorcycle for a ride around the lot. This was a serious honor: the only other person who had ever ridden the bike was simply moving it for him. Josh did not feel ready for this. He only sat on the motorcycle, feeling slightly goofy, while Dwight, disappointed, took his picture.

9

Room to Grow:
Mike and Abby

Josh kept up with many of his former students through Facebook. One night he saw a new post from Abigail Benavente. It was a photo of her with her hands cradling a round belly. Below were comments from friends. Michael Forbes had written, "Clearly we need to catch up!"

Josh felt stunned. Abby's college essay had told the story of her sister's pregnancy, and how it had compounded her family's struggles. Abby was the last person whom he thought would be a mother before she graduated from college.

Abby came to see Josh in her eighth month. She was round-faced and glowing, with a striped shirt and a black coat buttoned over her belly. Abby was excited and nervous about the prospect of giving birth. She was seeing a midwife rather than an obstetrician and was practicing ways to move while she was in labor. Because of her lupus, she had spent too much of her life in hospitals already and wanted to avoid a birth experience that was overly medicalized. "I'm not sick—I don't need to be in a hospital," she said. Like Ashley, Abby had watched the documentary *The Business of Being Born* in a college class. "I was like, I do not want to give birth in the hospital if I ever get pregnant. And then I ended up getting pregnant."

Abby told Josh that she had become pregnant during a lapse in her mother's health insurance, when she had stopped using birth control pills because they were too expensive to purchase out-of-pocket. "I didn't plan to get pregnant now. I always thought I would finish college, get a good job, *then* get married and have kids. I wanted to have my babies when I was ready, and I had my financial stability. I didn't want to be like my parents." But there was no question for her about whether she would carry the baby, and her family supported her. Their most immediate concern was her lupus. Women with lupus are no longer told they cannot have children, as had once been the case, but their pregnancies are considered high-risk.

Doctors met with Abby after a series of tests. Abby said that they had found no evidence that she had lupus. She was advised to discontinue treatment for the disease, and doctors speculated that many of the symptoms she had experienced in high school—vulnerability to fever, poor vision, and sensitivity to sunlight—were caused by Plaquenil, the drug she had been taking. "It was the pills. That's why I was getting sick. That's why I was always like that," Abby said.

For Abby, lupus had defined her teenage life. Now the worry and uncertainty that had hovered over health was lifted, and she was able to enjoy a healthy pregnancy. But it was hard to let go of the harm done by her misdiagnosis. Every couple of months, she said, she thought about what she had lost when she left Skidmore out of fear for her health. Her illness at college, her new doctors had told her, was unrelated to lupus and less serious than she had been led to believe. "What would have happened, how would my life had been different if I hadn't gotten sick? I probably wouldn't be pregnant."

The independence Abby had longed for was now out of reach, at least for the moment. She relied on her parents for food and housing. Her boyfriend, Quentin, was "not that dependable." Abby described him as someone who "still has the child mentality. He feels like he's free to do what he wants. He doesn't go out or anything, but he's very laid-back, with his video games and stuff. He's a guy who needs a push."

Abby described seeing Facebook posts from classmates like Daina, who had gone to Hobart and William Smith, where Abby was planning to go before she was accepted off the waitlist at Skidmore. Daina was spending her junior year abroad in Ecuador. "I could have done that, too," Abby said, "but I haven't, or I can't anymore, because of the place where I'm at. I guess that's why it's sad to think about. There are just things that not a lot of people experience, especially people like me. There's something I could have had, but it's slipped away."

Abby reflected wistfully on her high school years. "I wish I could go back to those days," she said. "They were so much easier, and everything came out so much the way it should be. I just felt more comfortable being in school than I did anywhere else. I felt like I was in the right place."

Josh and Abby shared memories of the long, difficult, college application process. Like Ashley, Abby refused to express regret that despite all the work and stress, she had ended up at home, attending the City University of New York. Just getting into colleges like Skidmore, Muhlenberg, and Hobart and William Smith, she said, had given her a sense of possibility that helped her to keep dreaming. Her big dream was to create her own school, "where kids learn out of their curiosity instead of learning how to pass tests."

This dream was now "far away." But it had not disappeared, and though she knew it would be a long path, Abby was resolved to stay in school as she raised her child. "Once I'm done with my bachelor's, I want to go on to my master's. I can't be working in retail or in a little office all my life. I want to help kids: that's the most important thing. I want to help kids who don't have as much privilege."

Mike started his sophomore year at Skidmore determined to pull his grades "way, way up." His freshman year GPA was a 2.6, and he realized that other students in the HEOP program were averaging 3.5. He chose his classes carefully, making sure he had enough study time in his schedule of activities and part-time jobs. These included his responsibilities as a resident assistant, a position that paid for his housing and gave him a private suite with a separate study room. He did "rounds" when he was on duty, "walking through to make sure things are running smoothly." If students were locked out of their rooms, he said, "they would come to me to gain access."

Mike was finally in control of his own space and in the position of responsibility that suited him best. He became known as the campus audiovisual expert, sought after for help by students and faculty in his work-study job in media services and as the campus representative for Apple Computers. He was elected president of SkidTV, which involved managing everyone, "making sure the club is continuing to grow, that operations are running smoothly, that things are getting scheduled." Alongside this independence and leadership came academic achievement: Mike earned a 3.5 the first semester of his sophomore year and a 4.0 the second.

Josh spoke with Mike at the end of his sophomore year about the success he had found at Skidmore. What was behind it? Mike said he realized "there's no point in being here unless I really try to push myself forward enough to make actual changes." He had a sense that this was his "one shot" at the kind of education Skidmore could provide. "I had to give it everything I had. I realized I'm not going to be in high school again—I'm never going to go to a fancy private school that's going to give me access to colleges like this, opportunities like this." Despite his complaints about the Opportunity Programs, he knew the message was, "We believe in you and we want to give you a shot at this." This was enough, he said, "to make me want to hold my own with other students who I'm technically competing against."

Though self-sufficiency was tremendously important to Mike, he recognized progress is not always possible without the support of others. To find success, Mike said, students in situations like his need someone to recognize their potential and help them see new possibilities for themselves. "It's not something that a student can do alone," he said. "Giving a person an opportunity that they may not have been given before can open new doors within that person." Kids need someone to "really work with them, to let them know that even though things haven't been so great in their life so far, they can go on to do great things."

Josh spoke about Mike with Susan Layden, who had previously directed Skidmore's Opportunity Programs and was now the college's associate dean of student affairs. Sue had read Mike's application, even though she was no longer officially working for the Opportunity Programs at the time he applied. After she left the Opportunity Programs, Sue had been distressed to find that many students of color, particularly young men, were being routinely screened out on the basis of grades and scores. One year, she said, in the first reading of files for program candidates, only female Asian students had been recommended for admission.

Despite having changed jobs at the college, Sue took on the role of reading all the applications from African American and Latino males for the Opportunity Programs and training staff in how to review them. Sue looked for qualities that are not readily apparent in students' grades and scores, like exceptional energy and motivation. She also encouraged admissions staff to try to understand the context in which students were living and learning and the obstacles that many faced.

Reading Mike's application, Sue recognized that the drop in his average when Mike left Georgia did not reflect ability or work ethic, but a catastrophic change in life circumstances. In his essay, list of activities, and letters of recommendation, she saw the resilience, maturity, and self-discipline that suggested what Mike was capable of achieving on campus, alongside students accepted through traditional measures of achievement. Now, Sue said, she saw these qualities borne out not only in Mike's high grades but in his impact on the Skidmore community. She had hired Mike to make a promotional video for the office of student academic services, and the result had a nuance and sensitivity that was vital to encouraging all students to take advantage of the psychological and academic support her department offered.

Sue remembered meeting Abby on the first day of the Summer Academic Institute and noticing her intelligence and enthusiasm. But because she was focused on African American and Latino males, Sue had not read Abby's application. When Josh told her why Abby had left, Sue was angry and upset. Right away, she said, those who read Abby's application should have flagged the fact that Abby had lupus. They should have made sure that the staff knew about Abby's needs and that Abby and her family were informed about the services available to them coming in.

Sue felt responsible for this oversight, even as she knew she couldn't anticipate or bridge every pitfall faced by the students she worked with. She had built the Opportunity Programs and the Summer Academic Institute to ensure that students like Mike and Abby were not passed over in the application process and that they were positioned to realize their potential at Skidmore. But Sue knew that the structures she built were stationed in a vast landscape of risk. Without a larger institutional and societal commitment, these students would continue to be vulnerable to the ocean of forces ready to knock them over or pull them down. In Abby's case, a missed sentence in an essay meant the loss of an opportunity that had barely begun.

About a year after his meeting with Abby, Josh attended a first birthday celebration for Quentin Jr., usually called Q J. The party was held in the Spanish Baptist church in Boerum Hill, Brooklyn. The social hall was decorated with a jungle theme: a cardboard lion, a sheet cake iced with trees and animals, and a table where kids were making animal masks from paper plates. Josh saw

Abby now as he remembered her from high school, surrounded by friends, including familiar faces from the Secondary School for Research and new ones from Hunter, and her large and supportive extended family. Abby wore a flowing black dress, big hoop earrings, and sparkly necklaces that Q J played with. He was a sturdy toddler with bright dark eyes and hair and soft round cheeks, nattily dressed in little trousers and a vest, staring seriously at the guests.

Abby's mother, a small woman in a flowered summer dress, exuded energy and warmth. She set out foil trays of Peruvian food: baked chicken with spicy potatoes and baby carrots, pasta with shrimp and tomato sauce, steamed vegetables and salad. Abby's father put on a CD of soft religious music. He had a lined face and black-rimmed glasses and wore a pressed white shirt that by the end of the evening was speckled with green and orange icing from carrying his grandson, who adored him. He was eager to speak to Josh, with Abby translating from Spanish. He told Josh with great pride that the next day, Easter Sunday, Abby would be baptized in the church. This was a choice she had made, as he had, to be reborn.

Quentin arrived late, having just gotten out of work. "It's been a hard year," he said when Josh asked how he was. "I moved out; I'm living in Jersey now with my dad." He said he was trying to put aside his sadness at the split with Abby, his anger and frustration. "Look at this," he said pointing to his spiky head. "Gray hairs, and I'm only twenty-three."

Everyone doted on Q J, especially his mother. Abby kept him as close as possible, talking to him in English and Spanish, hugging him, and playing peekaboo under the tables. She told Josh that she didn't mind the social limits motherhood placed on her life—she had always been "kind of a homebody." Her responsibilities, she said, kept her disciplined and focused. Having Q J had brought joy and meaning to her life. "I stayed in school because of him, and I aspire because of him," she said.

This semester, Abby was taking five classes and expecting to earn A's in three and B's in two. She had been elected vice president of Alpha Phi Omega, the co-ed fraternity and service organization at Hunter, making her responsible for arranging all the projects undertaken by the group. She was also working at a Victoria's Secret store thirty-nine hours per week. As Josh learned from other former students, many retail jobs offered hours just under full-time, so that employers would not be required to pay for benefits. Abby woke up at 5 a.m. to go to Manhattan, where she readied merchandise before the store opened. Abby's mother, who worked forty-eight hours per week as a home attendant, took care of Q J while Abby was at work.

The family had moved to a larger apartment in Bensonhurst, south of Sunset Park in Brooklyn, and Abby and Q J now had their own room. Abby's sister, Ruth, and niece, Valerie, had moved to Florida, where they lived with Abby's brother. Abby planned to move there, too, after she finished her bachelor's at Hunter. She could transfer to another Victoria's Secret in Florida and once she had established residency in the state, begin earning credits toward a master's degree at one of Florida's public colleges. Abby said that she looked forward to being in an environment where Q J could be involved in sports, where he would have more space to play and room to grow.

As Abby celebrated Q J's birthday, Mike was finishing his senior year at Skidmore and making plans for the next stage of his life. When Josh spoke with him after his freshman year, Mike had said his goal was to become a film producer. At the time this had seemed to Josh the unrealistic dream of an eighteen-year-old. But Josh was delighted to learn that the summer after his junior year, Mike had started his own video production company, with gigs filming a preschool graduation and college events. Mike was earning enough money from this work, and from his work for Apple, to start saving in an IRA. He had broken up with his girlfriend,

Jamie: she was attending graduate school for social work at Washington University in St. Louis and the long distance relationship had been too hard. He had a new girlfriend, Molly, who was staying in Saratoga Springs after graduation. Mike had loved the summers he spent there and was considering staying, too, and developing his business through local connections.

But Mike had also applied, along with many of his peers, for Teach for America, and was one of the few accepted. The two-year program offered the chance to give back and would provide a steady income in a difficult economy. Though he was tempted by the independence of striking out on his own, Mike decided to accept the position he was offered: teaching technology at the Maureen Joy Charter School in Durham, North Carolina.

Josh told Mike he was coming to the Skidmore commencement ceremony and asked if he could offer Mike's family a ride from Brooklyn. Mike thanked him. His mother, Ebony, had lost her car and her license since being pulled over by the police for illegally using her car as a taxi and for unpaid parking tickets. His brothers had never been to Skidmore.

Josh drove to the address Mike gave him on Flushing Avenue in Bushwick, on a block with Chinese toy warehouses, car dealerships, and buildings with broken windows. The beige cement building was another homeless shelter. As Josh had learned from Mike, his mother and brothers had lost their three-bedroom apartment. Someone's extension cord had shorted in the apartment above, and the family suffered through another fire.

Josh called Ebony from the car to tell her he had arrived. She and the boys emerged about twenty minutes later. Ebony wore a light blue shirt, jeans, and white slip-on shoes. Her eyes were large and deep set, her hair pulled tightly back. She was warm and talkative with a deep laugh like Mike's. The boys were both tall, with polite manners and cautious movements, still getting used to their adolescent bodies. Justin was finishing seventh grade, Anthony ninth.

Ebony explained that it had taken her some time to get out because the boys had been in bed, catching up on sleep. Ebony often did not arrive home until midnight, and Anthony and Justin were not allowed into their unit without her. Instead of going to childcare at the shelter, which cost money and which they disliked, they sometimes went to their grandmother's apartment in Lefferts Gardens, a Brooklyn neighborhood on the southeastern edge of Prospect Park. When they did this, they left their grandmother's after 11 p.m. to take the city bus back to the shelter to meet their mother when she came home from work. Ebony described her reluctance to let them take this bus ride. The neighborhood was largely barren and unsafe, though, she added, "white people were coming and buying the warehouses, turning them into lofts." She described, with a sense of wonderment, the young woman she sometimes saw riding her bike down Wyckoff Avenue at 2 a.m.

One night, Anthony and Justin had both fallen asleep on the bus and didn't wake up until they reached the end of the line, in Maspeth. It was the last bus of the night. To get home, they had to walk back to the shelter in the dark, after midnight. Ebony had been sick with worry, and showed Josh the MetroPCS phones she had bought afterward. "This is where we walked," said Justin, pointing out the window as Josh drove away from the shelter.

Throughout the drive to Skidmore, Anthony and Justin made frequent comments and observations from the backseat. "I like this area," Anthony said as they left behind New York City's asphalt for the green of Westchester County. "It reminds me of Georgia." He watched a hawk soaring and noticed, with sadness, a deer that had been killed in the road. He wanted to be a veterinarian and told Josh about how he was caring for a stray kitten. A man he knew had given it to his girlfriend, and when they broke up, Anthony said, the man "kicked out the kitten," which now lived in the street.

Justin peppered his mother with questions, beginning each with "Mommy, Mommy." Ebony was proud of Justin's curiosity and motivation to learn. She said he taught himself independently, looking things up on the Internet and reading books Mike brought home from college. Justin said that he was going to be a physicist. When Josh asked him about his school, he said that it was bad and that he would probably have to go to summer school because of repeated lateness: it was a long subway ride in the mornings and hard to get up when they got to bed so late.

Currently, Justin was interested in the economic relationship between the United States and China. "Do we owe China a lot of money because we buy a lot from them?" he asked Josh. "Are we going to get into a war with China because we owe them a lot of money?" He was reading about sweatshops in China and had watched an interview on YouTube with a boy his age who worked in one and who said that if he didn't have this job he would starve. "In America," Ebony said, "you might not eat what you want to eat, but you won't starve."

Ebony spoke to Josh about how miserable she was in New York City. She was determined, now, to get back to Georgia. This time she could do it because she no longer had fear. Fear, she explained, is something that you live with when you don't know where the bottom is. Now that she had already fallen so far, she was not afraid to take steps forward, no matter how risky they seemed.

Her plan was to save money through "penny auctions," which she had discovered on the Internet. She bought a certain number of bids, then bid on gift cards, iPads, watches, perfume, bed and bath sets, and other items that she then resold on eBay. She was saving up money in a PayPal account for a down payment on a house in Atlanta. She was already having conversations with a broker there about homes that were partly subsidized by the U.S. Department of Housing and Urban Development or in foreclosure.

Ebony hated living in the shelter on government assistance, but saw herself as trapped. She didn't see how she could save enough to rent her own apartment while she was paying for food, transportation, and childcare for the boys. The government, she said, paid thousands of dollars per month to the shelter to house her family, and $150 per month to the storage company where her belongings were now held. Wouldn't it be better to use that money to help her rent an apartment of her own? She used to resent people who received welfare checks and food stamps and believed they lacked the work ethic that had enabled her to support her family and save for the future. Now her attitude had changed, and she had grown cynical. Her poverty, it seemed, was somebody else's profit. "Maybe they want us here," said Justin, listening to her arguments.

The conversation turned to Mike and his many jobs and activities on campus. "How does he do all that? How does he have time to study?" Justin asked. To Justin, Mike's life, and the life of all the adults he knew, seemed like an exhausting grind. "You wake up, you drink coffee to get through the morning, and then you go to class and your professors yell at you. Or you go to work, and then you have to go home and spend time with your partner, make food, shower, then go to bed." Already, in seventh grade, he had to drink Five Hour Energy to get through the day. What did he have to look forward to? Josh tried to explain how fulfilling work and study could be and the kinds of choices Mike now had before him.

Mike had lived off-campus his senior year, in a house he shared with DJ, who had been his best friend since they were freshmen. Driving into Saratoga Springs, Anthony and Justin tried to guess which house was Mike's. "I don't think Mikey would have such a big flag out front," Anthony said of one. Mike's was brown wood, with a red roof and small balcony. Mike, in a white tank top, came out to wave to his family.

The house was spacious, with an open kitchen and big dining table, though the furnishings were mostly packed up. Mike introduced his girlfriend, Molly. Ebony had met her before and commented on her new spiky haircut. "I used to have hair like that. I would cut it myself."

Ebony seemed full of nervous excitement in seeing Mike, and Mike seemed subdued, not looking his mother in the eye. "I told him my whole life story," Ebony said when Mike asked her and Josh about the car ride. Anthony and Justin looked around the house, curious. It was clear that the family needed time together, and Josh left them alone.

Graduation was held the next day at the Saratoga Performing Arts Center. A long, slow line of cars drove through a forest of pine trees. Graduating seniors were lining up on the lawn, draping their gowns with multicolored scarves that indicated their areas of study and decorating the tops of their mortarboards. Bagpipers in tall fuzzy hats led the processional, the high whine rising above the hum of voices.

In his commencement remarks, Skidmore's president, Philip A. Glotzbach, addressed "the raucous chorus of contemporary cultural critics who portray liberal education as hopelessly detached from the requirements of practical life." In a world marked by "rapid, persistent, and unpredictable change," he said, Skidmore provided students with an "intellectual and ethical tool kit" that "represents the best guide to life that one could possibly seek." The historian and author Ron Chernow described the way his own failed attempts to become a novelist led to a career in journalism and spoke about the way life's "improbable plot twists" and "baffled intentions" could lead to "new syntheses and a much deeper fulfillment elsewhere." Life, Chernow said, "has a wonderful way of disrupting all our tidy plans and, just when we thought we had hit bottom, bringing something newer and fresher and better into being."[1]

After the ceremony Josh joined Mike's family as they were packing up to leave the house. Anthony and Justin wore sweater vests over polo shirts and jeans and seemed serious and fatigued. Josh asked them for their impressions of the college and the commencement. The day before, they told him, Mike had taken them on a tour of Skidmore's campus. It had been a long walk around "all the little locations Mike goes to": the bookstore, the library, the science lab, the theater, the art and music departments, the SkidTV studio. At graduation, Anthony was especially interested in the horses, ridden by two park rangers, and the sign language interpreter. Josh pressed the boys for more of their reactions to Skidmore, hoping to hear how this first visit to Mike's college affected their visions of their own futures. But Anthony and Justin were clearly less focused on the college itself than on having time with Mike. "It's great," both said when Josh asked them how it was to see their brother. "Everything's great about that."

The August after graduation, Josh received a call on his cell phone from Mike. Mike, his mother, and his brothers were in a U-Haul truck in the parking lot of a hotel in Durham, North Carolina. Just a couple weeks before, Mike explained, his mother learned that she and the boys would be transitioned out of the New York City shelter system. The family decided that Ebony, Anthony, and Justin would move with Mike to Durham. Though Mike had already made arrangements to live with another Teach for America fellow, he had quickly found a house where he and his family could live together.

The problem now, Mike told Josh, was that he could not yet sign the lease: the paperwork he needed from his new employer, the Maureen Joy Charter School, to prove he could afford the rent had been held up. Until the lease was executed, Mike could not be given keys to the house. The family had slept in the hotel the previous two nights while they tried to resolve the issue. They had spent all they could spare. The duration of their U-Haul rental had expired, and substantial fees would mount if they kept the truck any longer. It was Friday, and if Mike couldn't manage to get the paperwork he needed before the end of the day, he would need to wait until business hours on Monday to meet with someone at the leasing office for the housing development. Adding to all of the other complications, Mike didn't know what to do with his mother's car, which they had towed from Brooklyn on the back of the U-Haul. The car did not have valid plates or registration, and if they parked the car on the street, it might be impounded. If this happened, they would not be able to afford to get it back, and without a car, it would be almost impossible for Mike's mother to find work in the area.

Mike needed help thinking through this logistical nightmare. He and Josh talked together through each of the most pressing problems. Josh reminded Mike that in two days he would be arriving in Durham for the visit he had planned to see both Mike and Dwight and offered to help in whatever way he could. They touched base throughout the day and, later that evening, Mike called to say that he had received the keys and that his family was okay.

When Josh arrived in Durham, Mike and his family were settling into their new home. While Ebony was busy unpacking, Josh went out to eat with Mike, Anthony, and Justin. It was one of their first meals together since the move, and Mike took a stern, paternal tone with his brothers as he described the new ground rules. "Now that you're living with me," Mike said, "things are going to be different." Bedtime would be strictly 10 p.m., and they were going to eat well and exercise. He told them he was going to get them bikes and library cards, and that he would join the PTA at their school and keep careful watch over their performance.

Mike told Josh that he still felt anxiety about what his absence during college had meant for Anthony and Justin, and whether it was too late to make up for the time they had lost. He also knew that looking after them would be a lot to manage while he plunged into his new job, and that living with his family would mean giving up some of the freedom he had enjoyed at Skidmore. But he felt positive about the new beginning, which gave him the chance to once again act as a father to his brothers and help support his mother. It felt crazy, he said, the way things had come full circle.

10

Undocumented American Dream:
Aicha and Santiago

O n January 31, 2008, midway through Josh's second year at the Secondary School for Research, principal Jill Bloomberg received an e-mail message from the Department of Education ordering her immediately to cut 1.75 percent of her school's operating budget. This surprise midyear cut, in effect for all New York City public schools, came on top of the $324 million cut already in place for the budget for the following year. For Jill, this meant she would not be able to replace teachers who left, that class size would rise, and that she would have to choose programs and positions to cut. The *New York Times* reported that in response to rage expressed by principals, Mayor Michael Bloomberg remarked that the cuts would have "no impact whatsoever," adding, "I know of no organization where you couldn't squeeze out 1.7 percent, or even a lot more."[1]

At the Secondary School for Research, students, faculty, and staff experienced the cuts as a personal blow. Among the students, outrage was voiced most strongly by a junior named Aicha Diallo. As event coordinator for the Secondary School for Research student government, which she had helped establish that year, she took the lead in creating a group called Students Against the Department of Education Budget Cuts. She called city councilman Bill de Blasio, in whose office she had interned as a sophomore.

With the councilman's help, Aicha and other members of the student government formed a coalition with several citywide organizations and organized meetings in the John Jay building's auditorium. These meetings drew many families from PS 321, the highly regarded elementary school a few blocks away: a rare instance of worlds meeting as low-income students and middle-class parents recognized their shared stake in high-quality public education. The culminating event was the Broken Hearts Rally held on Valentine's Day. On the steps of City Hall, Aicha and other founding members of the group stood alongside city council members and state senators, in front of hundreds of other protesting students, parents, and activists. Aicha addressed the crowd with confidence and passion, asking why the city would choose to solve its fiscal problems by taking away from those who had the least.

In the essays she would write the following school year, Aicha described, in personal terms, why she and her peers felt so motivated to make their voices heard. "We wanted to let the city know, as well as our parents and teachers, how unfair these budget cuts were. How offensive and degrading they were. As poor students living in New York City, the last thing we want to feel is that we are hopeless and unworthy of knowledge and support. And that's what these budget cuts did: they made us feel that our futures weren't worth the investment." They had created their organization, she wrote, "to show the world that we, along with thousands of other public school students, deserve to be well educated, as well as respected, supported, and trusted."

Aicha attributed her indignation to her experience on both ends of the economic spectrum. Until she came to America at the age of ten, her family had lived a life of relative comfort and prominence in Conakry, the capital of Guinea, where her father was a successful textile merchant. In Brooklyn, Aicha lived in a small three-bedroom apartment in Crown Heights with her parents, her aunt, and her four younger siblings. Her father worked long hours as a driver for a car service, and the money he earned barely covered the family's basic needs.

Aicha's writing traced the ways her desire to help the less fortunate had evolved into a resolution to battle injustice. In Africa, she was aware of the poverty around her: "I saw it every time I stepped out of my home and into the unpaved streets; every time I visited the man in the small store who taught kids how to read the Q'uran; every time I said hello to the lady who sold food in front of my mother's store to support her family while her husband was in another region of the country; every time I stepped out of class and into the schoolyard, where vendors were trying their best to entice kids into buying rice or cakes." Aicha remembered feeling, as she got into her father's white Mercedes, that she wished that "all the neighborhood kids could come with me."

But, Aicha wrote, "shrouded by my wealth and all the preconceptions that came along with it," she was not able to imagine what it was like to be at the bottom of the socioeconomic ladder until she found herself there in America. "When you've had the comfortable life and have had to downgrade into a life of financial hardship and uncertainty, life becomes much more difficult and reality hits you like a ton of bricks."

Aicha became aware of how the privileged shield themselves by feeling, often unknowingly, that poverty reflects laziness or bad values. Getting past her own prejudices as she got to know her peers in America, she realized "that just because someone is poor, that doesn't mean others can think of themselves as better, because they're not." She also saw how those who are vulnerable are less likely to raise their voices in protest. "I know what it's like to have something, and I also know what it's like not to have anything," she wrote. "And these two things, I believe, give me an insight into what seem to be the two main categories in our lives. I want to change this; to help those who don't have anything and are helpless in standing up and saying, 'I have something, I am somebody.' "

Aicha and her brother had first come to Brooklyn to visit their father, who had left Guinea three years before. At the time, nearby Sierra Leone was torn apart by civil war. The American embassy was granting temporary visas, and like many others he saw this as an opportunity that he could not pass up, especially amid the violence and uncertainty that threatened his business. "When you grow up in a third world country," Aicha remembered, "America is like this huge gold palace you want to be in. No one in Africa would have ever said no to a chance to go to Europe or America." In her childhood imagination, America was a land of wealth and ease: "When I heard I was coming here, I could only imagine myself living in those skyscrapers in Manhattan. I thought I was going to have a huge house with many maids like everyone in the movies."

Aicha and her brother's visit was not meant to be permanent; they planned to go back home to their mother, who had stayed behind in Guinea. Her father's intention was to save money while in the United States, and return to Africa once the political situation stabilized in Sierra Leone. But, Aicha remembered, she couldn't bear the thought of being away from her father for another three years, and begged him to let her and her brother stay. She had little idea of the kind of change this would bring to her life. "As a ten-year-old kid," she wrote in an essay, "all it meant was spending time with my father, whom I adored dearly, and a chance to advance my education."

Aicha described the promise of educational opportunity in America as a powerful force in her family's decision to stay. "That's how you become a somebody in life," Aicha described as their attitude. "You have to be educated." In Guinea, her parents were dissatisfied with the schools, where Aicha remembered being "terrified of teachers who thought the only way to teach was with force, and beat us with big tire strips." Her mother had had only a few years of education and her father had attended a school where he learned to read the Q'uran. School in Guinea was expensive, and the money her parents spent "was becoming too much for an education they thought was mediocre."

Aicha's American education began in a Brooklyn middle school. As a new immigrant, she struggled to adjust to her changed economic circumstances and to learn English—in Guinea she had spoken Fulani at home and French at school. She did not know other children from Guinea and felt out of place among her African American peers as an African and as a Muslim. Aicha didn't socialize much, threw herself into her studies, and earned high grades. When, at the end of New York City's high school application process, she was placed at the Secondary School for Research instead of one of the better-known high schools to which she had applied, she said she cried for two weeks straight. "I felt like it had all been a waste," she said of her hard work.

Her first year of high school, Aicha said, "I wanted to get the hell out of that school." She sensed that other students saw her as stuck up, and her attempts at friendship hit roadblocks. "All of a sudden, people would stop talking to me." She remembered running down the hall in tears with a teacher running after her, and her father coming to pick her up. Her English teacher, Menucha Stubenhaus, recalled, in a letter of recommendation, that as a freshman Aicha was still "in culture shock" and that she "isolated herself from her peers, whom she thought had different interests and priorities."

At the same time as she felt alienated socially, Aicha formed strong relationships with teachers and advocated for herself with administrators. Jill, the principal, described how, when Aicha first began at the Secondary School for Research, she stopped Jill in the hallway, introduced herself, and asked if she could enroll in an anatomy course designed for seniors. Despite her initial reluctance, Jill agreed, and Aicha became one of the top students in the class.

As a sophomore, Aicha continued to impress her teachers but felt out of place and lonely among her peers. In the cafeteria, she said, she "didn't like the food, so I would be sitting by myself, not eating anything." When she discovered the new college counselor's office at the bottom of the stairs, she would stop there instead of continuing on to lunch. Not only was it a place where she could start planning for college, but it was an environment where she "didn't have to think about what person doesn't like me, about being alone when everyone else is having fun."

Josh remembered meeting Aicha that year, his first at the Secondary School for Research. He was still struggling to draw students to his office, which was three floors down from the rest of the school, and here was a sophomore who came in almost every day. Aicha had a round face, bright brown eyes, and a trace of an accent from West Africa. She chatted with Josh in her ebullient, confident way—calling him Steckel as she heard other students do—or sat at a computer to research enrichment programs. Aicha had an appetite for every opportunity that came her way. She kicked off the school's internship program with her position in Councilman de Blasio's office and, as a sophomore, she enrolled in a College Now course in precalculus at New York City College of Technology. During the summer, she was selected to participate in the first year of Syracuse University's Summer College in New York City, where she took courses in media and cultural studies.

By junior year, Aicha had grown more comfortable at school and had taken on leadership roles. Like Ashley the year before, she was selected as one of two student representatives on the School Leadership Team. Building from her activism around the budget cuts, Aicha organized student participation in rallies and led school fundraisers in support of just legal responses in the cases of Sean Bell, an unarmed African American shot and killed by police the morning before his wedding, and the Jena Six, a group of black teenagers in Louisiana given lengthy prison sentences after a racially charged fight that followed the hanging of nooses in the schoolyard. In her advocacy, Aicha allied herself with her African

American peers, whose futures were intertwined with her own. With a hope of one day becoming a lawyer, Aicha spoke about the role of race in law enforcement, and argued for the ways the Sean Bell and Jena Six cases gave the lie to the American promise of equal protection and equal treatment by the justice system.

In her college-level work, her proven leadership skills, and her extracurricular activities, Aicha, like Ashley, struck Josh as the rare student at the Secondary School for Research who would be admissible to one of America's most prestigious colleges. And unlike Ashley, who initially wanted to stay at home and follow a practical path toward her career goals, Aicha was eager to travel into the unknown territory of the residential campus experience. She understood that selective liberal arts colleges incubated America's leadership and was especially drawn to Wellesley, the alma mater of Hillary Clinton, whom she saw as a model of an outspoken, confident female leader.

It wasn't until the spring of her junior year that Aicha told Josh that she was undocumented. Her father had overstayed the term of his visa, which was not renewable. She had not revealed this to Josh earlier, Aicha told him, because she was afraid he would tell her he could not help her. During her time in America, she had gradually become aware of the limits her status placed on the opportunities available to her after high school, and knew that it would be hard "to get into college, period." She had been deemed ineligible for several enrichment programs and had grown to understand that "for everything in America, you need a Social Security number."

Still, Aicha believed that college would not be impossible. "It was like, I know this is going to limit me, but I'm pretty sure that there's a way I can go." Family friends mentioned scholarships that colleges and companies might award her if her grades were high enough, and it was this idea, in part, that drove Aicha to study so diligently. "I knew that my SAT scores, my transcript, my essays, everything had to be top notch." Aicha saw success as her responsibility to her family: "I didn't have a choice. I felt like so many people had sacrificed so much for me to be successful, so to fail or to slack off was not something I could even think about."

Josh had worked with two undocumented seniors the year before. Everything had been new to him in their application processes, and he felt he had not achieved satisfactory results. While he still lacked the knowledge he needed, now he at least had time to discover better options for Aicha and for the other student in her class he knew to be undocumented, Santiago Hernandez.

Santiago had begun coming into the college office the year before, as a junior. He often accompanied friends who were seniors, including Janet Wu, whose experience hearing her peers' college essays had transformed her perceptions of them. Janet, bilingual in English and Fujianese, had a quiet, watchful demeanor and a stubborn streak. Her Spanish teacher remembered that as a sophomore Janet had announced, "I don't like Spanish, I will never understand it, and I won't need it, since I don't plan on going to college, because I will be working in my father's restaurant." By her senior year, Janet had resolved to go to college and had become close friends with Santiago, who spoke only Spanish at home. Drawn by Janet's intense questioning and attention, Santiago began to open up to her in ways that were new to him, speaking about his family and his desire "to go to college, to have an education, to do something with my life."

Santiago told Janet, and later Josh, about how he came to America. From his early childhood in the village in Mexico where he was born, he remembered rows of little houses, dirt roads, and garbage. His father had a job that paid well, but left the family for another woman when Santiago was five. Unable to provide, Santiago's mother took her children to live in the house her own mother had abandoned when she moved to the United States ten years before. The house was half broken down, with curtains and plastic bags filling a gap in one of the walls. Santiago, his mother, his baby brother, and his aunt shared a bed. "For us to eat something, we would have a slice of tortilla with sour cream and salt. For dinner, a small bowl of scrambled eggs. We barely had any breakfast." When Santiago's grandmother heard about what they were going through, she saved up money to bring them to the United States.

Santiago remembered crossing the border. "There was this desert place. We had to run from a certain point to another point. We had to hide from the border patrol. I was six years old. My mom was carrying my brother, because he was really young. She couldn't hold both of us. I had to keep up with her, run after her, try not to get lost."

Then he remembered twenty adults crowding into a hot minivan, "squishing each other, kicking each other, just trying to get in." In the van, he said, "I remember crying, trying to stretch, and not being able to. It felt cramped and the trip seemed like days." He remembered being in an airplane and landing in New York City, where the family moved in with his grandmother. She shared a small apartment with his uncle, who worked in a shipyard. Santiago's mother found work as a babysitter and housekeeper, and Santiago attended elementary school and middle school in Brooklyn.

Like Aicha, Santiago was initially unhappy about attending high school at the Secondary School for Research, where he said he had been placed because of a clerical error. The school was only one floor, and it had only a basketball team, which was "not his kind of sport." But he found that the school's smaller scale helped him to get to know his teachers and to concentrate on his studies. In junior high, where he had had many friends and played sports after school, "I didn't care about school and I didn't want to study." At the Secondary School for Research, he would just "go to school, do my work, and go home, so I was actually more focused." Still, Santiago didn't see his grades as very important, anticipating that, like other members of his family, he would work in a low-skilled job after high school graduation, earning his living in the underground economy.

During the summer after his freshman year, Santiago, who

was tall for his age, obtained fake documentation that said he was twenty-one and joined his uncle in his work fixing army ships. They would wake up at 4 a.m. and drive to the dry dock. "There was this place under the ship where the water stays, some kind of tank. You had to go there and clean it out." The work was difficult and dangerous, and Santiago, though he was strong, struggled to carry the heavy tools. "It was really smelly, really dark. You couldn't see anything. You had to watch your step because there were holes and everything was slippery."

Santiago remembered that when he began, "I always just wanted to go home. I didn't want to have an accident, get injured, or worse." He knew this was not work for a fifteen-year-old. "Everybody was in their thirties. Everyone would talk to you like you were a man. They would rush us, and if we did it wrong they would scream at us, 'You're stupid, you can't be acting like this.' " Before working there, Santiago said, he was a "shy kid," always polite. The work toughened him up. He stayed shy, but his "mood started changing, and he started talking back to people."

Santiago remembered getting his first paycheck: $560 for a week's work. It seemed like a lot of money, and he was proud to have earned it. At the same time, it was depressing to imagine that this was all his future had to offer. He thought, This is me. I'm going to work for money.

When Santiago gave the money to his mother, her gratitude made the world seem less bleak. "She was happy I was earning money. Every time I came home from work she would tell me to rest, give me food, treat me nice." He would keep $160 for himself, and the rest went to sustaining the family. "We were fine the whole summer, because my mom had money to spend on me, my sister, and my brother. It was hard work, but it was worth it." After his sophomore year, Santiago returned to the shipyard for a second summer.

As he began junior year, Santiago began to think more concretely about what would happen after high school. Josh told his class that all were expected to apply to college, and the idea that he could continue his education began to take hold of him. Going to college, he believed, would give him self-respect and "make me feel like I'm accomplishing something, like I'm going to get somewhere someday." Santiago's mother had left school to work and depended on him to pay bills and make phone calls even when a Spanish translator was available. "I don't know what they're saying, it's best that you call them," she would say, sensing that people would take advantage of her. "If someone is an immigrant and doesn't know much, people talk about them behind their backs," Santiago said. "I didn't want to be looked at as a low person."

Santiago told Josh that his dream was to become a police officer. He knew that he couldn't pursue this kind of career without a Social Security number. But Santiago told himself that maybe someday he would have one, and he wasn't ready to give up. With the encouragement of Janet and other friends, during his senior year he asked Josh what options were available for an undocumented student.

As Josh had learned the previous year, the most obvious choice was to attend a college in the City University of New York system. At CUNY, citizenship status would have no bearing on admission. And through a policy unusual among public systems in the United States, students without Social Security numbers could be charged in-state tuition if they signed an affidavit stating that they were working toward legalizing their immigration status. Until the year before, any New York City public school student who graduated with an average of 80 or above—regardless of their citizenship status—was eligible for a Peter Vallone scholarship, which granted a thousand dollars a year toward CUNY's tuition. The scholarship had been slashed as part of the previous year's citywide budget cuts. Josh promised Santiago that he would look into other scholarships for undocumented students to help cover CUNY's fees.

For Aicha, whom Josh hoped could attend an elite residential college, the process would be very different. Most private colleges, Josh had discovered the previous year, are reluctant to work with undocumented students. This is due in part to the legal sensitivity of issues related to residency status, which some colleges work around by putting undocumented students in the international applicant pool. Mainly, though, the problem was funding: undocumented students are unable to apply for financial aid from the government. Given that most undocumented students have very high need, colleges generally must fund the entire cost of a student's education in order for it to be possible. Josh had learned that a small number of private colleges were willing to work with students in Aicha's situation, and he believed that Aicha was so extraordinary as a student and a leader that one of these colleges might be willing to admit and fund her.

Josh met with Aicha in the spring of her junior year to describe her options. He told her that CUNY would be the easiest choice. But Aicha was reluctant to give up on the idea of a private college. "I didn't want to go to CUNY," she remembered. "Maybe it's a little cocky of me, but I felt like I worked way too hard in high school." A residential college, she felt, would give her the chance to discover her passions, and to develop into the kind of leader she wanted to be. "I didn't want to live at home. I wanted to be independent."

Josh followed off-the-record leads to identify admissions and financial aid officers open to speaking with him about an undocumented student. It was clear that spots and funding were very limited. Aicha would be competing not only with other low-income students of color, but with both full-pay and full-need international students, whom elite colleges were increasingly recruiting. And even if she were admitted and funded, she would be unable to work in legitimate jobs during and after college. The more he learned, the more it seemed to Josh that the best way for Aicha to realize her dreams was to apply for asylum.

Josh sat down with Aicha and her father. A change in citizenship status, he told them, could make it possible for Aicha to attend one of the best private colleges in the country. Josh had spoken with a lawyer at Legal Aid, who could offer assistance free of charge. It was only after Aicha began the asylum process that it struck Josh what a tremendous risk they were taking. A family that had been under the radar would now be within reach of the law. If their petition were denied, they would be deported to Guinea. That he had urged them to do this as a route toward admission to elite colleges kept him up at night, wondering if his well-intentioned ignorance would lead to a family with shattered lives.

Aicha remembered that she and her father of course knew the risk, but "we were like, let's just try. Sooner or later we're going to have to do it." They had already spoken with friends who had been through the asylum process and based on friends' experiences, decided to retain their own lawyer.

As the process moved forward, Aicha took an increasingly active role in managing it. She spent afternoons "going to the law office to make sure I knew what was going on," reminding her father to file papers, and calling to ensure that the court had received them. Josh marveled at how much she managed, keeping up with the process through the summer as she took college courses in Manhattan and an SAT prep class at the school in Brooklyn, and in the fall as she began her college essays and applications. Aicha would shrug, saying that she just did what she had to do. "It's part of everyday life," she said. "It's just normal, I guess, to me."

One afternoon during the fall, Aicha came into the college office with a piece of writing she asked Josh to review. It was a statement she had written explaining that at the age of ten in Guinea, she had been "circumcised." This practice, known by its opponents as female genital mutilation (FGM), is widespread in Guinea; despite a law prohibiting it, 96 percent of girls are subjected to FGM.[2] Aicha's report explained that her father had protected her when he was still in Africa, but that her mother's extended family had made it happen during his absence.

Aicha's father did not want her to remain in Guinea after he learned what had occurred and feared that her two younger sisters, both born since her family's arrival in the United States, would be subjected to the rite if Aicha's parents were forced to return. In an article describing the experiences of West African girls in New York City, the *New York Times* reported that in some families, "parents oppose female genital cutting, but the decision about whether or not to have it done is not always theirs to make. Many elders in West African communities hold great social authority and do not seek parental permission to have it done to a girl."[3] Under U.S. law, FGM is a valid basis for an asylum claim, though with complications for those already inflicted with FGM. According to a 2008 congressional report, "the federal courts that have addressed this issue currently treat a past infliction of FGM as a basis for a well-founded fear of persecution. The BIA [Bureau of Immigration Affairs], on the other hand, has rejected this position, arguing that FGM is a one-time procedure, and that once inflicted, an applicant will not be persecuted with FGM again, and thus cannot act as a basis for an asylum application."[4]

In her senior year Aicha felt herself at a crossroads. She feared what her life would look like if her application for asylum were denied: "I came to this country, I forgot French. What do I do back in Africa?" At the same time, she found herself constantly thinking back to her lost African childhood, to the rainy days "spent running around with nothing but my underwear on," and "the sunny days I would walk my pet goat down by the meadow for an afternoon lunch."

Aicha opened her personal essay with an anecdote that captured the contrast between the life she remembered in Africa and her current life in America:

One day, when I was six or seven years old, my younger brother and I went around our neighborhood with masks. These were Halloween masks my father had sent us from the United States. And since no one knew about Halloween in Africa, the masks were a real fright to them. That day, we had nothing to do, so we came up with this crazy idea to put on our masks and ride around the neighborhood. We took maybe five turns and had every kid in sight crying. They were really scared. Their bodies were shaking, noses running, eyes closed. It was really bad, but of course my brother and I thought it was entertaining. Before long, we had a mob of parents running and yelling after us to stop. All of them were too frightened and confused to actually come near us and take off our masks. This was hilarious. My brother and I were on our bikes, barely breathing because we were laughing so hard.

After a couple more times around the neighborhood, we finally came home and put the masks away. Moments after we got home, our yard was filled with mommies and daddies and aunts and uncles ready to chew our heads off, but they knew better. As well-off and outspoken residents of the neighborhood, my parents had made it abundantly clear that their kids were not to be hit by anyone. The saying, "It takes a village to raise a child," really was the practice in my neighborhood, but my parents were not willing to allow other parents to discipline us. And so the parents complained to our mother. To most neighbors, we were two rich spoiled kids who had no manners and did whatever we wanted. That was not true; both my brother and I, along with the people in our house, knew better. Rude behavior, bad grades, and anything offensive would not go unpunished. But the neighbors didn't want to believe that. When the other parents left, my mom sat us down and scolded us. We never did it again.

The move to America, as Aicha's essay went on to describe, brought a sense of anonymity and insecurity, both physical and economic:

That was then, in Africa, when my father was a successful merchant who didn't have to drive a cab seven days a week, for twelve
hours a day, in order to pay the bills. When all I ever had to do
was walk down the road to school, instead of traveling an hour
every morning to get there. When I didn't know what pain in
my shoulders felt like, because I didn't have so many responsibilities, such as helping my mom cook after a ten-hour school
day, or washing the family laundry with a paper due the next day
and no computer access at home. It was before my parents forbid
me from going to friends' houses because they believe that parties and sleepovers will get me off track, lead me the wrong way
to drugs and sex and no future. Sometimes I think they don't
trust me, but I know it's not that; they just don't trust I'll be safe.
"This country is dangerous; you think you know someone, until
you hear they have killed someone on TV," they say. And suddenly, I remember laughing at my neighbors' fears back in Africa
and realize that I fear my neighbors here in America. That in
Africa, my parents didn't mind letting my brother and me wear
masks. That in America, they feel compelled to protect us from
the masks they fear everyone else is wearing.

Though she complained about her neighbors in Africa, Aicha
continued, "now I miss the community I had there." She described
how at the end of Ramadan, the city would shut down all major
highways so everyone could pray together. She remembered her
parents easily allowing her to spend long days with other families.
"As long as they knew who I was with and where I was, everything
was okay. I have never had that sense of freedom in America."

In America, however, she had learned about "different kinds of
freedoms." There would have been nowhere in Guinea, she wrote,
that she could be as independent and open-minded as she was today. "Africa teaches women to be housewives and mothers, but
America has led me to imagine raising a family, while at the same

time being a CEO at a developing company." In her country, "gays, lesbians, and bisexuals are persecuted. In America, I have friends who are gay and bisexual who don't care what the world thinks of their orientation."

Aicha concluded, "There would have been nowhere in my country that I could have learned to be as strong-headed and open-minded as I am today. America has taught me self-worth; it has taught me love and compassion. This great country has come to be the place I respect and that exemplifies what my dreams could become."

Josh pushed Aicha to finish her essays early so that they could be included in the pre-application packages he would send to colleges on her behalf. He knew from his work with Ashley that to make a low-income student from an unknown school visible, he needed to start early and be persistent. For Aicha, whose process would require even more legwork than Ashley's, this was especially crucial. Josh collected writing samples from Aicha and letters of recommendation from her teachers and spoke in as much detail as he could about Aicha, calling her "the most remarkable student I have ever worked with in my ten years in education, as a teacher and college counselor in private and public schools in New York City."

Josh learned that the elite, all-women's colleges known as the Seven Sisters recruited many international students and seemed more open than most to working with undocumented students. They were also very appealing to Aicha. In an essay, she wrote that "the idea of attending an all women's college with strong, independent, smart, and motivated women gives me a sense of pride that's hard to explain." Her mother and aunts, she wrote, "have had minimal education" and rely on their husbands. She wanted to be independent "both financially and emotionally" and show her four younger siblings that they could break free from "the gender roles that society places them in."

Josh received encouraging responses from Bryn Mawr College and from Wellesley, where an admissions officer wrote that Aicha's essay had made her cry. "This kid is amazing," she said. These positive responses encouraged Josh to widen his net to other elite liberal arts colleges. He spoke with Liliana Rodriguez, his contact at Williams, about whether the college might work with an undocumented student with an asylum case in progress and made similar inquiries elsewhere. Responses were cautious but open. Aicha assembled a list that included Williams, Amherst, Wellesley, Bryn Mawr, Swarthmore, Duke, Barnard, and Brown, all among the most prestigious colleges in the country. She also decided to apply to Brooklyn College, to Muhlenberg, and to Manhattanville, a small college in Purchase, New York, that Josh learned had fully funded an undocumented student from another New York City public high school.

The applications to these colleges required intense amounts of writing: in addition to the essays required by the Common Application, most included substantial supplemental essays, which were specific to each of the different colleges. Aicha e-mailed Josh drafts of these essays up through midnight on January 1, the submission deadline for most schools. On New Year's Eve, Aicha was finishing her essay for Williams, which asked the following question: "Imagine looking through a window at any environment that is particularly significant to you. Reflect on the scene, paying close attention to the relation between what you are seeing and why it is meaningful to you."

Aicha's essay began, "In a far away place there's a window that shows the past. Seldom do I ever look into this window, but today, I manage to." She then described what she found there:

As I approach, I can hear the *ra-ta-ta* sounds of gunfire. I don't remember this, but I hear the sounds loudly. I cover my ears as I reach the window and peer into it.

And I see . . . I see my mother, my brother and me, lying on our living room floor in Africa. We're sleeping on top of covers, to soften the hard, barren floor. I can't remember ever doing that, not ever. I remember our home as filled with furniture: couches, tables, and certainly beds. How then to explain this strange scene?

A moment passes, and I watch, with pleasure, the three of us sleeping. We all look so free of care. Yet the atmosphere is stressful and scary. I ponder an explanation for another minute or two, then suddenly, the sound of gunfire returns, even louder. A bullet, round and small, shoots down through the ceiling, its silver metal glistening in the African sunlight. It lands right next to my mother's head, leaving a scar on our tiled floor.

And suddenly my memory of this event from my childhood in Guinea returns. And I remember that I never really understood why the military was shooting and that my mother never really explained it to me. Usually she explained things, took her time and explained what had happened, but this time, she didn't.

The events were clear enough. There had been a coup in my country, and the military was deployed to put it down. Some of the most intense fighting took place in my neighborhood. A bullet penetrated our ceiling and almost killed my mother. The bullet had missed her by inches. Later, we learned, a huge grenade had landed in one of the flowerpots in our yard. I don't remember how my mother found it, but I do remember the soldier digging out the grenade, telling my mother that if the safety pin had been removed, our whole house, along with everyone in it, would have been destroyed.

I remember trying to imagine my mother dead. I remember hugging her. I remember that a couple of weeks later, things died down and everyone forgot about it.

And so I step away from the window, feeling different, stronger, perhaps. I feel like I have repossessed a moment I had chosen to forget, a moment during which my life could have been changed forever. And even though nothing is changed,

something is different, my heart is filled with sadness and wonder. And I can't help but to think of the many children who
weren't as lucky as me; all those children who saw their dear
mothers killed by bullets that were not an inch away from their
lives. All those children whose lives were destroyed by forces
outside of their own control.

Alongside the intellectual and emotional work her essays required, Aicha embarked on a financial aid process that was the
most labyrinthine Josh had ever encountered. He told colleges
that Aicha was on the road to citizenship, but it was unrealistic,
he saw now, to think that she might be granted asylum in time
to apply for federal or state government aid that year. In speaking with colleges, Josh received many different answers about how
Aicha should apply for aid, and he had the sense that the colleges
themselves were unsure of the process. Some asked her to complete the traditional College Search Service Profile, the College
Board's application for nongovernment aid accepted by most selective colleges; others asked her to complete the version of that
application intended for international students; others asked her to
complete both. In addition to the College Search Service Profile,
many colleges also asked students to complete separate applications for institutional aid; and again, colleges varied in whether
they asked Aicha to complete the version for domestic or international students. Without a Social Security number, she could
not submit a Free Application for Federal Student Aid, so some
colleges requested separate documentation of her family's income,
as well as records of the taxes her father was paying. Josh helped
her to complete a detailed report that listed her family's income
and expenses, including the value of her father's car, rent, utilities,
and legal fees.

As he worked with Aicha, Josh sometimes thought how much
simpler and less risky her process would be if she had been content

to limit herself to CUNY. In his work with Santiago, however, Josh saw that CUNY presented its own problems for an undocumented student. Santiago was working harder in school that year, earning much better grades, and expressing resolve to continue his education. But while Josh felt confident that Aicha would have choices, it was unclear whether Santiago would be able to get to college at all. Without need-based grant funding from the federal and state governments, the tuition at even the least expensive of the CUNY schools would be very difficult for Santiago's family to manage, and he would not be able to borrow funds through government student loan programs. As other students with academic records similar to Santiago's were completing their financial aid applications and applying to the State Opportunity Programs, Josh was giving Santiago lists of scholarships open to undocumented students to research online. Santiago clicked through them but found few for which he qualified. "I felt like I wasn't getting anywhere," he remembered. "I was fighting my way through it, but I kind of knew I was going to be stuck in one place." Josh felt guilty that he couldn't think of more ways to help Santiago, a student who, like Aicha, had absorbed the American dream of opportunity through education.

In early March, Aicha received news that a court date had been set for the following November. She would present her case to the judge, who would either grant her asylum or begin proceedings for deportation. Aicha felt both excited and scared. She thought about a time she saw a family emerge from their hearing smiling and hugging. She asked herself, "Am I going to be walking out of there smiling or crying? Which one is going to be me?"

For the college process, Josh felt hopeful that the clear timeline would help Aicha's chances. March was when colleges met in committee to make their final decisions and when he made another round of calls to advocate for students. Josh wrote to Bryn Mawr about the court date, saying, "It's worth knowing that this may mean she is eligible for government aid by this fall. I would also love to know if you have any more info about how she's looking at Bryn Mawr!"

Josh found several admissions officers receptive to his follow-up calls. He received a call back from Wellesley, Aicha's first choice, with an enthusiastic reading of her application, and had a positive conversation about Aicha with Williams. At the same time, he knew there were serious factors working against Aicha's chances. The financial crisis had ravaged university endowments; according to a *New York Times* article, from July 2008 to November 2008, the value of college and university endowments fell an average of 23 percent.[5] An admissions officer from Barnard described how much more competitive this new economic reality made admissions for students like Aicha, whom the college would have to fund entirely from its own budget.

Decisions began arriving in late March. Santiago got into his first choice: the John Jay College of Criminal Justice. He was accepted through the SEEK program, which promised academic and transitional support services and advising. But how Santiago would pay the tuition was unclear. Most SEEK students receive the maximum amount of need-based funding through the federal government's Pell Grant program and New York State's Tuition Assistance Program, which are not available to undocumented students. Josh had learned that Santiago should be eligible, through SEEK, for a stipend designed to help with the cost of books and travel. But when Josh spoke with aid counselors at John Jay College, they didn't know how to handle Santiago's situation. Though Josh had been told explicitly by an official at the New York State Higher Education Services Corporation that citizenship status does not affect eligibility for SEEK services or the SEEK stipend, the aid counselor said Santiago could not in fact enroll through SEEK if he couldn't submit a federal financial aid application.

Through March, as other students were receiving letters from colleges, Aicha kept checking for mail that did not arrive. Josh helped her to look up results online. By the first week in April, she learned that she was turned down at Duke, Brown, and Swarthmore. She was placed on the waitlist at Amherst, Williams, Barnard, and Muhlenberg. She was accepted at Manhattanville and at Brooklyn College.

Aicha felt anxious and discouraged. It seemed like "everyone else was getting their top choices" except her. Muhlenberg had accepted nine students from the Secondary School for Research that year, most of them with applications she knew were far less strong than hers. She understood that this was because of her undocumented status, not her merit, but this was little comfort.

Josh reminded Aicha that they still had not heard from Wellesley, her first choice, or from Bryn Mawr, where Josh thought she had the best chance. On April 6, Josh wrote to the admissions officer at Wellesley who had been moved by Aicha's essay, asking that she call his office to deliver a decision to Aicha. Aicha had no Internet access at home and no cell phone, and though the colleges had her correct address, the letters had been returned. "I can't imagine her going into the vacation still waiting for this news, and with the possibility that, as with so many of her other admissions decisions, the letter never arrives," he wrote. He sent an e-mail to his Bryn Mawr contact on the same day.

The admissions officers did not write back. But Josh was able to help Aicha access her results online before she left for vacation. She was waitlisted at Bryn Mawr and turned down at Wellesley.

Aicha remembered the day she found out that she didn't get into Wellesley as "a really terrible day." With the rejections from colleges came the sense that despite all her efforts, her future was out of her control. She had stayed optimistic throughout the college process, hoping she would get a Social Security number before financial papers were due, then hoping that one or more elite colleges would admit and fund her without it. Now, she said, "I felt stuck, trapped. I was like, damn, what am I going to do?"

Aicha didn't talk much with her father about how she was feeling but knew he understood. He reassured her, "You'll be okay. We'll figure something out." She knew her father's main concern was her "being admitted to college and being able to pay for it." She had been accepted to two colleges, though it was still unclear how they would afford either one. "To be honest, I don't think he cared where I went to college," she remembered.

But, Aicha said, "I cared. I cared a lot." She wanted to prove to herself, and to her father, that all they had gone through was worth it. "I felt like it would make him proud to say his daughter went to one of the best schools in the country," she said. "He worked so hard. I sacrificed some things, but he sacrificed, too."

Josh also wanted badly to see Aicha at a college that would give her the kind of experience she longed for and that would open doors for her in the fields she hoped to pursue, like international relations or law. Manhattanville was not a choice Aicha had seriously considered in the application process: the campus lacked the energy and activism Aicha sought. Aicha had been waitlisted at Williams, Amherst, Barnard, Bryn Mawr, and Muhlenberg. One of them might come through.

Of these five schools, Aicha identified Barnard as her first choice. Josh wrote to the admissions officer who worked with international students to get a sense of Aicha's chances. He understood, he wrote, that colleges often waitlist qualified students they can't afford to fund, and that this might be especially true given the current economic situation. If coming off the waitlist was not a real possibility, he wanted to know: "I don't want to ask her to endure this process further. It has been so hard on her, given how much she has accomplished and how clearly she understands that something outside of her control (her residency status) is preventing her from having all the options she deserves."

Josh did not hear back from Barnard, or from Bryn Mawr, where he made a similar plea. He had better luck at Williams with Liliana Rodriguez, with whom he had formed a strong personal relationship. She expressed surprise that Aicha was not admitted to the other schools. If Aicha had been a citizen, she said, she probably would have been admitted to Williams. But the college could not commit to funding her for four years without a contribution from the federal government. If the financial aid office understood that she was on the verge of being granted asylum, they might be able to approve an offer from the waitlist. At Lili's request, Josh spoke with Aicha's lawyer, who explained that every asylum hearing is also a deportation hearing. He offered a positive assessment of Aicha's case but was unable to give any guarantees.

Aicha had initially been uncertain about Muhlenberg, a less selective school than she had hoped to attend. Josh knew that the college's decision to waitlist her was partly a function of Aicha's lack of enthusiasm. After their experience with Kennetta's class, in which many of the accepted Secondary School for Research students did not choose to attend, Chris and Cindy wanted to focus on students who applied early decision or who had strongly conveyed their commitment to Muhlenberg.

Josh felt he could be completely open with Cindy, with whom he had spoken about Aicha in the past. He explained that the only real waitlist possibility was Williams, which was unlikely. They were waiting for a financial aid package from Manhattanville, but Aicha, he said, would much prefer Muhlenberg, if it were an option. Cindy told Josh, with regrets, that the financial calculus was not going to work: the college simply could not afford to provide Aicha with the funding she would need.

Josh still could not let go. Of the colleges where Aicha had been waitlisted, he had the weakest connections at Amherst. But Josh remembered that the SAT tutor who had worked closely with Aicha that summer was an Amherst graduate. When they spoke, the tutor told Josh he had a close connection with a member of the Amherst board of trustees and would be happy to contact him. After looking at Aicha's essays and letters of recommendation, the board member agreed to advocate with Amherst on Aicha's behalf. This was the kind of connection, Josh knew, that could move a waitlist. When Josh contacted the admissions officer with whom he had spoken previously about Aicha, he was impressed, and newly encouraging about Aicha's chances of admission.

In early June, on the evening of the Secondary School for Research prom, Josh accompanied Aicha to the Park Slope Civic Council year-end meeting. At the meeting, local leaders, including Brooklyn borough president Marty Markowitz, celebrated recipients of the scholarship the civic council awarded to students who had demonstrated extraordinary service to the community. Aicha was one of the winners.

Each student was introduced to the civic council members by a guidance counselor. Josh stepped to the front of the room to speak about Aicha. After describing her accomplishments, he told the audience that she had been accepted to Manhattanville College, but that she was hoping for an offer from the waitlist at Amherst. Aicha, in a ruffly purple satin dress, received her award and a long round of applause.

Santiago went to John Jay College several times during May and June to explore what sources of aid he might be eligible to receive, and what steps he needed to take to register. He encountered obstacles in each of the offices he visited. In one, he was turned away because he had no record of his mother's income, since she was babysitting and not paying taxes. In another, he was given a form that asked for his immunization records, including a meningitis vaccine. While Santiago had a copy of his health records, he had not received the meningitis shot. Not realizing that he could simply sign a form to waive this requirement and submit the records he had brought, he was unsure what to do, and the woman behind the desk was not helpful. "She sent me someplace, and they sent me to another place, and it was back and forth, back and forth. I kind of got tired. Nobody knew what to do with me."

On graduation day, Santiago had mixed emotions. He was very

proud to be graduating: neither his mother nor his uncles had a high school diploma. He was disappointed that his mother was too busy with work to come to the ceremony. He was excited to be with his friends, but it was hard to compare himself to his classmates. "I knew that everybody was going to go to college. They all had a plan, and I didn't. I felt like I didn't have any future." Santiago knew he would have to begin to work to earn money, but he wanted more than that. "I was disappointed. I wanted to be the first person in my family to go to college. My mom would have been happy for me and really proud. I was angry at myself, and at the whole system, about not being able to go to college because of documentation."

Santiago's senior year at the Secondary School for Research had been a time of hope. He had started to love school, and he wanted to continue his education. With Josh's help, Santiago thought he would find a way to get to college, but nothing had worked. After graduation, Santiago concluded that it wasn't going to happen for him. "I went back to reality. I had to stop dreaming."

11

Let's Change Lives:
Kennetta, Angie, and Rafael

Cynthia Amaya, the admissions officer who welcomed Kennetta Christian, Angelica Moore, and Rafael Padilla to Muhlenberg College, described herself as a "very shy person by nature," something that surprised students to hear. Cindy's job required the behavior of an extrovert: interviewing prospective students, traveling to high schools, convincing families that Muhlenberg was the right choice for their children. Cindy was twenty-nine when the three students from the Secondary School for Research arrived. She had wavy shoulder-length hair, wide brown eyes, and a comfortable laugh that made her shoulders bounce. Cindy was senior associate director of admission and coordinator of multicultural recruitment and worked closely with the dean of admissions, Christopher Hooker-Haring.

Cindy was a Muhlenberg graduate, class of 2001, and for her, the memory was still vivid of coming to campus as a freshman with "no idea of what I was getting myself into." She had been afraid to speak in class and was shocked when a roommate described approaching a professor with a complaint. In her work-study job in the admissions office, she was intimidated by the decision-makers in the upstairs offices. "I literally would just do my work. I talked a little bit to the ladies who were the administrative assistants, but they gave me a task, and I did it." Remembering her own difficulty adjusting, she said, "fuels me to help students out as much as possible."

Cindy's mother came from a family of nine and, together with most of her brothers and sisters, had immigrated to New York City to escape the civil war in El Salvador. Cindy's family lived in Queens until she was eight. When Cindy "started coming home with an attitude they didn't like," her parents "fought their way to leave the city and move to suburban New Jersey." Cindy and her cousins were part of the "first generation to go off to college, here in the United States," and Cindy, among the eldest, had few role models. "The process of what it took to apply to colleges was absolutely foreign to me."

Cindy first learned about Muhlenberg when recruiters scouted her school soccer team. "I started hearing from coaches, and all of a sudden it became a reality that I could play on a college team." Like Kennetta, Cindy was won over by the smiles and greetings she experienced during her first visit to the college. "I fell in love with the fact that people were so nice on campus and that they were so friendly and welcoming."

When she began in 1997, Cindy said, Muhlenberg was "just 5 percent diverse." In a class of roughly 500, that would mean 475 white students and 25 students of color, from the United States and abroad. Cindy felt out of place not only as a racial minority, but as a cultural outsider. She had had a sheltered, born-again Christian upbringing and didn't understand the "rules of engagement" in the college's social life. Cindy began on the premed track and struggled in her classes. It was "the same story that we've seen," she told Josh, of a first-generation college student trying to live up to the dream of becoming a doctor. Her parents had sacrificed so much for her, and when she spoke to her brother and sister on the phone, they would complain that all their parents would talk about was "Cindy's college tuition."

In her sophomore year, Cindy said, "by the time I got to organic chemistry, I was crying all the time. I was miserable. I didn't know if I was doing this for the right reasons anymore, and I didn't know what to do." Unsure where to turn, she sent an e-mail to the admissions counselor who had interviewed her and quickly received a call back. "She could have not responded," Cindy said, "but she did. She started navigating me around Muhlenberg, and connecting me with other people." The admissions counselor helped her find her way both academically and socially. Cindy decided to drop premed and discovered a love for sociology and psychology. She made close friends who offered emotional support and began to find life at the college fulfilling and fun.

Cindy had kept up her work-study job in the admissions office and, before she graduated, she was asked to interview with Christopher Hooker-Haring for a new position: assistant director and coordinator of multicultural recruitment. The college wanted to attract greater numbers of students of color, and, though Cindy was quiet, the higher-ups "saw very quickly that multicultural students were gravitating toward me to talk with them." Cindy accepted the job and became an important voice in conversations about diversity at Muhlenberg.

At the time she graduated, Cindy said, the college had more students of color on campus than when she first arrived. But the numbers were still small and morale among them was low. "It was a catch-22, because we knew that we couldn't recruit more students if the culture on campus wasn't fully engaged." Current students gave prospective students of color a bleak picture. "It was a struggle to bring a multicultural student to campus, and our own students were recruiting against us, saying, 'If you're thinking you're going to come to Muhlenberg, and there will be a lot of us here, you're wrong. It's not a happy environment.'"

In recruiting students, Muhlenberg also faced a problem confronted by other liberal arts colleges: given a choice, high-achieving students of color were more likely to attend colleges with greater name recognition. It was frustrating for leaders in the admissions office to invest time and budget resources for applicants who rarely came. Chris and Cindy looked into becoming a college partner of Posse, but the cost of bringing the program to campus did not make sense for the college's budget. "Chris was saying, where else? What else can we do?"

When Chris made the connection with Josh, whom he and Cindy remembered from Josh's years as college counselor at Birch Wathen Lenox, they thought, "This might be it." They recognized that in underfunded, unrecognized public schools across the country, there was a vast pool of talented, highly intelligent students who were invisible in the admissions process. In a partnership with the Secondary School for Research, they saw access to what Chris had called the "under-the-radar" students whose race and economic status disconnected them from pathways to selective liberal arts colleges. "If this is another population we should start tapping into, that's awesome," Cindy said.

The college would depend on Josh to identify students he thought would do best at Muhlenberg. Josh would also function as a crucial bridge between families and the college. Cindy knew from her own experience that "in this demographic, it takes a huge leap of faith for a student to say, 'Mom, Dad, I'm leaving home and going to college.' " To make the leap required either a student "who has that innately in them to say 'I'm leaving,' or a counselor who's saying to parents who are letting go of their first child, 'I trust that college, and I know that they're going to do right by you.' "

Cindy knew the college would also have to take a leap of faith in admitting students whose academic preparation was weaker than those in its regular applicant pool. She expected that other admissions staff would balk at the students' uneven writing skills and grades and would question their qualifications. To prepare their staff to read applications in a more nuanced way, she and Chris had arranged, during the previous year's overnight visit, for every admissions counselor to meet individually with one of the seniors from the Secondary School for Research.

Her colleagues, Cindy said, had been smitten with them. "The stories that the kids told in their interviews were so powerful. I remember everybody coming back together afterward, and going around the table: this person told me that, and that person told me that." At the conclusion of the meeting, the staff expressed a shared sense of purpose. "Let's see what we can do here," Cindy remembered as the attitude. "Let's change lives."

As with "starting any new endeavor," Cindy said, "we knew that this was going to be a lot. Obviously we didn't know how much 'a lot' this was going to be." The responsibility for advising and supporting Kennetta, Angie, and Rafael initially fell to Cindy. It was unusual for an admissions officer to play this role. Bates was an exception with its "swing dean" system, in which the admissions counselor who recruits multicultural students one year moves over to the office of the dean of students the following year, working with the same group of students to ease their transition to college. Cindy's position was less formal and harkened back to her own ongoing relationship with an admissions officer when she was an undergraduate. She was told, "Cindy, you've worked with them. Help them through their first year."

In a lighthearted e-mail during the fall of his freshman year, Rafael wrote to Josh about how much he relied on Cindy: "I always go to her and complain about all the work and tell her I'm going to drop out and she ends up trying to throw things at me but her aim is very bad. . . . Lol." But Cindy described the emotional intensity of what the students were experiencing and its effect on her: "There were times where Kennetta would come in, and be like, 'I need to go home. I'm tired.' I remember saying to her, 'I'm not letting you give up.' I think because I poured so much of myself into them, that their struggles became my struggles."

Cindy remembered her own "darkest moment" on the night of her thirtieth birthday. The staff had "invited thirty multicultural students, who were my kids, to show up randomly throughout the day, and hand me a rose." Later that evening, she went out to celebrate. "But it was also when Kennetta was having such a hard time letting go of premed and finding something else. I felt that it was my fault. I didn't feel like I was helping her enough. I just remember crying my eyes out that night."

All three Secondary School for Research students experienced the transition to Muhlenberg as a shock. On the picturesque campus that Rafael had imagined as a place of peace, he found that as a student of color, "you stick out like a sore thumb." The friendliness that had struck him during his visit to Muhlenberg now seemed forced, and he grew tired of dealing with people "smiling in your face, pretending to want to be your friend" alongside the "blank stares or the immediate stereotypical comments." Rafael was frequently stopped by campus safety officers, who doubted his assertion that he was a Muhlenberg student. "I managed to keep my cool and show them my ID," he said.

Rafael described his sense of unease living on a campus that felt so isolated and unreal. Where were the homeless people, the pregnant teens? He missed, from Brooklyn, the everyday grit of urban life, the *bachata* music blaring from bodegas. Rafael described walking around the streets of Allentown—where Muhlenberg students were told not to go—so he could hear Spanish spoken and find foods that reminded him of home. Being in downtown Allentown, he said, "made me feel whole again." It was a place where "what you saw was what you got," where he could escape from the "hypocrisy" of the Muhlenberg environment.

Angie said that she started at Muhlenberg with her guard up. "I went into college knowing I wasn't trying to make friends. I was going to get in and get out." But she underestimated the extent to which she would feel not only isolated, but embattled. "At Muhlenberg, you interact with a lot of ignorant people, overall. They're not used to being around black people, Hispanic people, minorities period. The comments that are said, it's just very offensive. There are professors who are the same way—they're no better than the students. It takes a toll. You can't live life that way. *I* can't live life that way."

Angie described walking to a party thrown by the Black Students Association, and overhearing a girl outside say, "That party's only for black people. They're playing so much black music." Almost more rankling than the dismissive tone was the phrase "black music." "What makes music black?" Angie said as she told Josh about the incident. "There isn't a genre—there's pop, there's R and B. That is part of the black culture, but that's not black music. If you had any intelligence you would know that you don't say stuff like that." She heard from another student that his roommate said to him, "Oh, your mother's black, right? So she must be like that big black lady from *Madea*"—referring to the outsized personality played by filmmaker Tyler Perry. Angie was a big fan of Tyler Perry, but she was disgusted by students who didn't know enough to separate stereotype and caricature from reality. "Because of what you're seeing on TV, you're thinking that everybody's mother and grandmother is like that."

During her first year, Angie lived in a room that her two suitemates needed to pass through to get to theirs. As she recounted, they would often "stroll in with their friends," drunk at 4 a.m. while she was trying to sleep, being "loud and obnoxious." Angie felt constantly frustrated that her roommates were "not showing me the respect I was trying to show them."

Finally, she said, "there was a time when I was loud, disrespectful, and obnoxious" to them. In response, her roommates complained to the resident assistant, an older student. The resident assistant, after speaking with Angie's roommates, referred their issues to Residential Services.

It outraged Angie that her roommates did not confront her directly. She did not want to attribute their avoidance to racism. But her sense that her roommates saw her as threatening echoed Nkese and Ashley's descriptions of the way urban women of color were perceived on their campuses. "It was, 'Let's go talk to the resident assistant instead of talking to her, because she's too loud.' But when *you're* loud, it's okay. You're drunk, so that's your excuse. You're stumbling on my stuff, you're going in my room to use my microwave and my food, but then you can't have the decency to talk to me because you think I might have an anger problem?"

The final insult for Angie was her roommates' complaints, during one of the meetings that followed, that when Angie had an asthma attack in her room, she didn't ask them for help. "They just heard a knock on the door and saw EMS coming into the room. They got offended because I didn't talk to them. Why would I try and ask you for help when the whole semester, we did not talk? I'm supposed to be knocking on everybody's door struggling to breathe? No. I'm going to calm myself down, and I'm going to call campus security so I can go to the hospital to get what I needed checked out."

Josh kept in touch with Kennetta, Angie, and Rafael throughout their time at Muhlenberg and visited campus often. By the summer after their junior year, it seemed all three had found places within the community where they felt at home. Kennetta had co-founded a group called God Ordained Dancers, which performed "praise dance," the expressive form of worship she practiced at her church in Brooklyn, and she had a serious boyfriend. Angie was active in the Black Students Association and the Theta Nu Xi Multicultural Sorority. Through Muhlenberg's Office of Community Service and Civic Engagement, she was hired as student director for the IMPACT Project, which provides mentoring and programming for Allentown youth in the juvenile justice system. Rafael had made a diverse group of friends and had discovered passions for creative writing and Latin American history. When, during Kennetta, Angie, and Rafael's sophomore year, ten new students arrived as the second cohort from the Secondary School for Research, Rafael became a mentor and caretaker for them.

But Josh's conversations with Kennetta, Angie, and Rafael,

and with the faculty and advisers who worked closely with them, revealed how severely he had underestimated the difficulties that the three would experience as the first cohort in the partnership between Muhlenberg and the Secondary School for Research. Though he had known the transition would be hard, he believed that ultimately the college would be a respite from life in Brooklyn, that it would be a place where they could focus on their intellectual and personal development. At Muhlenberg, Josh learned, Kennetta, Angie, and Rafael still struggled with the problems of home, but now from a distance. Though they had found advocates, on the whole the college lacked the structures to support them effectively. On top of this, Muhlenberg introduced the Secondary School for Research students to a new kind of stress, as they felt, beneath surface friendliness, that they were perceived by their peers and professors as threatening strangers who did not belong. Combined, these factors made it hard for the students to maintain their emotional equilibrium and concentrate on their studies.

Angie described "a lot of scare moments at the school" when her mother and aunt fell ill back home. Angie knew that her coursework would suffer if she missed classes, but could not stand the idea of being away at these crucial times. When Angie's mother had to have major surgery, Angie went home to "make sure that everything was okay, talk to her doctors, take care of her, and cook her food. School is important to me, but family is more important to me. If there's anything I can do, even if it's just being by their bedside, I'm going to be there."

Angie recognized the way her fear for the health of her loved ones affected her performance in classes. "I was just tired, and constantly thinking about them, and not thinking about myself. It was weighing me down." Angie remembered Cindy telling her, "You gotta remember, your mom is sick now, but she doesn't want you failing out of school because you're worrying about her." Angie said she knew Cindy was right, but "just because it's being said and you know it in the back of your mind, it's hard to make that transformation. I'm always going to worry about my mother, because she's all I have."

Kennetta and Rafael were both spending the summer after their junior year on campus taking courses they needed to stay on track to graduate in four years, making up for semesters when they had failed a class or taken a reduced load. Kennetta told Josh, "The main thing that I still carry here from my family is the money issue. I'm always worrying, did my family eat today? Were my parents able to pay the bills?" Kennetta had just been home, she said, "and there was no food, really, in the house. My mom was just like, 'Yeah, I'm sorry that I didn't get to cook. It's just a really low week, Kennetta.' " Her mother said that she and Kennetta's dad were going to try to go grocery shopping that week. Then, Kennetta said, she had to ask for $125 for a book for one of her summer classes. "I'm feeling really guilty—I know that I potentially took their last grocery money for the week."

When Josh spoke with Rafael, he expressed excitement about his academic path. That year he had dropped his business major: he was earning poor grades in accounting and other required courses, and he was not enjoying them. He had fallen in love with Latin American history and took all the courses offered "with the only professor who taught them, Dr. Cathy Ouellette." Professor Ouellette, he said, was "smart, witty, and open to discussion inside and outside the class." Though she was not Hispanic, she became someone he could speak with about issues he faced as a minority on campus. Rafael was working with Professor Ouellette and with Professor Charles O. Anderson, director of the Africana studies program, to try to establish a Latin American and Caribbean studies major. He still imagined a future as an entrepreneur, but now, he said, "I want to find a way to leverage my knowledge of history and culture in the business world to make bigger change."

Though Rafael spoke positively about his experience at Muhlenberg, Josh knew he was on the edge there. That July, the federal government had implemented a new requirement that colleges set standards for "satisfactory academic progress" that must be met in order for students to continue to receive federal aid. Cindy told Josh that if Rafael did not achieve at a certain level in the three classes he was required to take that summer, he would not meet these new requirements and his aid would not be renewed for his senior year. Rafael could not continue at Muhlenberg without aid. Already, he was working several part-time jobs to pay his tuition, including a job with a moving company that often required him to work early in the morning or late at night. Josh also learned that Rafael, the son of an alcoholic, often spent long nights partying and then would go to bed drunk, only to wake up the next morning for a long day of work and classes. Rafael still held tightly to his principle of self-reliance and was reluctant to seek counseling or ask for help. And although he acted as a mentor to the young men from similar backgrounds who came to campus after him, there were few men of color on staff to whom he could turn himself.

Josh spoke about his students' first three years at Muhlenberg with psychology professor Kate Richmond, who was assigned as Kennetta and Angie's adviser during their freshman year and who joined Cindy in the work of being their advocate and counselor. Kate, like Cindy, was a Muhlenberg graduate, from the class of 2000. Though she was white, she came from a working-class background and felt she could relate in some ways to Angie and Kennetta's experience of feeling out of place and academically underprepared at Muhlenberg. But like Josh, she had underestimated the extent to which the social, emotional, and financial challenges the Secondary School for Research students faced at Muhlenberg would undercut their ability to achieve to their potential. More significant than the ways these students were not prepared for Muhlenberg, Kate believed, were the ways that Muhlenberg was not prepared for them.

During regular check-ins with Angie and Kennetta about

their academic progress, Kate saw the pervasive impact of non-academic issues on their performance. Both students lacked access to resources most Muhlenberg students took for granted. When Kennetta was sent to the emergency room because of severe pains in her chest, "there was an assumption that she had health insurance. Or that if she had health insurance, she wouldn't be underinsured." Kate remembered that Kennetta's family, on the edge of eviction, was sent a bill for several hundred dollars for a chest x-ray conducted during her visit. Trying to void this bill took months of work. Faculty and staff, Kate said, rarely recognized the obstacles students faced. "I've heard faculty say, time and time again, that the students don't have their books in class. Well, they don't have their books in class because the book costs ninety dollars and it's already been checked out at the library." Problems getting home and communicating with their families caused guilt and anguish for both Kennetta and Angie; often, they could not afford to pay for the cell phone minutes they needed to keep in touch or for cab fare to the bus station so they could travel back to Brooklyn.

In response to these problems, those involved in supporting the students advocated with the college to put some fixes in place. To ease the burden of the cost of books, Kate said, the college set up a system in which students could take out an interest-free loan at the beginning of the semester to buy their books and repay it through work-study over the course of the term. The college purchased two cell phones that were kept at the admissions office and, during designated hours, students with need could sign them out. The college also recognized, from conversations with students of color, that many felt uncomfortable seeking peer tutoring in part because all the tutors were white. In response, Kate and others "made a very conscious effort to recruit students of color" as tutors.

Kate described her own learning curve in understanding how best to support Angie and Kennetta. When things were going badly for them, she realized that "they're not going to check in with me, I have to check in with them." Kate recognized how important a sense of connection and accountability could be. During their first two years, she would send them a weekly e-mail, and with Kate's encouragement Angie often wrote her papers at a computer directly across from Kate's office.

Kate could see how difficult it was for Angie to maintain the mental clarity she needed to develop her ideas in writing. Most college students struggle to muster the self-discipline necessary to complete essays as they manage busy schedules and sleepless nights. On top of their academic work, Angie and Kennetta faced relentless challenges to their personal and economic stability, without a safety net of family and financial support. At one of Angie's lowest points, Kate said, "I think she wrote one sentence in four hours." During these times, Kate believed, it helped to be in the presence of someone who cared.

The work of advising Angie and Kennetta, Kate said, was difficult and time-consuming. "You're managing crises, and it's never predictable. If you ask Cindy, it really feels like once a crisis with Kennetta has been resolved, Angie has one. And then once Angie's is resolved, it's Kennetta." Something would usually happen, Kate said, "when I'm behind on my grading, or when I have a thousand letters of recommendation to write." Out of her fifty advisees, Kate had dedicated as much time to Angie and Kennetta as she had to the other forty-eight combined.

Kate also said that of all her work at the college there was perhaps nothing else that she felt made a larger impact on the campus and on her own development as an adviser and as a professor. In particular, Angie and Kennetta helped Kate to see how crucial it was for the college to recognize the ways socioemotional and economic factors could affect students' ability to study and learn. This understanding, though particularly essential for helping low-income students, was important for supporting students from all backgrounds.

In the classes Kennetta and Angie took with her, Kate said, their insights reshaped class discussions, and changed how she taught and how she chose assigned readings. She began to understand more concretely "how all students could benefit from taking more African American studies and more women's studies courses" and how to encourage students to question received wisdom and to speak their minds. Angie and Kennetta, she said, "pushed me to understand their perspective and my own perspective and constantly challenge it. As an educator, that's the goal: to be involved in this process of discovery."

In speaking about their academic experiences at Muhlenberg, all of the Secondary School for Research students called attention to the fact that, like its student body, Muhlenberg's faculty was overwhelmingly white. During Kennetta, Angie, and Rafael's first two years, Charles O. Anderson, associate professor of dance and founder and director of the Africana studies minor, was the only African American professor on campus.

It was in class, Kennetta said, that she found offensive comments hardest to handle. "There's a professor there, and if they're not understanding where you're coming from, you don't want to come off as, I'm the black person, be sympathetic for me." She described a flare-up in her Introduction to Sociology class, which was taught by a white man. In a discussion of race, a white student commented, "You just have to know your place. When I go into certain neighborhoods, like black neighborhoods, I know I'm not welcome there."

Kennetta jumped in. "What do you mean?" she recalled saying. "That's not necessarily true." The student, she said, then "started to tell a story about this incident, where he was driving in his car in Harlem and stopped at a red light. There was a group of 'them'— he was referencing black people—sitting on the stoop in front of their house." The group "started making comments, saying 'What are you doing here?'" They started getting up to approach the car, the student said, and he "got really scared."

Kennetta raised her hand and asked the student, "Was this your first experience of racism?'" When he answered yes, she

continued, "Well, that's one compared with every day on this campus. We black people, we experience racism, but that doesn't stop
us from coming to Muhlenberg. Just because you go through one
bad experience, you shouldn't take that out on an entire race."

The conversation became heated. There were three other
black students in the class, and they spoke up, too. One pressed
the young man further about his experience in Harlem. It turned
out, Kennetta said, that of the taunters, one was black, one Latino,
and one white. When asked if any of them actually came close to
the car, he said, "No, but I knew that they were going to." When
he "told the truth," Kennetta said, other white students jumped
on him as well. After class, they approached the black students,
saying, "We're so sorry. That's so embarrassing, for us, as white
people. I can't believe that you guys have to go through this."

But Kennetta did not see the incident as either a victory or valuable learning experience. Following the class session, the professor
sent the entire class an e-mail Kennetta remembered as communicating that "when somebody makes a comment in class that's offensive, there's a certain way that you should handle the situation."
She understood the message to be a reprimand directed at her.

Kennetta e-mailed him back. "I hear what you're saying," she
remembered writing. "I probably could have stayed calmer, but
you're not gonna tell me that I have to sit in class and listen to
a white person make racist comments about black people, and I
can't express how I feel." Kennetta felt she was being held responsible for sensitivity in a way others were not. "Why is it that black
people have to watch how they respond, but you don't say anything
to white people about how they come off to black people?" she
remembered telling the professor. "How you're coming off is like
you're taking his side."

Kennetta told Josh that when she first arrived at Muhlenberg
she had stayed quiet in class when people made offensive comments, worried that "these white people would look at me like this
angry black girl." But after a while, "I was just like, no, I shouldn't

have to change who I am just to make other people feel comfortable, when I don't feel comfortable half the time." She knew she sometimes came off as angry, but it was hard to voice her reactions in a measured way, she said, "especially when you're looking around the classroom, and you're the 'only.' "

Kennetta and Angie both spoke about how their roles in class discussions evolved during their time at Muhlenberg. Coming into the school, Angie said, "everybody thought I was really aggressive and I'd be quick to yell at you or pick an argument with you." But as time went on, she learned to modulate her responses. "I just try to set the record straight. That's when my professionalism comes in. I could be as angry as ever, but I know that this is a classroom setting." She would try to address the issue, "and then hopefully the professor would take on the rest." If she did not feel the professor made an appropriate intervention, she might follow up with a conversation after class and at least know that she had taken action in a positive way.

Charles O. Anderson became a mentor for all three of the students from the Secondary School for Research. Kennetta described how he taught her constructive ways to navigate conversations about race, showing her that she could interrogate her peers' troubling remarks, instead of attacking them. In his classes, "if a white person made a racist comment, or an ignorant comment," he "would question it, and not in a bad way." Some students, Kennetta said, were clearly just taking his Introduction to African American Studies class to fulfill Muhlenberg's diversity requirement. But when students left the class, "their mind-set was totally different."

Kennetta did not, however, lose her tendency toward confrontation. One day a Jewish student in the class angrily objected when the professor compared slavery in America to the Holocaust. The professor challenged her, and Kennetta jumped in. "You want us to sit here and listen about Jewish people went through this, Jewish people went through that?" she remembered saying. "I'm not knocking that. But that is just so rude for you to be in an African

American studies class and say that black people don't matter, because Jewish people went through worse. There's no worse or better. They're both bad."

When the girl tried to respond, Kennetta interrupted her: "You need to shush and listen. How would you feel if this was a Jewish studies class, and you had me in the class, saying, 'Well you know, black people, we had to go through slavery, and even here on this campus, we have to go through discrimination'? That doesn't feel too good, does it? Because that's what you're doing right now." The girl started crying, Kennetta said, and walked out of class.

Kennetta's harsh response reflected her sense that the class was a rare space where issues facing African Americans were a focus and where it was safe to address them. Kate Richmond's multicultural psychology class was another space like this. Kate, Kennetta said, "would tolerate no type of sexual discrimination, no type of racial discrimination. She'll say something." More often, though, in thinking back on class discussions that dealt with race, the students described attitudes from professors that ranged from insensitive to deeply offensive. Angie recounted how a visiting professor, who was black, asked students to "interview an African American." They had to provide a physical description. "Describe the hair," Angie recalled as one suggested question. "Is it straight or nappy?" During her final semester, Angie took an independent study on African American literature with a white professor who, Angie said, constantly asked her if she could relate to the characters who were slaves.

Kennetta, Angie, and Rafael were aware of, and involved in, the college's attempts to increase diversity among its faculty. As a leader of the Black Students Association, Angie was an active member of the hiring committee for a new professor of Africana Studies, a process that began in her sophomore year. "They came to us, the BSA," she said, "and said it was really important to have your input on who should be hired, because this professor will be interacting with you as well as with the rest of the community."

In Angie's account, the first round of candidates taught sample classes, and students on the hiring committee gave their feedback. Both students and professors agreed on a white man as their top choice. He was "beyond qualified," Angie remembered, and had a focus on law that many found appealing. Angie was frustrated when the college president rejected their choice. But in the next round of candidates, Angie met Kim Gallon, a historian of African American life "with special interests in gender, mass media, and sexuality in the late nineteenth and early twentieth centuries."[1] Kim was hired and would become Angie's academic and personal mentor.

When Kim arrived at Muhlenberg, at the beginning of Angie's junior year, members of the Black Students Association were thrilled. "We had two black professors, for two whole semesters. We were like, *yes*. I'm so excited." But at the end of the school year, Charles O. Anderson broke the news that he had accepted a tenured position at the University of Texas. "A lot of the students were crying," Angie said. "Even me, I teared up a little."

Had Muhlenberg been a positive choice for Angie, Kennetta, and Rafael, despite all the negative experiences they faced there? When Josh asked Kate Richmond this question, she said that although the college had a long way to go in serving students like those from the Secondary School for Research, she felt that it was an "exceptional choice" for them. Her primary reason, she said, was that Muhlenberg, like other liberal arts colleges, "values relationships." She knew from her work as a psychologist that "in therapy, the number one variable that creates change is the relationship," and she believed this to be true in education as well. The relationships students built with faculty, staff, and one another would help them to grow and equip them to cope with realities that could be "unpredictable and sometimes scary."

Angie, reflecting on her Muhlenberg experience as she prepared to enter her senior year, echoed Kate's focus on relationships. "When I compare Muhlenberg to universities I could have gone to, I know I wouldn't have had the same one-on-one feeling that I get a lot with different people here," she said. "When people say Angelica Moore, they know who I am. It helped a lot that when I had problems, people actually showed me that they cared. Nobody gave up on me."

Angie found this support at many levels and learned to marshal it at crucial moments in her own development. When she had to decide whether to accept a nomination as president of the Black Students Association, she consulted with Cindy, Kate, and with Kim Gallon about how the leadership role would affect her schoolwork, and she ultimately declined it.

Angie also found unexpected support from the financial aid office during one of her most difficult moments at Muhlenberg. When she returned to the college for her junior year, she told Josh, she learned she had lost the Broad scholarship. The award, which she won as a high school senior, was worth $2,500 per year, and renewal of funds each fall was contingent on a student's maintaining a cumulative GPA of 2.5. Angie's sophomore year was her most challenging, as she dealt with her mother's and aunt's illnesses and the fallout from a car accident she was in, and her overall grade point average fell to just below the minimum requirement. Without the Broad funding, Angie could not afford to pay the remaining balance of her tuition. Her only choice would be to withdraw from Muhlenberg, at least temporarily, and find a job. She went to the financial aid office, she said, "and the secretary told me that there was nothing they could possibly do, it was just too late."

Angie described walking out of the office, picturing having to pack up her things, and asking herself how she would tell her mother. "That little five minute walk to my room from the office was like the walk of a lifetime," she said. She felt that all her hard work "was just going down the drain now. But oh well," she told herself, "you're going to have to do what you gotta do, so that you can continue to move forward."

When Angie arrived back at her room, the phone rang. It was

Greg Mitton, the director of financial aid. Greg, with whom she had worked in the past, asked her to come back to the office. When she told him she had lost her scholarship, he responded, "Well, you're covered." Muhlenberg would provide the missing funds as part of her aid package.

When she heard this, Angie said, "I just cried more, and I'm not a crier. I just didn't understand why he was helping me." Greg said that he was supporting her the way he would any other student and told her to stop crying. Angie responded, "I can't. This is too nice. You don't have to do this." It wasn't Greg's job, she said, "to give me extra or help me out because I'm having problems. That's my problem." She felt, then, that Muhlenberg was not going to let her fail. This gave her "so much more hope."

Starting her senior year, Angie said, "the expectation for me to achieve was much higher," and she had confidence she would. "I refuse to give up on anything that I put my mind to. I was like that before a little bit, but it's stronger. I'll take a million failures before I say I can't take it anymore." The obstacles she had overcome so far at Muhlenberg "weren't just little things. They were huge, explosive things." Muhlenberg, she said, "has given me more courage."

Kennetta was also entering her senior year at Muhlenberg with a sense that she was stronger and more confident than when she began. She reflected that during her college experience so far, "My main thing has been getting me better. Trying to be the best person I can for myself and for my family." Her academics, she said, were "still a work in progress." She was worried about staying on track to graduate, "but I can't really stress about it. I just need to stay focused."

Speaking with Josh about high school was painful, and she did not remember some of the moments he recalled, including the suicide note she wrote in his office. "I know that I have changed," she said. "Before, my self-esteem was really low—about where I come from, about everything that involved me and my life and my family. Even knowing what I used to say, how I used to think, that does bother me, because I feel like, how could I have been so low?"

Kennetta had very low points at Muhlenberg, too. She was depressed through her sophomore year, she said, sleeping only three hours each night and suffering from panic attacks. "I felt like my life was just ending."

At Cindy's urging, as a sophomore Kennetta began to use the college's counseling services. It was helpful, Kennetta said, that the therapist she met with was black and that she was a Christian, "so she understood when I wanted to talk about faith. She grew up Pentecostal, and I'm Pentecostal, so that was even better." They started by talking about Kennetta's relationship with her father. But after a while, Kennetta said, "I didn't really feel like sitting there and talking to her all the time. I don't know if maybe I wasn't open enough. I just didn't feel like I was getting the help that I was looking for."

On top of family, financial, and academic issues, Kennetta had begun an intense new relationship in the fall of her sophomore year. She had met her boyfriend, Josh Foss, the summer before. Josh was a sociology major with a minor in Africana studies. He was white and grew up in a suburb of Allentown. The relationship had emotional highs and lows as both struggled with past issues: Josh, Kennetta learned, had battled drug addiction through his late teens.

As their relationship grew more serious, Josh got to know Kennetta's family and was drawn to Pentecostal worship. Though he did not have a religious upbringing, Kennetta said, in his recovery from addiction "he knew that something more powerful than himself had helped him." During the summer after sophomore year, Josh was baptized: dressed in white, he was dunked into the tide at a Long Island beach by Bishop David C. Wallace, the spiritual leader of Kennetta's church.

Kennetta's boyfriend also became part of the healing process within her family. Over Christmas vacation during their junior year, he came to Kennetta's family's apartment in Brooklyn. One day Kennetta and her father launched into a familiar fight with Josh on the couch between them. "Nobody in this family wants to admit that they're still hurting from past stuff," Kennetta told her father. "We need to talk about it and get it out, or we're all going to be stuck in it."

"No, it's just you that's stuck in the past," her father responded. "You're the only one that always has something to say about it."

"You guys are still sitting in this hellhole," Kennetta shot back. "When you're sitting in something, you can't see the bigger picture. I left. When I come back, I see what a mess it is. I'm telling you that something's wrong."

Kennetta started crying and left the room. Her boyfriend followed her. He told her, "Kennetta, you need to approach everything in a different way. You're always arguing back with your dad—that's never going to accomplish anything. You can't change your father, but you can change you."

Kennetta spent twenty minutes with Josh, calming herself down. Then she went back into the living room. She said to her father, "Dad, I want to ask for your forgiveness. I didn't mean to yell at you and be disrespectful. I need to learn how to get what I feel off my chest without exploding."

Her father, also calmer now, told her he was grateful. "You finally, for the first time, changed your reaction," he said. "Now I'm willing to listen to you."

Kennetta told her father that she always just wanted him to acknowledge her feelings. He told her that even if what he did was wrong, he still wanted her to treat him with respect. "Then he told me sorry," she said, "and we hugged." Following this encounter, Kennetta said, she and her father sometimes spoke on the phone, and "when we go home, and there's nobody at the house, he sits down on the couch, and we watch TV together, or have a conversation."

Rafael did not earn the grades he needed in his summer courses to continue on as a senior. At the end of the summer, Cindy had to break the news to him that his financial aid would not be renewed. "That was another night that I think I cried," Cindy said. "How do you say, I stood here your freshman year telling you I'm going to be here when you graduate, and then say, 'You're going to have to take a year off'?"

As Angie and Kennetta entered their senior years at Muhlenberg, Rafael moved back to Brooklyn. It was difficult for him to speak about this transition. "I did hit a depressed point where I realized that I was back home and no longer in school," he said. Rafael did not want to talk about what he went through at this time, except to say that the experience of being out of college "opened my eyes," and showed him, "I needed to get myself back in line to actually graduate."

During his leave, Rafael started to work at a temp agency, thinking that making connections with companies could help him with networking in the future. "It was a lot of data entry, mail room, and receptionist work," Rafael said. "But it was all within the business field and the medical field." If he went on to earn a bachelor's degree, Rafael believed, he could use these connections to find better paying jobs.

Professor Cathy Ouellette played a crucial role in helping Rafael to pull through this difficult time. Rafael was also supported by Jess Taylor, who had graduated from Muhlenberg three years before and was living in New York City. Jess was African American and grew up in Brooklyn, though she had attended a private high school on the Upper East Side. At Muhlenberg, Cindy had asked Jess to serve as a mentor for incoming freshman, and Jess and Rafael had become close. "It was easy to develop a connection with her because she listened," Rafael said. He appreciated that Jess understood where he was coming from and that she could share "her own stories about her time at Muhlenberg, and how she managed to get through it."

Josh came to Muhlenberg for the weekend of Kennetta and Angie's graduation. The evening before, he met Angie on campus after the baccalaureate ceremony. She was dressed up, wearing a flowered dress and yellow platform shoes. They drove to a nearby TGI Fridays, where Angie ordered a sizzling chicken and shrimp and a Long Island iced tea. She told Josh that she loved to cook and spoke about an interest in culinary arts. It was something she might pursue when she was older, she said, after a career working with children.

Angie hoped to spend a year working at a nonprofit and then to apply to graduate school for child psychology. She was looking at job openings through the website Idealist and had sent out some résumés. She described a phone interview that she thought had gone well: the job was almost identical to her experience as a program coordinator and mentor for troubled teenagers at IMPACT in Allentown. Angie had received an award from the mayor of Allentown for this work, and it had been one of the most fulfilling parts of her college experience.

Josh asked Angie if, during her four years at Muhlenberg, she thought the atmosphere on campus had changed for urban students of color. "You see minorities trickling in," Angie said, "though the population is not growing the way I or any other minority would want it to grow." Angie did not think the presence of more students of color had done much to affect the larger campus community. She voiced frustration at her sense that while she had been part of hiring committees and invited to dinners at the president's house, she did not feel she had been heard. She had changed and grown a lot while at Muhlenberg but felt that the college as a whole had learned little from the multicultural students it had worked so hard to recruit.

After the graduation ceremony the next day, Josh found Kennetta on the quad. That January, Kennetta and her boyfriend had gotten engaged. Both their families surrounded them. Kennetta's mother, Annette, wore plastic-framed glasses and buzzed with energy. Kent, Kennetta's father, had an intense and friendly manner. Kennetta, in her black cap and gown, gave Josh a tearful hug.

Josh spoke with Cindy on the quad as well. She was filled with emotion and very proud that Angie and Kennetta had graduated. Reflecting on the Secondary School for Research partnership, she said, "I think it's been a success in that it's changed some lives. It's definitely changed the conversations that we're having on campus."

The main shift, Cindy said, was that there was now a wider circle of faculty and staff invested in the students' success and well-being. After the first year, those around Cindy were aware of how much weight she carried as the students' main support. When ten students arrived the second year, she remembered hearing, "Cindy can't do ten." Another admissions officer, Melissa Falk, took on a group of her own and served as a partner for Cindy within the admissions office. The team also included the director of the multicultural center, the dean of academic life, the director of the academic support services center, and the chair of the biology department, who became the mentor for three students who had won grants from the National Science Foundation. It made a big difference, Cindy said, to have more people who "were willing to partake in this wraparound mentoring to see the students get through." After the third year of the partnership, the college piloted an initiative called Emerging Leaders, which gathered the various support structures already in place into a formalized program that included a summer pre-orientation, mentorship, and efforts to connect students with leadership opportunities on campus.

Cindy told Josh that she was feeling hopeful about Rafael. Earlier that spring, he had approached Cindy, saying, "I'm ready. I want to come back." If, in the three summer semester courses he was asked to take, he performed at a high enough level to demonstrate "satisfactory academic progress," they would be able to renew his financial aid so that he could graduate the following year.

One year later, Josh attended his second Muhlenberg graduation. Rafael was in the processional, along with eight other students from the Secondary School for Research. Rafael would officially graduate in October, after he had participated in and earned credit for a three-week trip to Spain and Morocco that was the culmination of a spring semester course, Ethnic and Religious Diversity in Spain. The course had been co-taught by Professor Cathy Ouellette, who would also lead the trip. Rafael had been saving for a year to make this trip possible.

Professor Kim Gallon presented commencement speaker Isabel Wilkerson, a journalist and the first black woman to win the Pulitzer Prize. Wilkerson's book, *The Warmth of Other Suns*, traces the journey of African Americans from the South to the North during the Great Migration. At the end of the speech, Wilkerson read the lines, written by Richard Wright, from which she drew the title of her book. To Josh, the Wright quote resonated with the way his students spoke about their lives, and what it had meant for them to come to Muhlenberg. Introducing the quote, Wilkerson said that Wright "wrote these words about a decision he made when he was about your age, as he was embarking on his own journey as part of the Great Migration":[2]

> I was leaving the South to fling myself into the unknown . . . I was taking part of the South to transplant in alien soil, to see if it could grow differently, if it could drink of new and cool rains, bend in strange winds, respond to the warmth of other suns and, perhaps, to bloom . . .[3]

12

The Will to Aspire:
Aicha and Santiago

In June 2009, Aicha Diallo, one of two undocumented students from her graduating class, sent an e-mail to Amherst College expressing her hope that she would be offered a place off the waitlist:

> I can see myself at Amherst. As an international student coming from a high school with 75 seniors, it is very comforting to know that I would be able to have one-on-one conversations with my professors, that the professors would know my name and not just my face, and that I could reach out to them for support. I want to be able to meet people who are as committed as I am to their work and ideas, who are politically active and involved in their communities. Amherst seems like a place where people can disagree, but still have respect for one another's opinions; like a place where students have intellectual discussions on a Saturday night, and that's not nerdy; like a community that cares about issues in the world outside of campus and that values participation in the political process. Amherst seems like a place where I would fit in.

When, in July, Aicha still had not heard from the college, Josh confirmed with the admissions office that nothing had changed. Aicha had held on to her spot at Manhattanville College, where she had been offered a funding package of $42,000 in institutional scholarships and grants out of the college's $46,500 total cost. Aicha had received one-time awards of $1,500 from the Park Slope Civic Council and $500 from the College Access Consortium of New York. That summer she tried to find babysitting work—her best option since she could be paid off the books—to help her father cover the remaining $2,500, along with the costs of books and travel.

When Aicha moved into her dorm at Manhattanville the next fall, she remembered her first priority as making friends. In her senior year at the Secondary School for Research she had finally felt like a real teenager and had enjoyed hanging out with other students. Now, she looked forward to dorm life and to parties. Though she did not drink, she pictured herself dancing and having fun. But as at the beginning of high school, Aicha had difficulty forging relationships. "I had people that I spoke to, but no one that I was really close with." Sometimes friendships would seem to begin, then "dwindle off."

Aicha, who the previous year had often stayed at school until 8 p.m. for drama or student government and then returned home to a host of responsibilities, found herself bored in college. Her classes were challenging, as was adapting to new academic routines. "I was trying to figure out the whole system. You have to make sure that you register for classes, you constantly have to look at the syllabus." But the college schedule, with its increased independence, left her with free time she wasn't sure how to handle, and campus life lacked the energy and inspiration she had hoped to find in it. She worked a few hours each week as a set and scene assistant in the dance and theater department, painting and climbing ladders to hang lights, but did not enjoy the job.

At the same time as she felt aimless and disconnected in school, Aicha felt guilty for leaving her parents and four younger siblings. Her father had to work more hours to pay her tuition, and she could no longer help her mother manage meals and housework. As she traveled back and forth for immigration proceedings, Aicha wondered if it might be better for her to be at Brooklyn College, since the residential experience was not proving to be the space for growth that she had imagined.

In her second semester, Aicha's social life began to improve. She met two African students, who, she said, "took me up as their little sister, because I was a freshman, and they were sophomores." She was impressed by the activities and internships they described and began to see the ways Manhattanville, though a less active campus than she desired, could connect her to her aspirations. She decided to major in international studies and was excited about taking a course taught by the United Nations ambassador to Pakistan.

That spring, Aicha had to attend her final asylum hearing with an immigration judge who would determine whether she could stay in the United States. About two weeks later, she received notification of the result: she had been granted asylum.

For Aicha, the sense of exhilaration and relief was quickly followed by the questions her new status raised about her educational choices. As an asylee, she was immediately eligible for federal aid and would be able to apply for status as a permanent resident and eventually for citizenship. Now Aicha thought, "I could get into some of the other schools that I really wanted to go to." It would be easier to justify everything—leaving her home in Guinea, her father's long work hours, all her own work and sacrifice as a high school student, all the time, money, and anxiety involved in moving her and her family's case in immigration court toward a decision—if she were attending one of the country's most elite colleges. In May, Aicha wrote an e-mail to Josh asking, "How would I go about transferring to another college, and is it too late?"

Aicha told Josh she wanted to try again for Amherst and also apply to Barnard. She was also considering moving back home to attend Brooklyn College, though this was a choice she would make more out of a sense of responsibility than desire.

Because it was too late to apply for the fall, Aicha decided to return to Manhattanville for her sophomore year. At the same time, she planned to work with Josh on transfer applications for the second semester or for junior year. She believed, as did Josh, that it had been her status that had limited her to the waitlist at so many schools. Now, she thought, some of those closed doors might open.

Santiago Hernandez remembered going home after high school graduation with the sense that, as an undocumented immigrant, he had no real prospect of attending college. At first, he said, "I just sat there thinking about what I was going to do next." A week passed, then two, and he knew he had to find a job. A friend of his mother's told him about an opening at a ninety-nine-cent store near Eighteenth Avenue. Santiago organized supplies, brought up merchandise from the basement, and helped customers. He was paid in cash.

The following spring, Santiago decided, reluctantly, to accept his uncle's standing offer to return to the shipyard where he had worked for two summers in high school. Santiago had hated the work. But his mother had stopped babysitting after his graduation, and he was the only source of income for his mother, brother, and sister. At $560 per week, the pay was far higher than what he was earning in the store.

Though at eighteen he was "already old," Santiago said, "it was still scary to go back there." Some days he worked high on scaffolding, supported by a harness, to make repairs to the sides of the ship. He heard about a time when a harness broke, and the worker, who was cleaning seaweed off the hull with a pressurized water gun, fell and broke his arm and leg. Other times, he worked in the dark ship bottom, pumping out bilge water. Workers were sometimes required to stay through the night and into the next day to meet a deadline. Santiago once again used false documents, and this heightened his fear as well: "I was just scared about getting caught, getting myself in trouble, getting deported."

After several months, debilitating kidney pain interrupted Santiago's work. Santiago had first become aware of his kidney condition toward the end of eleventh grade. One day after school, he had been playing basketball with friends in the gym at the Secondary School for Research, when he started to feel feverish. He stayed home for several days thinking he just had a bad cold, but the pain worsened, and sweat soaked his sheets. At the emergency room, the doctor told him that he had developed kidney stones and that his kidney had swollen to twice its size. If he had waited longer, it could have burst. They would try to remove the stones, the doctor told Santiago, but if this did not work, Santiago would have to have his kidney removed.

Santiago remembered waking up from his first surgery with intense nausea and pain in his back. The doctors explained that they had inserted a long needle through his back to his kidneys. The surgery had been successful in removing the stones, but the condition did not go away.

Though the work at the shipyard exacerbated Santiago's kidney problems during his first year out of high school, he kept returning. "I kept telling myself I didn't want to be here, but I had to go," he said. He was providing for his family, but losing hope that he could build a better future for himself. Whenever he got sick again, he said, "I would stop working for a period of time. I had to go through surgery after surgery." He described his experience of the anesthesia, the whole world spinning as he went under. "I kind of liked that part," he said. "My life shut down for a while. I felt relief, getting away from everything." Then, "I would wake up, and feel this pain all over my body."

In the summer of 2010, Santiago stopped working at the shipyard. "I couldn't stand it anymore," he said. He spoke with friends who knew people who worked for drug dealers. "It was a way of having money, but an easier way. You just have to go to certain houses and distribute some weed." But Santiago never followed up with the leads his friends gave him. "How can I say it? I always thought to myself that I was better than that. I shouldn't be doing something like that even though I wanted to, and even though it was a good way to get money, fast."

Whenever he could, Santiago played soccer in the park near his home. He had known many of his soccer friends since middle school. Like him, most were immigrants who worked in manual labor or temporary jobs. "I have a lot of friends who graduated from high school but didn't go to college, and they're still working, trying to see what they can find. Some of them are my age, some older." One of Santiago's friends, who was twenty-six and worked on a construction crew, told Santiago he would ask his boss about a job. About a week later, he called Santiago and told him they could use a helper.

Santiago began renovating apartments alongside his friend. They worked in Brooklyn, Queens, and Rockaway Beach, knocking down ceilings, hanging dry wall, and tiling floors. His boss, Santiago said, "knew I wasn't experienced with construction, so he would teach me." This relationship was a welcome change from the daily insults and reprimands from supervisors at the shipyard. The team of three got along well, and Santiago enjoyed the work. "It was kind of hard, but not as hard as working on the ships," he said. "I liked building stuff with my hands." He was paid in cash, bringing home $80 to $100 each day.

Santiago often spoke with another friend from soccer, an immigrant who "has documents," went to college, and had recently begun work in a law office. Hearing about this work, Santiago felt a combination of jealousy and pride. Among their group of friends, "he was the only one that actually did something for himself." Santiago started to think, "Why can't I be doing something like that? I should be going to college and trying to work in a better job."

That fall, Santiago began spending more time with Janet Wu, who had graduated from the Secondary School for Research the year before him. Janet told Santiago about the problems she was having with her boyfriend, and Santiago "would support her and talk to her." Santiago, who usually kept his feelings to himself, talked to Janet about his rekindled desire to go to college. "I would tell her about my hopes, and she would listen," Santiago said. Once, Janet came to visit Santiago while he was working. She had planned to just stop by and eat lunch with him, but when she saw him alone, painting, she picked up a brush and they finished the job together.

Santiago began to set aside cash from his construction job to save for college. He knew from his work with Josh that as an undocumented immigrant, he could get into a CUNY college but could not receive government financial aid. By springtime, he had saved about two thousand dollars, enough for a semester's full-time tuition. Santiago called Josh, who briefed him on the next steps for applying and enrolling and told him to keep in touch.

At this time, Santiago's crew was in the midst of a two-week job covering a backyard with concrete. "We gutted the whole thing out, carried heavy bags of sand, and mixed and spilled concrete." With the strenuous work in the hot sun came kidney pain. Soon after his phone call to Josh, Santiago once again had to stop work and admit himself to the hospital for surgery.

Up through the age of eighteen, Santiago's surgeries had been paid for by Child Health Plus, a state-subsidized insurance plan that does not require beneficiaries to provide a Social Security number. He had turned nineteen that winter and aged out of Child Health Plus. Others in his income bracket could transition to another program, Family Health Plus, but this plan required a Social Security number for enrollment. The surgery cost $1,700, and without insurance the money Santiago had saved for college "kind of flew away."

Janet would not let Santiago give up. She had broken up with her boyfriend and, at the end of June, the two became a couple. Janet began staying up late, setting aside her own schoolwork to pore over the CUNY website for Santiago. She researched the least expensive options, advising him to complete all his prerequisites at the cheapest college, then transfer to another school for his major.

Josh spoke with Janet and Santiago together a year after their relationship began. He asked Janet about what motivated her to work so intensely to help Santiago get to college. Janet was a student at Queens College, majoring in elementary education and mathematics. She said that she used to bring Santiago to campus and introduce him to her friends, who would always ask him where he went to school. She knew how much Santiago hated the question. "I work. I can't go to school," he would respond quietly, and Janet would try to change the subject. When she was helping him, Janet said, "it made me feel better. It was something that he really wanted also. He has every right to go to school, just like everybody else."

Santiago kept trying to save, but the money he earned in his construction job quickly disappeared between paying for another surgery and the costs of groceries and rent. His mother spent her time caring for Santiago's baby sister, whose father, Santiago's mother's boyfriend, provided little besides diapers.

Because she was born in the United States, Santiago's sister was eligible for the Supplemental Nutrition Assistance Program, the new name for the federal government's food stamp program. Santiago's mother had submitted an application. Late that spring, she received a follow-up call asking if she had any information about Santiago's father, who had abandoned the family when Santiago was five and his brother three, leaving them in destitution in Mexico. "My mom said she had no idea," Santiago said. "She told them she just had his name, his date of birth, and the last place she knew where he was."

About two months later, Santiago's mother received word that Santiago's father had been found in California and served a summons for unpaid child support. "That's when he started coming back into our lives," Santiago said.

Santiago tried not listen when his mother spoke to his father on the phone. "My mom would try to make me talk to him, and I didn't want to. I was angry. I didn't want to know anything about him, because he left us. I didn't need him in my life." When, one day, his mother told him that his father wanted to pay his tuition to go to college, Santiago immediately refused. "I didn't want to accept his money," he said. "I've been through so much. I can take care of myself now."

Santiago told Janet about his father's offer and his own response. Janet tried to convince Santiago to accept the money. "I told him that his father owes him," Janet said. "Raising a child costs what, $300,000? His dad didn't spend anything on him." This wasn't the best way to get the money, she remembered saying, "but it's still for you to go to college, and that's what you've always wanted."

After several days of thought and with intense ambivalence, Santiago called his father to tell him he would accept his offer. "I didn't feel so proud of myself for that," he said. "I was using him, just to go to college. To me, going to college was everything, even if it meant talking to someone that I'd hated for so long."

The conversation was as difficult as Santiago expected. "He was trying to convince me that he didn't abandon us, that he was trying to look for us. I didn't believe him at all. I know he has another wife, some other kids. There were so many things I wanted to tell him. I wanted to curse him out, but I couldn't. He's my father, I have to have some respect for him. If I had him in front of me, I don't know what I'd do."

Janet urged Santiago to push aside his feelings and focus on getting enrolled for the fall. The cheapest college, according to her calculations, was the Borough of Manhattan Community College (BMCC). Anyone with a high school diploma was eligible to attend. Janet had made a list of all the documents Santiago needed and helped him gather them. On a sunny August day, the two of them traveled to the campus in lower Manhattan to begin the admissions process.

Both Janet and Santiago felt buoyant as they got out of the

THE WILL TO ASPIRE: AICHA AND SANTIAGO

subway, walking past the columns and archways of the Tweed Courthouse, the green plazas around City Hall. "It was a happy moment for me, and for her," Santiago remembered. "I imagined myself getting off the train, going to school, studying, and hanging out outside. I had all my papers, I was ready."

"I was hyper," Janet said. "I was more hyper than him. I was pushing him like crazy. It was so much research, staying up late. It was something he wanted to do for a long time. Finally, finally, it was happening."

Janet had timed the journey to BMCC from Santiago's home. "This is actually not that far," she remembered telling him. As they walked to the campus, she pointed out a Dunkin' Donuts—"I know he needs his morning coffee"—and a Subway, where Santiago could get a healthy lunch. Near the main building was a green yard, where a show was going on. "There were little kids there, and there was laughter," Janet said.

The main building of the college spanned four city blocks, and, according to the BMCC website, "was designed with the Hudson River harbor in mind—shaped like a ship with its helm pointed to sea."[1] Janet and Santiago wanted to walk around more, but the admissions office was right up the stairs from the main entrance, so they went in. A desk separated the waiting area from the offices in the back. Santiago signed his name on the sign-in sheet, and he and Janet sat down in a row of empty chairs to wait.

When the lady called Santiago's name, he went up to the desk and gave her all his documents. After looking through them, she said she would begin entering his information into the computer. She asked for his name and date of birth and then for his Social Security number.

Santiago experienced the feeling that he always did when he was asked for his Social: "I don't know what to say. I freeze for a second." Then he told the lady that he didn't have one. "You don't know it, or you don't have one?" she said. "I don't have one," he repeated. "I don't have a Social Security number."

Santiago remembered that the lady stayed quiet for a little while. Then she said, "Well, we can't really do anything for you." Santiago told her he would pay out of his own pocket and that he didn't think you needed a Social Security number to go to BMCC. "I need your Social to register you in the computer so people can see you," he remembered as her response.

Santiago asked if he could speak with an admissions counselor or anybody else from the back offices. "I can't allow you to go inside," she told him. She handed him a paper and circled the address of the CUNY website, telling him he could try applying online.

Janet, always impatient, came up to the desk to see what was happening and began asking questions. The lady did not respond. She just pushed the paper toward Santiago, looked over his shoulder, and shouted "Next, next," though nobody was waiting.

Janet remembered that she and Santiago "went out laughing," but with outrage and disbelief, not with humor. "What the hell just happened?" they said to each other. The paper in Santiago's hand simply sent them to the website Janet had spent the summer studying. "I knew everything about the website," she said. "We didn't come for her to give us a paper with a circle on it." Going in, Janet told Josh, she and Santiago were expecting to find "a person kind of like you"—someone who would understand Santiago's situation and try to help him. Instead, they had been rudely kicked out of the office. "Shouldn't they hire someone who's nice and encouraging, or gives advice?" Janet said.

Santiago felt angry and humiliated. "At the moment I was just thinking she was a racist person," he said, though the woman was black. "I don't have a Social, I'm Hispanic, there's a lot of reasons. I was mad and put down at the same time." Though he knew he had a right to apply to BMCC, the experience of being turned away was another sign that the doors to college were literally closed to him. When he was still in high school he had been accepted to college, but that was not enough. "What do I have to do to get *inside* a college?" he asked. Even Josh had not been able to make that happen, after months of their working together.

As Santiago was trying to apply to CUNY that spring, Aicha was finishing her sophomore year of college and her first year as a legal resident of the United States. She had abandoned her plan to submit transfer applications and decided to stay at Manhattanville.

Josh visited Aicha at the college in April. The campus was self-enclosed, with a gate where a guard asked Josh for the name of Aicha's dorm before letting him drive in. The large parking lot was half empty at 11 a.m. on a Sunday morning. Squirrels ran along a green lawn that was bright from the previous night's shower. Aicha emerged from her dorm wearing warm-up pants and her "Seniors" T-shirt from the Secondary School for Research, with "Keepin' It Brooklyn" in graffiti tag lettering. Her manner was still open and ebullient, though she seemed to have an edge of insecurity that Josh did not remember in high school. She stepped gingerly along the concrete path. "When it rains, all the worms come out," she said.

Josh commented on how quiet the campus was. Saturday night, Aicha said, everyone goes into New York City and gets back late. Sundays were for sleeping, cleaning, and homework. Aicha had gone into Manhattan the day before with a friend, getting her hair braided then eating at an African restaurant. Most weekends she went home to Brooklyn and stayed over Saturday night. Her mother had a new baby, and Aicha helped with her younger brothers and sister.

Josh followed Aicha into her dorm, a stone building called Founders Hall. Aicha shared a small room with Ahanu, her closest friend, who was at church at the time. "Ahanu's side is way more personal than mine," she said, pointing out the photos of family and friends around her roommate's desk. Aicha's desk was piled with her course books, which included *Multilateral Diplomacy* and

The Caribbean Pleasure Economy. Posters marking African causes covered most of the room's wall space, one advertising a film about child soldiers, another reading REMOVE JOSEPH KONY.

Aicha and Ahanu had begun that year as co-presidents of Uja-maa, the college's African student club. During her freshman year Aicha had attended meetings of Ujamaa, which she said were poorly attended and mostly arguments. In getting involved, Aicha and Ahanu wanted to focus the organization around education about Africa. Aicha was very proud of the event they had planned with the advocacy group Invisible Children, to raise awareness about child soldiers. It had been held in March, in the main hall of Reid Castle, the imposing stone centerpiece of the campus, and more than one hundred people had attended. Aicha was currently planning an event in collaboration with the campus club Seeds of Peace, trying to solicit donations from local businesses, and organizing a bake sale.

Josh accompanied Aicha to the dining hall to meet Ahanu for brunch. "People are starting to come out," Aicha said, looking at a table of young men in baseball caps. Ahanu was tall and muscular with deep dimples, wearing a head scarf and a white button-down shirt over black leggings. "She stalked me," Ahanu joked when Josh asked how she and Aicha had met. Aicha remembered saying, "I like your hair" to Ahanu as they were getting on a bus, trying to make a gesture toward friendship. "She was so busy rushing to basketball practice she didn't even pay attention to me."

As she filled her tray, Ahanu commented that the college had recently begun serving Fair Trade coffee, something she and Ai-cha both appreciated. Recently they had watched a movie in their Global Studies class called *Black Gold*, about the abuse of workers in coffee production. "Afterward we all just got up and left silently, feeling horrible," Aicha said. Both Aicha and Ahanu were passionate about global human rights and were looking for internships that would be stepping-stones to careers in international relations or law.

Aicha had decided against transferring once the year began because, she said, she had finally made friends and did not want to have to start all over again somewhere else. She described her core group: "There's this girl who's really hip-hop. She dresses like a boy." Another friend was "a real girly-girl, always in a cute little outfit." Then, she said, "there's me, somewhere in between."

Aicha appreciated meeting different kinds of people and did not feel like she stuck out on campus as a student of color. Most of her friends were black and from a variety of backgrounds. Among African students on campus, some were wealthy international students, including the son of a former prime minister of Tanzania. Others were from immigrant families, like herself and Ahanu, whose family was from Nigeria. The school was small, and in some ways like high school: "Everybody knows everybody. If there's a new person on campus everyone will ask, who's that? It's kind of like boarding school."

As she showed Josh around the campus, Aicha spoke about her classes. She was majoring in international studies, with concentrations in global justice and international management. "Why management?" Josh asked. "It seems like something that will help me get a job after I graduate," Aicha said. "And management will help me with nonprofit work. I think I have good leadership skills."

Aicha told Josh she felt challenged by her classes and liked hearing what the other students, not just the professors, had to say. "Some of the people here are really smart. I was listening to this girl talk, and her vocabulary—I needed a dictionary." There were others who would "just talk normally," but whose writing impressed her. "There are people who can make an argument that sounds like what you'd read in the newspaper." Aicha said that she usually sat in the back. "I'm more subtle here," she said. "It's not like at the Secondary School for Research, where I was always in the front, talking all the time."

Though most students took four or five classes, Aicha was registered for six, and had started off the year seeking permission to register for seven. "I thought I could do it all . . . I'm superwoman," Aicha said. She had trouble narrowing her choices and thought it might save her money by helping her to graduate early. Now that she was a permanent resident, her financial aid package included government grants, but also student loans. Part of her goal was to keep these as low as possible.

Aicha had found a variety of on-campus jobs and worked up to thirty-five hours each week. She began a work-study position as a library circulation assistant, working from 8 p.m. to midnight, or from 10 p.m. to 2 a.m., two or three times each week. In the fall, her library shift immediately followed her work as a phona-thon assistant in the office of alumni affairs. When the phona-thon ended in December, she added more hours as an assistant in the admissions office, where she gave campus tours, followed up with applicants, and entered student information into the da-tabase. Sometimes she canvassed for a local politician, earning $75 per day.

Josh asked about how life was different since she had been granted asylum. "I feel like the doors have opened up a little wider," Aicha said. Though she knew there were "crazy forces at work in the world," she felt that "if I really apply myself, and I take advantage of everything I'm being taught in class, and everything I'm learning from different people, that I have a good chance of being anywhere I want." With this new sense of possibility came pressure: "I feel like if I mess up, it's all on me. I don't have an excuse. Before, I felt like it was resting on that one thing: oh, it's because I'm illegal."

When Josh asked about her vision of success, Aicha responded that it would mean "having a good job, being able to support my-self, and being able to support my family." She imagined "being able to put ten grand on a credit card, and just give it to my dad. I want him to be able to retire, stop working, travel, live a good life. I can never repay my parents, but that would be me saying thank you."

At the same time, Aicha's ambitions clearly went far beyond economic security. She compared her own activities to the accomplishments of her classmates, especially their impressive internships. "School and work is not enough," she said. She was especially awed by a friend who was the daughter of an African representative to the UN, and whom Aicha described as "extremely independent, extremely smart, and opinionated when she has to be. And tall. She's way taller than me." Aicha's friend "had interned at J.P. Morgan Chase and at a huge record label with this African artist. She started her own camp for children in her country. She would tell me all of these things that she has done, and I'm just like, what am I doing? I need to do amazing things, too, because I want to be successful." With legal status, Aicha said, "everything is available to me, depending on how hard I work for it. Now, the real work begins."

Santiago and Janet agreed they would never again set foot in BMCC. But Janet would not allow Santiago to let go of his dream. "I'm stubborn, so I gotta get him into college," she said. She went back to her computer "to find out the next cheapest college" and came up with Kingsborough Community College.

Janet was uncertain about sending Santiago to Kingsborough. She had heard negative stories about the college from friends who had transferred from there to Queens College, "that people don't do as much work as they're supposed to as college students and that professors still treat people like high school students. I knew he wanted a college experience, not a high school experience over again." But Santiago, convinced to give college a last try, told her he didn't really care where he went. "If I was going to be there I would try my best," he said.

Kingsborough held a late registration session at the end of August. Once again, Janet timed the journey, about an hour from Santiago's home to the college's campus on the eastern end of Coney Island. The concrete buildings and redbrick rotunda were bordered by Manhattan Beach, which on this humid afternoon was dotted with sunbathers and kids playing in the waves. Janet could picture hanging out there with Santiago and pointed out a pizza place, Chinese restaurants, and a store where Santiago could buy his textbooks.

Janet and Santiago were directed toward a building where a large group of incoming freshmen waited in a stuffy auditorium. Janet remembered that after signing in, Santiago was a little shaky. "I was getting stressed," Santiago said. "It was too hot. I was like, what if they don't let us in? What if the same thing happens?"

When Santiago was called up to the desk, he was relieved to find that the person there seemed nice. "She listened to me. She kept asking me questions. If I didn't understand something, she would explain it to me." He gave her his high school diploma, his birth certificate, and his Mexican passport and ID card.

When the lady asked him for his Social Security number, Santiago remembered answering under his breath, as though hoping she couldn't hear him. "Just give me a second," she responded. Then she told him she would enter him as an international student. First, however, he had to complete an online CUNY application form at one of the computers, listing Kingsborough as his first choice. Santiago did this with Janet's help and returned to the desk.

Santiago waited to be told the next step. "She was on her computer for five, seven minutes," he told Josh. "It seemed like a really long time, because all these flashbacks came back. I was just thinking about everything I went through."

Finally, the lady handed Santiago a paper with his CUNY ID number and an appointment to register for his classes in two weeks' time. "That's it?" he said to her. "That's it," she said.

Santiago remembered thinking to himself, God, thanks. In all his efforts, "there was always this certain spot where I got stuck, and it's my Social, or the money." Now he was in the system, with a way to pay. "I'm going to be able to go to this school. I'm going to be a college student."

Janet and Santiago ate pizza and walked along the boardwalk. "It was a happy moment," Santiago said. "I remember seagulls passing by." Janet, always eager to move forward, called Josh on her cell phone to tell him that Santiago needed a copy of his high school transcript. Josh, who had not heard from Santiago since the phone call the previous spring, was delighted to hear that Santiago was about to start college, two years after high school graduation.

Before his appointment to register for fall classes at Kingsborough, Santiago had to complete a series of tasks, and he and Janet returned to campus three or four times. He obtained and submitted his $65 money order for the CUNY application. At the advice of a financial counselor, he completed and had notarized an "affidavit of intent to legalize immigration status," which would enable him to pay in-state tuition. Because of the time that had elapsed, he had to retake two placement tests in reading and writing. He passed the reading but missed the cutoff for writing by a point, which would mean he would be placed in a remedial class. His math tests, which he had passed, were still valid.

When the day came for his registration appointment in early September, Santiago gathered with other incoming freshmen in another auditorium. A man got up on stage to address the group. He was sorry to tell them, he said, that all classes were filled except for history. To enroll for other freshmen requirements, they would need to wait until the following semester.

A moan of protest went through the auditorium. "Everybody was like, damn, why did you guys make us come all the way here? Why didn't you just send us an e-mail, or let us know when we were coming back and forth before?" Santiago remembered.

Santiago himself was not upset, though it was frustrating to have to wait again. "I knew I was in. I just had to register for classes." He received a paper with a new appointment date and went back to work in his construction job. His boss, who was sensitive to his health condition, helped him avoid heavy lifting. Janet kept him on top of the phone calls and paperwork he still needed to complete. In January, he returned once again to Kingsborough for spring semester registration.

Janet had skipped her history class to accompany Santiago but was not allowed to come with him when he was called to a back office, which made Santiago anxious. Once again, he was asked for his Social Security number. When Santiago said he didn't have one, he was told to provide his CUNY ID number. "From now on, that's your Social Security number," the adviser said.

"I got a smile on my face," Santiago remembered, "and I was like, 'That's not a real Social, right?' "

The adviser said it was just a number that would enable them to look up his information on the computer, but Santiago "was still smiling." Now, when asked the question he dreaded, he could give a valid response. At least in the school, he said, "I felt about the same as everybody else."

After looking at his transcript and test scores, the adviser helped Santiago choose his classes. Finally, she printed out his schedule and bill, which at $1,800 was less than he expected.

Once again, Santiago felt a sense of accomplishment. Having made it through the door, he was now "climbing up," and "felt for the first time in a long, long time, that I was going to reach my goal, after so much trying."

Josh had dinner with Aicha the August after her junior year. She joined him after dusk to break her Ramadan fast and described how she enjoyed the holiday, with its celebratory late nights eating with her parents, cousins, brothers, and sisters. Her favorite dish was her mother's chicken couscous: chicken sautéed in caramelized onions with a side of mixed vegetable couscous. Aicha remembered how, when they lived in Guinea, her mother and aunt would always make this dish to celebrate holidays or when they welcomed a new child, making extra to give to their friends and colleagues.

Aicha reflected that her childhood in Guinea seemed more distant to her than it had during her senior year of high school, when she focused, in her essay, on the contrast between her African privilege and American poverty. Now, after a summer at home with her family, she described being pulled between her Fulani community's traditional expectations and the American values that seemed equally hers. "You are expected to do everything you're supposed to from Fulani culture," she said, and take only what her community considered the "best of America."

Josh told Aicha about Ashley's recent engagement to a Fulani man. Aicha and Ashley had been friendly in high school, and Aicha expressed surprise and some anxiety on Ashley's behalf. For Aicha, marriage seemed both worlds away from her life and frighteningly close; by nineteen or twenty, many young women in her community were already married. She had recently been at a garage with her father and heard someone say that a friend of hers was a virgin before her marriage. This gossip was very upsetting to Aicha. It angered her that this was what people valued in her friend and that somebody talked about it. "If I heard, then everyone heard," she said. She wrote a rant, inspired in part by what she had learned in a gender studies class, about her community's attitude toward female sexuality. "I had to get out my manifesto," she told Josh.

Junior year had been hard for Aicha. First semester, her friendship with Ahanu had ended. The two roommates had known that they were going in different directions—Aicha wanted to be more social, while Ahanu was increasing her focus on church and on schoolwork—but each had agreed to support the other. The breaking point came one Saturday when Aicha convinced friends to accompany her to an art exhibit she wanted to see in Harlem. After dinner, all her friends, including Ahanu, backed out, and Aicha went to the exhibit alone.

Aicha not only felt betrayed by her best friend but upset at what seemed to be a recurring pattern in her relationships where, she said, "I'm always overextending myself and not getting the same thing in return." She felt lonely and constantly preoccupied. "I couldn't even concentrate in my classes," Aicha said, "because I was so wrapped up in myself, analyzing my friendships."

It was this emotional turmoil that finally convinced her to visit the college's counseling center, something Josh had been urging her to do since freshman year. Aicha met individually with a counselor in the first semester, and during the spring semester, she joined a group. Group counseling with her peers proved transformative for Aicha. "Everyone at my school acts like they're straight-A students, and they don't have problems," she said. Going to the group, and hearing other students say, "I'm having trouble, too," made Aicha feel better, and showed her she was not alone. She felt that other students in her group were honest and genuine, and "when I shared some of my stories, they helped me out. I would explain something that happened to me, and they would try to help me see it a different way."

As she worked through relationship issues during second semester, Aicha began to remove herself from campus life. She was selected for an internship with the Police Reform Organizing Project in lower Manhattan, a two-day-per-week commitment with a small, grassroots team. Aicha appreciated the opportunity to write, help plan events, and develop fundraising ideas for an organization that was doing work that mattered. During her weekends in Brooklyn, she worked as a tutor for a program funded by the New York City Department of Education, earning $15 per hour to meet with students in their homes. Her time at Manhattanville was mainly spent attending classes and working in the library. "People were like, 'You're never on campus,' and I was like, 'I know, I don't want to be on campus.' "

Aicha had hoped to spend a semester abroad—something that

was expected of students in her major—and had been accepted to a program in Capetown, South Africa. She felt an intense desire to return to Africa, in part to find an experience that would be a release from her daily stress. "I just needed a different environment, to understand things better. I needed to be more spontaneous, instead of always planning. I wanted to be able to do this crazy adventurous thing, because this is the only time I'm going to be able to do it."

But the plans fell through. "Part of it was that my dad really didn't want me to go, and I didn't feel comfortable going against his wishes," Aicha said. Her father was afraid for her safety in a country with a high crime rate and anxious about her being so far away just as her status in America had become more secure. There were also logistical issues—she didn't get her passport in time, and the cost of the plane ticket would leave her without spending money.

Aicha still held on to the idea of returning to Africa, perhaps in the role of an American social entrepreneur. She had seen a documentary that showed young people in Guinea studying in the streets at night, relying on the light of the street lamps because their homes had no electricity. She told Josh about her idea for establishing a solar-powered community center where students could pursue their education without fear for their safety. She was speaking with her aunt, who had returned to Guinea, to explore how she could get this project off the ground.

Josh was tempted to tell Aicha that this sounded too big to take on, at least for now. She was already exhausted and caught between many commitments. But Aicha was a dreamer, and Josh did not want to tell her, or any of his students, to stop dreaming. A passage from Sonia Sotomayor's memoir, which describes her childhood in a Bronx public housing project and her path to becoming the Supreme Court's first Latina justice, voiced powerfully for Josh why dreams are so important:

The idea of my becoming a Supreme Court Justice—which, indeed, as a goal would inevitably elude the vast majority of aspirants—never occurred to me except as the remotest of fantasies. But experience has taught me that you cannot value dreams according to the odds of their coming true. Their real value is in stirring within us the will to aspire. That will, wherever it finally leads, does at least move you forward. And after a time you may recognize that the proper measure of success is not how much you've closed the distance to some far-off goal but the quality of what you've done today.[2]

Santiago called his father to tell him that he was registered for school and that he now needed the money to pay. The easiest way for Santiago to receive the money, his father said, was to open a bank account, something Santiago had never done despite his years of work.

The first bank Santiago and Janet entered was Chase. Santiago asked if he could use his CUNY ID number in place of a Social Security number. When the answer was no, Santiago suggested his tax ID. The bank officer told him that he didn't advise this—the account would not be secure. "The best way for you to have a safe bank account," he told Santiago, "is to have your Social."

Next they went to Citibank, where many of Santiago's friends had accounts. There, without objections, he was able to open an account using his tax ID and Mexican passport. After his father deposited money into the account, Santiago wrote a check for the first time, at the Kingsborough bursar's office.

Santiago remembered entering his first college class, a one-credit course called Student Development, aimed at helping freshmen make the transition to college. "As soon as I stepped into a classroom as a student, with a whole bunch of other students who were actually in college, I got this feeling of something being accomplished," Santiago said. He was asked for his name, and when he gave it, "they were like, yeah, you're in the right class." Santiago sat down, and "felt like I was somewhere that I belong." He said it was hard to explain his emotions: "It was like having your first baby, something that you wait for so long, and as soon as you get it, it's big."

Santiago's first assignment for the class was a personal essay, a daunting task for him after being out of school and out of the habit of reading and writing for almost three years. The professor "wanted to get to know us and our background." Santiago wrote the essay with Janet's help. In it, he described his struggle to support his family while pursuing his own dreams. "I had the school life, and I had the family life, and I had to carry both of them at the same time." It was hard, he wrote, "to have to walk, to take a step, with all of this weight on my back."

Santiago's family responsibilities were still heavy, but his health was stable, and now that he had made it to college, he found in himself a greater sense of mobility. "Before, I felt stuck. I felt like I wasn't going to go anywhere." His strength, he said, came from knowing he wasn't alone. "Janet was with me. She had my back."

Janet and Santiago clung fiercely to each other and to ideas of their futures that clashed with their immigrant families' values and expectations. Janet and Santiago were both loyal, devoted children who played crucial roles in their households, Janet in caring for her young nieces and nephews, Santiago in acting as the breadwinner and handling all his family's bills and paperwork. But both had developed, in their American educations, a desire to fulfill individual passions in ways their practical-minded parents didn't understand. Both were also the first in their families to date outside their ethnic group.

Though Santiago's mother was happy for him to take his father's money, she and Santiago's aunts and uncles had trouble understanding his intense drive to get to college. "What's the point of you going to college if you don't have any papers?" they would tell him. "First, you should go get married, get citizenship." Santiago said that he wasn't ready for that, though he had received offers from several young women. "There were people that wanted to help, but I didn't want to use someone," he explained to Josh. "I didn't want to take the easy way out."

Janet held on to the hope that someday she and Santiago would be able to marry. For this to happen, they would need to get past Santiago's principles and her parents' objections. In her family, Janet said, "Chinese people stick with Chinese people. There's no mixing." When Santiago came over, most of her family would try to avoid him. This was difficult in the crowded apartment, where Janet lived with her parents, grandparents, two sisters, brother, and five nieces and nephews. Janet had also rescued and adopted two dogs and recently took in a third to foster. Under city regulation she could not adopt more than two, so she registered the new one, a Chihuahua, under Santiago's name. Thinking that it was Santiago who had brought yet another dog into their crowded home, Janet's sister had exploded at Santiago. "She punched him right here," Janet said, pointing at Santiago's right shoulder.

Her parents, Janet said, were also suspicious that Santiago was just after her papers. As an immigrant family, they were very familiar with marriage as a path to legal status. Janet's two older sisters had both married men from China in traditional arrangements that brought citizenship for the groom.

Janet had refused to take this path to marriage herself and had also rejected the career choices her family wanted her to make. Her parents had finally accepted that she would not join their restaurant business as her two older sisters had done, but could not understand why she was going to college to become a teacher. "Recently, my dad saw something about how teachers were getting laid off, and don't make a lot of money," Janet said. "He's telling me to be a doctor. My brother is studying to be a pharmacist, and my sister's planning to be a physician's assistant. They earn way more than teachers." Janet found it difficult to hear how many people undervalued the teaching profession. Her English professor made similar remarks: "With your grades, you could be a lawyer or a doctor."

Janet found comments from doubters frustrating, but she knew they were nothing compared with what Santiago experienced. Santiago described how people constantly questioned why he would invest in an education that, without documents, was unlikely to lead to better opportunities. "They ask me that all the time, every time I go register for something." When he told his adviser at Kingsborough he was interested in nursing or criminal justice, she responded, "Why would you do that? Maybe you should do something like culinary arts, where people won't ask you so much for citizenship."

Though he knew she was just trying to give him practical advice, Santiago felt offended by the suggestion that he should keep his expectations low. For Santiago, going to college was more than a path to a better job. He hoped that one day he might have documentation. But even without it, a college education would give him self-respect. "I still want the knowledge," he said. "I still want to have something that I accomplish for myself."

Santiago finished his first semester at Kingsborough with a grade point average of 3.6. That summer, his father told him he would no longer be able to pay. He had been working two jobs, including one at a market that was closing for renovations, cutting his income by more than half. During their conversation in July, Santiago told Josh that he was looking for work and hoping to enroll in at least one class in the fall. He was determined to continue his progress toward a college degree. "I have to take a small step at a time. I know it's going to take me longer than other people, and I'm going to have a harder time, but I'm going to get there."

Josh spoke with Santiago and Janet again the following May, four years after Santiago's high school graduation. Santiago had not been back to Kingsborough that year. He had again developed painful kidney stones and again had to spend his savings on surgery. He and Janet learned that the reason for his condition was a narrow ureter, a problem that could have been corrected with surgery when he was in high school and still insured through Child Health Plus. Now that he was over eighteen, this surgery was too expensive. Josh tried to help Santiago, connecting him with a community-based organization in his neighborhood that provided health care advocacy and services. But without documentation, there was little that anyone could do.

During the spring semester of her senior year, Aicha called Josh to tell him she had been selected as an intern for the Clinton Foundation. This was the badge of honor she had been waiting for: a prestigious internship at a foundation doing work in international aid.

Two weeks later, Josh heard from Aicha again. She was very upset. She had just been called in for a meeting with her department director, who questioned her commitment to the internship. Aicha had been late several times and had stayed home in Brooklyn during a snowstorm without calling in to the office, which was located in Harlem. The supervisor reminded Aicha that she was expected to commit a minimum of twenty-three hours each week to the internship and asked if this was something Aicha was prepared to do.

The meeting had taken Aicha off-guard. She hadn't realized she had messed up, though she knew she was having trouble holding her schedule together. Since the fall, she had been working at a Starbucks in Grand Central Terminal on Fridays, Saturdays, and Sundays, from 6 p.m. to 2 a.m., for a total of twenty-four hours. Because of work-study requirements, she also continued working at the Manhattanville library, spending four hours each week there. Together with the twenty-three hours required by the Clinton Foundation, this added up to fifty-one hours she needed to dedicate to her internship and jobs. Aicha was also taking five classes that semester. On top of this, she still needed to complete sixty hours of community service in order to graduate. Her parents continued to rely on her to help with her younger siblings at home in Brooklyn, where she usually stayed. "Why did you think all this was possible?" Josh asked Aicha. "Josh, this is my normal," she said.

Josh tried to help Aicha figure out how to make the internship work. The Clinton Foundation had agreed to pay her a stipend of $1,000 for the semester. Couldn't she quit the job at Starbucks? Aicha said that she needed both sources of income to cover the expenses of food, professional clothing, and travel to and from the internship. The MetroNorth rail line had recently raised its prices from $7.75 to $8.50 for a one-way, off-peak ticket from White Plains, the closest station to her college, to Manhattan, and subway fare was $2.50. "Now round trip is almost twenty bucks, and if I'm going back and forth several times a week, I'm spending a minimum of sixty bucks, on transportation alone."

Aicha decided to compromise by cutting ten hours off her Starbucks shifts. She hoped this would also free up time for things she enjoyed, "because I'm finding that all I do is work." Maybe reducing her Starbucks hours, she said, "can help me do something that will keep me sane. There's this poetry café that I've been meaning to go to for a while."

When Aicha spoke with Josh at the end of the semester, she told him that her internship had turned out to be a success. In her evaluation, her supervisor told her that, while her beginning was rocky, she had more than made up for it and that her writing and communication skills were very strong. In early May, Aicha changed her Facebook profile picture to a photograph of herself with Bill Clinton. Aicha, in a white button-down shirt and black blazer, looked professional and proud. "I am so happy and humbled that I got to meet President Clinton. . . . He is AMAZINGGGGG and a GREAT INSPIRATION," she posted.

Aicha graduated from Manhattanville on May 18, 2013. "I can't believe I made it," she told Josh as they gathered with her family after the ceremony. Aicha wore a traditional West African outfit under her gown, with a long embroidered shirt and pants. She seemed centered and happy. Aicha's mother looked like her, with a round face and big eyes. Her father was trim and handsome, clearly very proud of his eldest daughter.

Josh asked Aicha how, in the end, she felt about her four years of college. "My experience at Manhattanville has been far from what I expected college to be," she said. "It's been somewhat disappointing." She had enjoyed the small classes and academic challenges. But she had thought campus life would be "fun and adventurous, and free." Instead, she found herself saddled with responsibilities and, toward the end, disconnected from her peers.

This was in part because of the character of the college and in part because of choices she had made. But the largest factor, she said, was financial. "When it comes down to it, the hardest thing in my college years was tuition," she said. "Paying off the remaining balance of my tuition was hard, every semester." The many hours she spent working had made it difficult for her to engage in the process of self-discovery she craved and which she knew she needed.

Aicha said that in some ways she thrived on being busy. "I've always had something to do, and when I'm not doing something, I feel like I'm wasting my life." But she knew that she had a tendency to overcommit herself and that sometimes she didn't realize things were falling apart until she was "at the edge."

Aicha said she also felt that she needed to get used to a hectic schedule, "because to be successful, you have to work hard. You can't be taking time off. It's not just for academics, it's for everyday life. If you really want great things to happen you have to be proactive." Aicha told Josh that despite all the hours she worked, "I honestly feel like I'm a huge slacker. I have so many different ideas, but I never implement them. My study habits suck. I always wait until the last minute. My professors tell me, 'You're talented, but come on.'" Managing all these jobs and responsibilities, she said, was "sort of like boot camp. I'm training myself, improving my stamina."

Aicha saw her "training" as geared toward something bigger now than it had been in high school, when she was focused on the daunting task of getting into a top college as an undocumented student. Now, as a legal resident with a college degree, she was trying to develop the self-discipline she knew would be required by the world-changing work she wanted to do. "I'm connecting it to something," she said of her hard work. "I'm doing it because I want to start projects that are going to be successful, and because I want to be successful in my life." She saw herself as "someone trying to take advantage of everything she has had, someone trying to achieve something good, something great."

Conclusion:
College Material

Josh is often asked if college is for everybody. He sometimes responds with an anecdote. At the age of five, his nephew Noah asked his parents, professionals with elite educations, "Do I have to go to college?" When his mother said no, Noah said, "If I don't, will you tell them I'm not coming?" Noah, only in kindergarten, had a sense that a college was actually holding a place for him, as if he had a reservation that his mom had to call in and cancel.

Most of the students Josh has worked with in the public schools have internalized the opposite message: that there is *not* a place for them at college and that to secure one would require extraordinary measures. Those who do expect to go to college usually have limited information and rarely understand the range of choices available to them. In too many cases, choices are made for students by adults who believe—without examining their own biases—that they can determine who is "college material" and who is not. "I can tell by fifth grade which students will go on to college," a longtime guidance counselor at a highly regarded elementary school told Josh.

Not every student needs to go to college, and fulfilling alternatives to college need to be available for students from all demographics. But when the question "Is college for everyone?" is asked in relation to young people who have never seen college as a real possibility, it has a very different force than when it refers to students who have always assumed that college is a choice. In

America, college is broadly understood as a time dedicated to growth, learning, and preparation for making a meaningful contribution to society. When Josh tells students, "I believe you can go to college," what they hear is, "I believe you have a future."

Stories of students who "make it out" are often read as heroic narratives, testament to the remarkable character of the protagonist. Josh, though constantly awed by his students' strength and grit in the face of so many obstacles, was also struck by the element of chance at work in all of their outcomes. Nkese's success at Bates had its roots in the qualities she demonstrated in high school and that Bates saw in her application: her sophisticated analytical ability, her effectiveness as a student leader, her sensitivity to issues of equity and justice. Sometimes a student like Ashley took on "the odds" with a degree of self-discipline and drive that far exceeded what should be expected of anyone during adolescence. But twists of luck shaped students' choices in dramatic ways. Success depended, for many, on chance encounters with people who saw their stories differently than the teacher who told Nkese's eighth-grade class about the dismal fate of "kids like them."

In a 2012 study, University of Pennsylvania professor Shaun Harper researched factors that led to success for 219 black men who were defined as "achievers" at a variety of colleges. More than half were from low-income and working-class families. Many of those he interviewed, the author reports, "claimed it was serendipity, not aptitude, that largely determined which Black men succeeded":

> Participants did not deem themselves superior to or smarter than their less accomplished, disengaged same-race male peers. In fact, most believed lower-performing Black male students had the same potential, but had not encountered people or culturally relevant experiences that motivated them to be engaged, strive for academic success, and persist through baccalaureate degree attainment.[1]

Educational leaders and policymakers can reduce the element of chance in which students make it to, and through, college. Every high school should have a college counselor who can offer individualized support for students and families. The landscape of American higher education contains a broad array of private, public, and for-profit options, from the four-year "ivory tower" experience at a residential, liberal arts college to certificate and associate's degree programs that provide vocational and technical training to the evolving field of online education. For most first-generation college students, the terrain is riddled with pitfalls and virtually impossible to navigate without help. A knowledgeable counselor can help students identify and access choices that are a strong fit, that provide powerful networks of support, and that offer sufficient funding.

In the world of admissions, leaders need to examine the criteria by which aptitude is judged and adopt successful methods, such as those devised by the Posse Foundation and the New York State Opportunity Programs, to identify potential among populations usually excluded. Sources of government funding for low-income students, including the Pell Grant program, need to be significantly expanded. Individual institutions must reassess their priorities and commit the funds necessary to open their doors to students with high need. Colleges must also ensure that these students can get through college without being overburdened by part-time jobs and without graduating with debilitating debt. Financial aid counselors should be real counselors who seek to understand where students are coming from and help them to manage the complicated, high-stakes process students must undertake in applying for aid each year.

Undocumented students deserve the opportunity to build positive futures for themselves. In 2012, the Deferred Action for Childhood Arrivals program began allowing qualified undocumented individuals who came to the United States as children to work legally. But Congress must pass the DREAM Act and provide undocumented youth working toward a college degree with a pathway to citizenship.

On campus, colleges need to create and improve structures that enable students to succeed, such as Skidmore's Summer Academic Institute, Bates's swing dean system, and the wraparound services Muhlenberg has begun to develop. For students at community colleges, where graduation rates are alarmingly low, these kinds of services are especially important. In the City University of New York system, a smaller cohort model where students are known and supported by advisers, counselors, and faculty already exists through programs including College Discovery, Accelerated Study in Associate Programs, and CUNY Start. The Stella and Charles Guttman Community College (formerly called the New Community College) was explicitly designed with this model in mind. These programs, which serve a relatively small number of students, should become the norm for instruction and support.

In academic and residential life, colleges need to work with all faculty, staff, and students to help them engage with difference in the kind of depth that Josh's students ultimately valued and that is central to the role of education in a democracy. For all of the students in this book, the challenges they faced in their college experiences were intertwined with the value they brought to campus, in their coursework, leadership roles, and relationships. Their struggles—to discover their interests, passions, and abilities; to balance responsibility to others with self-fulfillment; to make sense of the roles of race, class, and gender in shaping their identities—reflect big questions colleges claim to address about individual development and social change. If colleges are to do more than replicate the status quo, they need the voices of many more individuals whose experience and insight can transform a society where gross racial and economic inequality undoes the dreams of so many young people.

For Josh, the most important skill he has learned has been how to set aside his own assumptions and listen. He found he could help his students to see the choices ahead, but only if they felt he was at least trying to understand where they were coming from and that he believed in them. His understanding of the role he might play crystallized when he heard an interview on National Public Radio with civil rights activist, historian, and religious leader Vincent Harding. Harding described a conversation with a young drug dealer who spoke about how he and many other young people were "operating in a situation where they felt it was just very, very dark all around them." What they needed were some lights, "live human signposts," who would stand with them in the darkness. These relationships, Harding said, had the power to open up possibilities they couldn't see, except "through human beings who care about them."[2]

In following his students' experiences in college, Josh saw over and over the way this dynamic was repeated on campus. Students most often described moments of positive change as catalyzed by relationships—with admissions counselors, professors, friends, boyfriends, and girlfriends who served as the lights to help them see a way forward.

Josh began his job at the Secondary School for Research with the hope that in helping his students get into college, he would help them get out of poverty. It is still too soon to assess what college will bring them in the economic terms most often used to measure the value of an academic credential. But in following the lives of the ten students in this book through their college years, Josh saw the value all found in their own search for meaning. Each explored, in highly personal ways, how they could be themselves and give to others. The road to this fundamental human quest should be open to everyone.

A NOTE TO MY STUDENTS

To the students in this book: You inspire me more than you could possibly know. Thank you for trusting me to tell your stories, as in high school you trusted me to help you imagine your futures. It has been a tremendous privilege to be with you as your adult lives unfold, and I have great faith in all that you have to offer the world. It was very hard to decide where to end your chapters, and I know that they do not always reflect your most recent accomplishments and the new directions you are heading. Special mention is due to Dwight Martin, who successfully completed the Guilford Technical Community College Firefighters Academy, graduating at the top of his class; Abigail Benavente, who has found new career opportunities and pathways to economic independence; and Santiago Hernandez and Janet Wu, who are engaged to be married.

To all my students: This book is really about all of you. Every year I am inspired by your extraordinary stories and by your tremendous courage, persistence, intelligence, and faith in what is possible.

—Joshua Steckel

ACKNOWLEDGMENTS

We were overwhelmed by the generosity of the families we got to know in writing this book. Thank you to Peggy Farrell and Ebony Jones for including us in the celebration of your children's graduations and sharing your own incredibly powerful stories. Each is a book in itself. Thank you to Karleen Jones for inviting us to celebrate your daughter's wedding; it has been a privilege to be part of your family's remarkable journey. Thank you to Jaime and Angie Benavente for your hospitality and kindness, for welcoming us into your home, where we were always fed the most delicious Peruvian cuisine, and for inviting us to share in the happiness of birthdays, baptisms, and reunions. Thank you to Annette and Kent Christian for welcoming us into your lives. Your faith, strength, and belief in the potential of young people is inspiring. Thank you to Linda and Harold Foss for hosting us at Kennetta and Josh's graduation party, and thank you to both families for giving us the opportunity to share in the joy of their wedding. Thank you to the parents of Aicha Diallo for putting up with all of our late-night conversations with Aicha over the past three years and for letting us join your beautiful family to celebrate her graduation.

Thank you to Candice Frazer, who as a student at Birch Wathen Lenox helped catalyze Josh's transformation as a counselor. It is so moving that you are now working yourself to help students pursue their dreams.

Thank you to the amazing individuals "on the other side of the desk" who are fighting to bring equity and justice into the world of admissions and higher education. Phil Smith, from Williams

College, has been a mentor to Josh from when he first began as a college counselor. To Nat Smitobol: thank you for your friendship, for your passion, and for your enthusiasm about this book from the beginning. Marylyn Scott and Liliana Rodriguez are models for how to do this work right. To Jason Patterson, thank you for "hitting the pavement" and finding the Secondary School for Research. Thank you to Mary Lou Bates and everyone at Skidmore who supported this project. Sue Layden and Sheldon Solomon shared wisdom from years of experience with Skidmore's Opportunity Programs and gave us the chance to shadow students in the Summer Academic Institute. What if all students could participate in programs like yours? Thank you to all who helped at Muhlenberg College; in particular to Christopher Hooker-Haring for having a vision, and to Cynthia Amaya-Santiago and Kate Richmond for your tireless advocacy for the students and for speaking with us so candidly about your experiences.

Sarah Goodman, an amazing educator, colleague, and friend, has offered support and guidance at every stage of this book, from its original conception while our families were on vacation together to editing the final draft. We could not have done it without you.

Thank you to Jill Bloomberg, principal of Park Slope Collegiate (formerly the Secondary School for Research), for your vision and dedication, and for giving Josh the opportunity to work alongside and learn from so many caring and talented educators. Special thanks to Menucha Stubenhaus, college essay teacher extraordinaire.

Cathleen Bell, and Beth's parents, Joseph and Tela Zasloff, read our book proposal and offered invaluable advice. Jeremy Steckel took time out of his busy work schedule for brotherly pro bono work to help get this book off the ground.

A summer grant from Fund for Teachers made it possible for Josh to travel and record interviews that have informed his practice as a counselor and provided valuable material for the book.

Thank you to Sit and Wonder Café, and to the Brooklyn Public Library, where most of this book was written.

LynNell Hancock gave us a crash course in journalistic practice that helped us through some eleventh-hour decisions.

To Alyce Barr: everyone needs an advocate, thank you for being Josh's.

We have felt so lucky to have Diane Wachtell as our editor. Thank you for believing in this book from the start and for your insights into how to manage the many stories we tell. Jed Bickman was also an amazing editor: thank you for engaging so deeply and thoughtfully with the text and for helping to keep us on track. We are thrilled to be publishing with The New Press.

This book is the collaboration of the parents of three children who, as it was being written, ranged in age from newborn to nine. Writing it would have been impossible without the support of our parents as well as our brothers and sisters and their families: Rebecca and Mark Brauning; Jeremy Steckel; Anne, Eva, and Karen Zasloff; Michael Adler; and Henry Kandel. Special thanks to Barbara and Steve Steckel for swooping in to help with child-care during our final stretch of writing, and to Shayna and Benji Kandel-Zasloff and Eytan and Noah Adler for your enthusiasm and help. Thank you also to Alice Kandel-Zasloff and to Nathan, Andy, and Scott Brauning.

To our kids, Gigi, Naomi, and Leo: We love you. Thank you for being so patient; for all your questions; and when students came to our house for interviews, for making sure there was fun along with serious conversation.

To our parents, Joseph and Tela Zasloff and Barbara and Steve Steckel—where to begin? Thank you for your love, support, encouragement, and help, for all you've taught us about writing, education, and trying to make the world a better place, and for making it possible for us to pursue our dreams.

NOTES

1: Riding Backward

1. In 2011, the Secondary School for Research changed its name to Park Slope Collegiate, and a fourth school, Millennium Brooklyn High School, opened in the John Jay Building.

2. Amy Waldman, "Neighbors Ask if John Jay Gets Too Many Troubled Youths," *New York Times*, April 26, 1998.

3. From "comments" on review of Park Slope Collegiate on inside schools.org/high/browse/school/692, accessed August 18, 2013.

4. A.P. Carnevale and D.M. Desrochers, *Help Wanted . . . Credentials Required: Community Colleges in the Knowledge Economy* (Princeton, NJ: Educational Testing Service, and Washington, DC: American Association of Community Colleges, 2001).

5. A. Sum and R. Taggart with J. McLaughlin, N. Pond, and I. Khatiwada, *The National Economic Downturn and Deteriorating Youth Employment Prospects: The Case for a Young Adult Jobs Stimulus Program* (Boston, MA: Center for Labor Market Studies, Northeastern University, 2001).

6. Douglas Braddock, "Employment Outlook: 1998–2008: Occupational Employment Projections to 2008," *Monthly Labor Review*, November 1999, revised May 2000.

7. Anthony P. Carnevale and Stephen J. Rose, "Socioeconomic Status, Race/Ethnicity, and Selective College Admissions," in *America's Untapped Resource: Low-Income Students in Higher Education*, ed. Richard D. Kahlenberg (New York: Century Foundation Press, 2004), 106, Table 3.1.

8. Toni Morrison, *Song of Solomon* (New York: Knopf, 1977).

9. "Mission" on the Posse Foundation website, www.possefoundation.org/about-posse/our-history-mission, accessed August 18, 2013.

2: With Whom Do You Make Your Permanent Home?

1. The Common Application is described in this chapter as Mike and Abby experienced it in 2007. It has since been revised several times, though the account we offer of the form's structure and content remains largely accurate. In its newest generation, CA4, the wording of some questions has changed, the number of activities students can include has increased, and the "activity essay" is no longer a required piece of writing for all colleges.

3: Take the Brooklyn Out of You

1. Elaine Tuttle Hansen, "Room for Ideas," 2007 Bates College convocation address, www.bates.edu/past-presidents, accessed August 18, 2013.

2. The article Nkese read was by Miliann Kang, who later published a book on the subject: *The Managed Hand: Race, Gender, and the Body in Beauty Service Work* (Berkeley: University of California Press, 2010).

4: Someone to Step Up and Pave the Way

1. From the "Welcome" statement for the Sophie Davis School of Biomedical Education on the City College of New York website, www.ccny.cuny.edu/sophiedavis/, accessed October 9, 2013.

2. "About Questbridge" on the Questbridge website, www.questbridge.org/about-questbridge/mission-a-vision, accessed August 18, 2013.

3. "Mission" on the Posse Foundation website, www.possefoundation.org/about-posse/our-history-mission, accessed August 18, 2013.

4. Ibid.

5: Away from the Madness

1. Data on grade point average from "The Opportunity Programs at Skidmore College," a fact sheet presented at a faculty meeting in 2005–6, Skidmore College website, www.skidmore.edu/dof-vpaa/meetings/faculty/2005-2006/documents/10-07-05facultymeeting_heop.pdf, accessed August 18, 2013.

2. Susan Layden, Ann Knickerbocker, and Monica Minor, "Bridging the Gap Between Achievement and Excellence: The Skidmore College Summer Academic Institute and the Skidmore College Opportunity Programs," www.skidmore.edu/opportunity_program/documents/Bridge_Chapter1.pdf, accessed August 18, 2013.

3. Alfred North Whitehead, "Universities and Their Function," in *The Aims of Education and Other Essays* (New York: Macmillan, 1929), 91–101.

4. Allan Bloom, *The Closing of the American Mind* (New York: Simon & Schuster, 1987).

7: Finding the Best Fit

1. "Summer Science Program," Williams College website, science .williams.edu/summer-science-program/, accessed August 18, 2013.

8: Forward Movement

1. "About Us," Eleanor Roosevelt Legacy website, www.eleanors legacy.com/about, accessed August 18, 2013.

2. This information is drawn from the Bates College website's section "Diversity and Inclusion," www.bates.edu/diversity-inclusion/recruit ment-and-transition, accessed August 18, 2013.

9: Room to Grow

1. Transcripts from speeches for Skidmore College's Commencement 2012, www.skidmore.edu/archives/2012/index.php, accessed June 1, 2012.

10: Undocumented American Dream

1. Elissa Gootman and Jennifer Medina, "Budget Cuts Raise Wrath of Principals," *New York Times*, February 1, 2008.

2. United Children's Fund, "Female Genital Mutilation/Cutting: A Statistical Overview and Exploration of the Dynamics of Change," UNICEF, New York, 2013.

3. Nadia Sussman, "After School in Brooklyn, West African Girls Share Memories of a Painful Ritual," *New York Times*, April 25, 2011.

4. Yule Kim, "Asylum Law and Female Genital Mutilation: Recent Developments," Congressional Research Service Report for Congress, February 15, 2008.

5. Katie Zezima, "Data Shows College Endowments Loss Is Worst Drop Since the '70s," *New York Times*, January 26, 2009.

11: Let's Change Lives

1. Kim Gallon's Muhlenberg College faculty biography, www .muhlenberg.edu/main/academics/history/faculty/KimGallon.html.

2. Text of Isabel Wilkerson's Muhlenberg College 2013 commencement address, www.muhlenberg.edu/pdf/commencement/Wilkerson Address.pdf, accessed August 18, 2013.

3. Richard Wright, *Black Boy* (New York: HarperCollins, 1945), 414.

12: The Will to Aspire

1. "Campus and NYC," Borough of Manhattan Community College website, www.bmcc.cuny.edu/about/page.jsp?pid=1004&n= Campus%20and%20NYC, accessed August 18, 2013.

2. Sonia Sotomayor, *My Beloved World* (New York: Knopf, 2013), viii.

Conclusion: College Material

1. S.R. Harper, "Black Male Student Success in Higher Education: A Report from the National Black Male College Achievement Study," Center for the Study of Race and Equity, University of Pennsylvania, 2012.

2. "Transcript for Civility, History and Hope with Vincent Harding," *On Being*, August 25, 2011, www.onbeing.org/program/civility-history -and-hope/transcript/534.

PUBLISHING IN THE PUBLIC INTEREST

Thank you for reading this book published by The New Press. The New Press is a nonprofit, public interest publisher. New Press books and authors play a crucial role in sparking conversations about the key political and social issues of our day.

We hope you enjoyed this book and that you will stay in touch with The New Press. Here are a few ways to stay up to date with our books, events, and the issues we cover:

- Sign up at www.thenewpress.com/subscribe to receive updates on New Press authors and issues and to be notified about local events
- Like us on Facebook: www.facebook.com/newpressbooks
- Follow us on Twitter: www.twitter.com/thenewpress

Please consider buying New Press books for yourself; for friends and family; or to donate to schools, libraries, community centers, prison libraries, and other organizations involved with the issues our authors write about.

The New Press is a 501(c)(3) nonprofit organization. You can also support our work with a tax-deductible gift by visiting www .thenewpress.com/donate.